International Socialism 107

International Socialism 107
Quarterly journal of socialist theory

Editor: Chris Harman   Assistant editor: Sally Campbell

Editorial advisers: John Rees, Alex Callinicos, John Molyneux, Lindsey German, Colin Sparks, Mike Gonzalez, Peter Morgan, Mike Haynes, Judy Cox, Jim Wolfreys, Megan Trudell, Mark O'Brien, Michael Lavalette, Sam Ashman, Rob Hoveman, Mark Thomas, Jane Hardy, Gavin Capps, Hussain Ismail, Anne Alexander, Rachel Aldred, Gareth Jenkins, Paul McGarr, Neil Davidson.

Published July 2005
Copyright © International Socialism
Distribution/subscriptions:
International Socialism, PO Box 82, London E3 3LH
Phone: 020 7538 3308
E-mail: isj@swp.org.uk
American distribution: B de Boer, 113 East Center Street, Nutley, New Jersey 07110

ISBN **1905 192 05 3**

Printed by Cambridge Printing
Typeset by Sally Campbell
Cover image: Getty

Subscription rates for one year (four issues) are:
Britain and overseas (surface):
individual   £22
institutional   £30

North America/Europe   £24
Rest of world   £26

Contents

Notes on contributors

Gavin Capps teaches development studies at the London School of Economics and co-edited *World Development: An Introduction*

Hazel Croft is a socialist activist in north London and a frequent contributor to *Socialist Review*

Peter Dwyer works at the Alternative Information and Development Centre in Cape Town

Simon Gilbert lived in China throughout 2002 and last year completed an MA in Chinese studies at Leeds University

Mike Haynes is author of *Russia: Class and Power 1917-2000* and (with Rumy Husan) *A Century of State Murder*

Claudio Katz teaches at the University of Buenos Aires and is the author of *El Porvenir del Socialismo* (The future of socialism)

Charlie Kimber works on *Socialist Worker* in London

Esther Leslie teaches at Birkbeck, University of London and is on the boards of *Historical Materialism* and *Radical Philosophy*

Hassan Mahamdallie works for the Arts Council England, is active in Unite Against Fascism and has written previously in this journal on racism in Britain (IS 95) and William Morris (IS 71)

Paul McGarr lives in London's Isle of Dogs and is training to be a teacher

Jacob Middleton wrote on class in Britain in the last issue of this journal

John Newsinger is author of the book on Dublin *Rebel City*, and has written numerous articles in *Science and Society*, *New Left Review* and elsewhere. He teaches in Bath.

Dragan Plavsic recently co-edited *The Balkan Socialist Tradition* with Andreja Zivkovic

Helen Salmon used be on the executive of the National Union of Students and is now an active socialist in the West Midlands

Tony Staunton is a social worker in Plymouth

Megan Trudell has written previously for this journal on the Russian Civil War (IS 86)

Votes of no confidence

Chris Harman

The 'no' vote in the French and Dutch refendums. The loss of a million votes by New Labour in Britain's election. The defeat of Germany's social democrats in the state election in the Ruhr. One simple fact emerges from them all. Europe's rulers are failing to find a popular constituency for neo-liberal policies at the centre of their agenda.

There were, of course, particular factors in each case. The scale of opposition to the Iraq war was, of course, central to New Labour's lost votes and to the Tories' failure to pick up more than a small fraction of them. By contrast the main beneficiaries of disillusionment in Germany have been the conservative right, although the newly formed Wahlalternative did pick up enough votes (2.2 percent) for former economic minister Oscar Lafontaine to suggest it lay the basis for a wider left alliance. Right wing xenophobic feeling may have been behind a few of the 'no' votes in France, but it was very few, despite the media coverage in Britain (opposition to Turkish membership came seventh out of eight in the list of reasons people gave).

But what emerges clearly is the enormous gap between the neo-liberal policies to which social democrat and conservative governments alike are committed and the expectations of the mass of people, even if these are not always articulated clearly. Yet these policies are the only ones that meet the needs of Europe's capitalists in their competitive struggle with rivals in East Asia and North America.

During the election the mainstream parties attempted to paper over the gap by disguising their commitment to neo-liberalism. Chirac in France pressured the European Union to drop, temporarily, its Bolkestein directive liberalising services. In Germany, Schröder's party resorted to what the *Financial Times*'s Bertrand Benoit saw as 'an anti-capitalist campaign resurrecting arguments and imagery reminiscent of early 20th century class war rhetoric'.[1] New Labour in Britain moved the neo-liberal reformism zealot Alan Milburn away from the centre of its campaign, dropped Tony Blair's picture from most of its local propaganda and called in trade union leaders and veterans of its left (even Tony Benn) in an effort to get its vote out.[2] And the campaign of Britain's Tories was quite different from Thatcher's heyday: they tried to present themselves as the best defenders of the National Health Service and sacked a parliamentary candidate who spoke of savage cutbacks in government spending. The only tactic left to them was to try to outdo New Labour in authoritarianism and covert racism.

Worried candidates effectively told both parties that the mass popular reaction against neo-liberalism that tore apart the Thatcher and Major governments in the 1990s and brought Labour its sweeping victory in 1997 has not gone away. In much the same way, the mood that swept Labour-type governments to power in the mid-1990s in Italy, France and Germany still exists even after disillusion has allowed conservative parties to return to office.

Yet all the governments know they now have to forget what they said in the campaigns. Blair was quick off the mark, dropping his talk about 'listening to the electors' and preparing for neo-liberal assaults on disabled benefits and (once an inquiry by the former head of the bosses' CBI reports in October) pensions, as well as engaging in more authoritarianism. Schröder was no different, announcing that he was to campaign vigorously for neo-liberal 'reforms' even as he called for early national elections. The near unanimous response of 'mainstream' opinion to the referendums is to demand a pushing through of the 'reforms' embodied in a European constitution even if the French and Dutch votes mean it is formally dead.

But this cannot happen without encountering resistance which does not only take an electoral form. Ten years ago, as he spoke to striking rail workers at Paris's Gare de Lyon, the sociologist Pierre Bourdieu said they were involved in the 'first strike against globalisation'. There have been many ups and downs in the struggles across Europe since. The growing alienation of people from mainstream political structures means that bitterness expresses itself in different ways, sometimes flowing to the right, not the left, and sometimes not visible at all. Every time there is a lull, there are those on the left who say that a 'cycle of struggle has come to an end'. The huge demonstrations against the war in Italy, Spain, Greece and Britain, the public sector strikes in France two years ago, massive unemployed protests in Germany a few months ago, the most recent elections and referendums, all show that this is not so.

We can expect new explosions of anger as those who failed to convince people at the ballot box proceed to implement their measures anyway.

Britain's election

Four things stand out in voting in Britain's election:

● The long-term decline in support for the mainstream parties. Labour got the support of only 22 percent of those eligible to vote (compared with its peak of 40 percent in 1951) and received fewer votes than when it lost to the Tories in 1987.

● Unlike the pattern with previous Labour governments (see our last issue), the right were not the beneficiaries of disillusion with Labour. The Tory vote only rose marginally, with five out of six people who deserted Labour voting for parties which were seen as being on the left because of their opposition to the war.

● There is enormous electoral volatility. The far right populist party, UKIP, did very well in the European elections last year. This time it and the Veritas split from it suffered humiliation everywhere. The Nazi BNP has continued to pick up worrying votes in some places, particularly the old textile towns of the north and the outer London borough of Barking. But it has so far failed to consolidate its bases in areas it has done well in before.

● The success of Respect, not just George Galloway's victory in Bethnal Green and Bow, but the 20 percent of the vote achieved throughout the east London boroughs of Tower Hamlets and Newham, the 27.5 percent won in Birmingham Sparkbrook and votes of between 4 and 6.5 percent in six other seats. This is the first time that forces to the left of the Labour Party have won a seat in Westminster elections since the Communist Party in 1945. The impact was shown within ten days of the election results, when George Galloway went to Washington to confront the US Senate in front of the whole of the world's media.

There have been attempts to disparage the Respect vote by claiming it was a 'Muslim vote'—and some Respect supporters have accepted this line. There is nothing wrong if a party standing against war, racism and attacks on the working class wins votes from people who have been on the receiving end of oppression because of their religious background. But the reality is that the Respect vote was not a 'Muslim vote'. As Salma Yaqoob points out, 'There were three other Muslim candidates in this constituency. My result shows that there is no such thing as a Muslim block vote—every vote cast for me was a positive vote for Respect.' Lindsey German, who came second in West Ham, makes the same point:

> The majority of Muslims did not vote Respect in three of the four east London constituencies, and possibly not in Bethnal Green and Bow either. George Galloway, like Salma Yaqoob, was opposed by Muslims standing for the Liberal Democrats and the Conservatives. In my constituency New Labour went round Muslim areas telling people not to vote for me because I was not a Muslim and around white areas saying Respect was a Muslim party.

Those of us who went canvassing in the area found many white former Labour voters who were voting for Respect. A geographic breakdown of the East End vote shows that Respect's vote was highest in the poorer areas, and lowest in the yuppie area along the Thames. It was because Respect combined opposition to the war and to Islamophobia with a class approach that it won votes which all too easily could have gone to the Liberal Democrats, as 'Muslim votes' did in most other places.

The strong feeling among Muslims about the war, the occupation and Palestine helped create the critical mass necessary for Respect to seem more than a marginal force and votes for it not to be seen as 'wasted', but only because so many Muslims were drawn into a massive anti-war movement, most of whose supporters were not Muslims. Respect could not have achieved the breakthroughs it did without attracting large numbers of votes from non-Muslim whites, Afro-Caribbeans, Africans and so forth.

The Respect breakthroughs showed that the left can begin to seem like an alternative to people—but only if it learns to relate to their concerns, to campaign over issues like the war that worry them deeply, but also over the class issues that affect their every day lives.

The task for Respect

The left in Britain has great responsibilities in this situation. It has to seize the opportunity to build Respect on a much bigger scale than the left has known in many years. We must reach out to all those who have been thrilled by the election successes and the publicity received after Galloway's performance in Washington, and draw them into Respect as a living force in each locality.

This means not sitting back and waiting for next year's local elections, but taking up issues that present themselves. The war will continue to be one of the key issues. Resistance to the occupation will not go away, however much the Blairites and Brownites would like it to. But it will not be the only issue, or even, at times, the one that most concerns people and produces mass activity. All the class issues we've mentioned before can suddenly provoke new waves of agitation.

One thing is clear from the pattern of struggle internationally over the last five years. Protests suddenly take off over issues when people least expect them. Just as static electricity discharges as lightning in unpredictable ways, so does the widespread alienation from official politics suddenly find a way to express itself.

We have to turn Respect into a focus which people naturally turn to each time they are moved to act. This means working now to make it the political gathering place for the best activists in each struggle and each locality.

Revolutionaries and Respect

Respect is a coalition of forces from different backgrounds, brought together by opposition to the war, racism, Islamophobia and New Labour's attacks on working class people. It is not yet an explicitly anti-capitalist organisation, still less a revolutionary socialist one. No one should feel ashamed of this. We have always insisted in this journal on the need to build a revolutionary socialist party—that has been the burden of the polemics in a number of the debates in our pages in recent years.[3] But a revolutionary party is not built by proclaiming itself. Rather its precondition is full-hearted participation in struggles against the horrors of the system alongside others who as yet have different notions of how society can be changed. Only then can the comradely discussions take place which are necessary if people are to be won to a genuinely revolutionary perspective.

The discussions are important. Issues will arise at various points in the future which do not immediately seem as clear-cut as hostility to the Iraq war or an all-out attack on civil liberties or pension rights. In those situations activists who have not been won to a revolutionary perspective can find themselves confused and bewildered. But if such confusion is widespread, the responsibility will lie with those socialists who have stood back from building Respect and engaging in the discussions it raises. Not for the first time in the history of the international socialist movement, sectarians who turn their back on new forces drawn into activity would be leaving them prey to the confused ideas that dominate existing society.

Respect provides the left with the opportunity to avoid two mistakes made in Europe in the last decade. One is sticking to a sectarian ghetto with little impact on the large numbers of people who are radicalised every time new protests erupt. The other is simply dissolving itself into wider movements and so losing its capacity to argue against those who would divert the mood of resistance into the creation of new neo-liberal governments with a vague left colouring .This happened in France when sections of the left joined the government led by Jospin in 1997; it is in danger of happening in Italy as Rifondazione Comunista's leaders place their hopes in participation in a government led by Prodi; and there are those who want it to happen in Britain through 'reclaiming Labour' behind Gordon Brown. We cannot avoid the arguments. But through Respect we begin to win them and shape a new left.

NOTES

1: *Financial Times*, 19 May 2005.

2: *The Guardian*, 4 May 2005.

3: See, for instance J Rees, 'The Broad Party, the Revolutionary Party and the United Front', *International Socialism* 97 (winter 2002); and the reply by Murray Smith, *International Socialism* 100 (autumn 2003).

How France's referendum caught fire

Jim Wolfreys

Dominique Strauss-Kahn, former finance minister in Lionel Jospin's 'plural left' government, no doubt spoke for most of the Socialist party leadership when he remarked in January 2005 that, 'This referendum is bloody stupid. We were bloody stupid enough to ask for one and Jacques Chirac was bloody stupid enough to call it'.[1] By 29 May, when nearly 55 percent of the electorate voted to reject the new constitutional treaty for the European Union, virtually the entire political class in France must have felt the same way. All the mainstream parties—the Socialists and the various components of the ruling right-wing UMP coalition, along with the Greens—had taken a position in favour of the constitution. They all expected opposition to come predominantly from the nationalist and fascist right. Such illusions were to be brutally uprooted by a dynamic, informed and relentless whirlwind of a campaign organised by the anti-neoliberal left.

Mainstream complacency was graphically illustrated by a photograph which appeared in March on the cover of *Paris-Match* magazine (an upmarket version of *Hello!*) showing Socialist Party leader François Hollande and his Gaullist counterpart Nicolas Sarkozy besuited and smiling like two smug provincial bank managers after a particularly good lunch. The sub-heading, 'Hollande and Sarkozy face the angry French', spoke with unwitting eloquence of the gulf the campaign had exposed between the arrogance of a pro-market political establishment and the simmering rage of those whose lives had being pulled apart by two decades of neo-liberal rule.

The radical left's reaction was scathing. The global justice association Attac reproduced the photo on a leaflet with the words, 'OK… I understand. For a democratic and social Europe I'm voting No'. 'The neo-liberal twins,' ran the editorial in *Politis*.[2]

This was the pattern of the whole campaign. The broad consensus around neo-liberal values shared by mainstream parties of right and left found itself under attack on every front. Against all expectations the future of the constitution was put in jeopardy. The debate lurched to the left. Everyone, from the president down, began wringing their hands about the effects of unfettered competition. 'Ultra-liberalism,' Chirac told fellow heads of state at the March EU summit, 'is as great a menace as communism in its day'.[3] The Socialist Party leadership found its embrace of the market subject to the most serious challenge it had faced in over 20 years. A decade after the public sector strikes of December 1995 had signalled a deep-seated rejection of neo-liberalism in French society, and three years after the Trotskyist left had won 10 percent of the poll in the presidential elections, the anti-neoliberal left—its trade unions, grassroots associations and parties—had found the means to punch its weight. This article is about how and why the left was able to take on the neo-liberal orthodoxy and win.

The campaign

On New Year's Eve 2004, when Chirac announced that France's referendum on the draft constitutional treaty for the EU would be held the following spring, few could have predicted how different the debate on its ratification was going to prove in comparison with the dreary and stale discussions that took place around the 1992 vote on the Maastricht treaty. True, the campaign may have begun with the media assuming that figures like Jean-Marie Le Pen and the nationalist aristocrat Philippe de Villiers would have a role to play in the debate. And discussion did focus for a while on right wing opposition to Turkey becoming part of the EU. But by March it was clear that the real debate was elsewhere, with the left and its 'joyful' No. As it unfolded the campaign, in its optimism and thirst for ideas, was more like the European Social Forum than the Maastricht debate: its significance made most sense in the context of the Seattle protests against the World Trade Organisation (WTO) in 1999, the anti-capitalist movement's defence of José Bové in Millau in 2000, and the derailment of the WTO's Cancun ministerial conference in 2003. By May those involved in the campaign were reaching for other comparisons: the historic Socialist election victory of 1981, the May 1968 revolt, the birth of the Popular Front. What is certainly true is that the depth and breadth of the campaign can only really be understood in the context of the mass uprising against neo-liberalism underway in France since the mid-1990s.

The draft constitution was first published in June 2004 and signed by the 25 EU member states in October. On 1 December, the Socialist Party held an internal vote on the question. Once the leadership had won its mandate to back the constitution it was expected that the 41 percent of members who voted against it would lie low. But there was more at stake than just the constitution. In April 2002 the party's candidate in the presidential election, Lionel Jospin, had been beaten into third place by Le Pen. Many felt that this debacle had been caused by Jospin's embrace of the market (he had privatised more public services than both preceding right wing governments) and by his failure to campaign on a socialist platform. Those who had campaigned hard within the party against the constitution realised the stakes were very high. Even before Hollande's photo shoot with Sarkozy it was clear what kind of bed the leadership was making for itself: the same one as in 2002.

Thousands of Socialist Party activists were members of Attac, the association originally set up to call for a 'Tobin tax' on financial speculation which had become a significant part of the movement for global justice. Many simply joined Attac's mobilisation around the No campaign. Nouveau Monde, a current on the left of the party led by former ministers Henri Emmanuelli and Jean-Luc Mélenchon, pitched into the campaign in defiance of the leadership. Mélenchon became the most active Socialist Party figure in the No camp. But it was the presence, discreet at first but more and more prominent as the campaign gathered momentum, of a third leading Socialist, former prime minister Laurent Fabius, which confirmed that it was not simply the fate of the European constitution that was at issue, but the future of the French left too.

According to one of Fabius' closest advisors, Claude Bartolone, the referendum had given rise to the biggest opposition movement on the left of the Socialist Party since the debate over the abandonment of the Mitterrand government's nationalisation programme in the early 1980s.[4] But whereas in the 1980s most Socialist activists felt they had nowhere else to go, things were very different now. In October 2004 an anti-neoliberal think-tank, the Fondation Copernic, had launched a petition against the constitution in the name of left unity against neo-liberalism. The 'Appeal of the 200' was signed by figures from associations, trade unions and political parties from across the spectrum of the left. It ended with a call for its initiative to be followed up in every town and every sector of society by the establishment of unity collectives. By early March, 150 such committees had been set up. By mid-April there were 500. When the referendum came around at the end of May, 1,000 committees had been established across France.

As Frédéric Lebaron of the left wing Raisons d'Agir association noted, there were three main elements to the No campaign: resistance, hope and collective action.[5] Resistance took many forms. Throughout the spring school students continued their protests against the Fillon education reforms which they rightly saw as an attempt to impose a logic of profit and competition on schools. Public sector workers took the fight to employers over pay and conditions. In January postal, transport and electricity workers, civil servants, teachers and hospital staff took action. Over 300,000 demonstrated across France on 20 January. One postal worker summed up the mood, 'They're doing everything to turn the postal service into a business like any other. But it goes much further than just the post. We live in a society where only profits count. We can't go on like this'.[6] The protests escalated. School students demonstrated in their tens of thousands all over France. Police repression—over 400 students were held in custody during three months of protests—further radicalised the movement.

Meanwhile, mobilisations were escalating in both the public and private sector over pay and conditions. With wages frozen since the Jospin government introduced the 35-hour week, Raffarin was now planning attacks on that as well. On 5 February half a million workers demonstrated in over 100 towns. On 5 March a national demonstration was held in Guéret, a small town in the Creuse department where 250 local councillors and mayors had resigned the previous year in protest at cuts in public services. When François Hollande turned up, demonstrators (many wearing No badges) pelted him with snowballs.[7] Five days later a million workers, from public and private sectors alike, took part in marches across France in defence of their pay and conditions. When the European Trade Union Confederation (ETUC) demonstrated in Brussels against the Bolkestein directive on the deregulation of public services on 19 March, the 30,000-

strong CGT contingent left no doubt that it was implacably opposed to the neo-liberal constitution, in marked contrast to the attitude of ETUC's own general secretary, John Monks.

Unlike the demonstrators, Chirac could not fight on all fronts. He urged Fillon to drop part of his education reform and opened talks with the unions on wages. At the Brussels summit of EU leaders at the end of March he made great play of his opposition to the Bolkestein directive, as if he had been unaware of both the directive's existence and his own support for it over the preceding 12 months. The directive sought to remove obstacles to free competition in the service sector across the EU. It would have allowed employees from a member state where wages were low to be employed in another at the same rate, simultaneously undermining whatever social legislation was in place and pitting workers against each other. Chirac's 'anti-neoliberal' performance at the summit was a tribute to the way the No campaign had put the government on the defensive. Resistance, then, was also highly political. Both Attac and the Fondation Copernic had produced lengthy analyses of the constitution, demolishing any notion that it could further a social Europe.[8] *L'Humanité*, the Communist Party's newspaper, alone among dailies in calling for a No vote, was relentless in its coverage of the referendum and became an important tool of the campaign. The seriousness with which activists took the issue was underlined by sales of the copies of the constitution produced by *L'Humanité*, which topped one million. As Yves Salesse of the Fondation Copernic remarked throughout the campaign, the No camp's first victory was in imposing a genuine debate on the mainstream media and politicians alike, neither of whom were prepared for the educated vehemence of their opponents.

The sharpness of the campaign's political focus, combined with the militancy of the school students and the labour movement, made for a powerful combination. So much so that when millions of workers ignored the Raffarin government's cynical demand that they give up the Whitsun bank holiday Monday in solidarity with the old and infirm, the pro-constitution *Journal du Dimanche* complained that the outrage and militancy provoked by the government would require the remaining fortnight before the poll to be spent 'de-Whitsun-ising' the campaign.[9]

The unity forged among activists from the various currents of the left was crucial in building the movement for a No vote. Activist networks from previous strikes and protests were reactivated and plugged into the existing networks of the parties and associations participating in the campaign—Attac, the Ligue Communiste Révolutionnaire (LCR), the Green and Socialist left, the trade union movement, the Communist Party (PCF), and the myriad grassroots groups of the so called 'social movement'. As the LCR's Olivier Besancenot told a 6,000-strong meeting organised by the Communist Party in Paris on 14 April, 'We've come across each other so many times in struggle that it's only right we should work together now.' The unity committees, organised from below and open to all on an individual basis (as opposed to structures based on organisational affiliation) drew in significant numbers of people new to political activity. This was the fluid organisational shape of what PCF national secretary Marie-George Buffet referred to as the No camp's 'human chain'. This formed the core of a much wider word-of-mouth phenomenon, as millions defied what the establishment expected of them.

In the 20th *arrondissement* (district) of Paris, the call to form a unity committee was launched by a local Committee to Defend Public Services, itself set up on the back of the 2003 strikes against Raffarin's pension reforms. All the currents of the anti-neoliberal left participated in the group, but around a quarter of its 200 members were new to politics. A core of around 50 activists attended the committee's weekly meetings for three to four months, discussing the issues thrown up by the campaign before organising their activities for the week ahead. The committee drew up six or seven different leaflets during the campaign, and distributed 40,000 copies of them in the local area. Even taking into account the inevitable unevenness of the national campaign, the existence of around 1,000 such committees demonstrates the remarkable level of organisation and commitment achieved by the movement. The campaign in all its aspects can therefore be seen as the concentrated expression of the accumulated experience of more than a decade of struggle against the neo-liberal agenda of the mainstream.

The proposed constitution

One of the principal weapons at the service of the No camp was the constitution itself. The most powerful argument deployed against the document was that it would facilitate the dismantling of public services and the welfare state. Part I of the document sets out the values and functions of the EU, emphasising basic principles like respect for freedom, democracy, equality, tolerance and justice. Article I-3-2 states, 'The Union shall offer its citizens an area of freedom, security and justice without internal frontiers, and an internal market where competition is free and undistorted.' This commitment to 'free and undistorted' competition is translated into concrete measures elsewhere in the document. Other commitments are less precise. 'Peace', for example, appears as an objective (rather than a value) of the Union, but the document also commits member states 'progressively to improve their military capabilities' (I-41-3). European defence is specifically aligned with NATO policy (I-41-2).

Part II of the constitution (the Charter of Fundamental Rights first adopted at the Nice summit in 2000), frequently cited by the Yes camp as a step forward in social and democratic terms, is similarly short on specific commitments to basic rights and values. Indeed, the Charter confirms that it does not 'establish any new power or task for the Union' (II-111-2). It grants the right to work, but not to a job. It grants the right to help with housing, but not to a home. It claims old people should lead a dignified and independent life, but has nothing to say about retirement rights. Likewise, the need to ensure equality between men and women is stated, but few concrete measures back this up. So the right to marry and to found a family figure in the Charter, but not the right to divorce. The right to life appears, but not the right to contraception or abortion. Workers are granted the right to strike, but so are employers. In contrast to most social legislation in force across Europe then, the treaty would make the lock-out a constitutional right.

Nowhere in the draft constitution does the principle of 'public service' appear either as a value or as an objective of the Union. Where it does feature, it is almost invariably subordinated to the imperative of 'free and undistorted' competition. In Part III, the most controversial aspect of the constitution, the political and economic framework established for the EU by previous treaties is recapitulated. It is, to all intents and purposes, a neo-liberal manifesto for Europe.[10] Restrictions on free enterprise, and on the free movement of capital are 'prohibited' (III-138, III-156). This would rule out, for example, measures to prevent or inhibit the relocation of industry or any kind of Tobin tax on financial speculation. Public services, renamed 'services of general economic interest', are subjected to EU competition rules (III-166-2). State aid which 'distorts or threatens to distort competition' is considered 'incompatible with the internal market' (III-167-1) and the European Commission is granted powers to abolish it

(III-168-2). The text itself therefore gives the lie to Chirac's claims to oppose the principles behind the Bolkestein directive. Along with persons, goods and capital, the constitution also guarantees the free movement of services, abolishes restrictions on the freedom to provide services across the Union and calls on all member states to undertake the liberalisation of services beyond the extent outlined in the existing EU legislative framework, should the economic situation permit (I-6, III-144, III-148). Part III also confirms the independence of the European Central Bank along with the measures outlined in the EU's Stability Pact, which exert downward pressure on public spending and borrowing.

The treaty, in other words, enshrines free market capitalism as a constitutional principle.[11] Here, perhaps, was the most mendacious aspect of the Yes campaign. Its leading proponents frequently claimed that the measures contained in Part III were less important than the generalities outlined in Parts I and II. Valéry Giscard d'Estaing himself, responsible for overseeing the drafting of the constitution, constantly attempted to downplay the significance of Part III, while the Socialist former Euro-deputy Olivier Duhamel was not alone in publishing a version of the constitution which omitted it altogether. Yet far from simply recapping previous treaties, Part III (along with the rest of the constitution) supersedes them, as the protocols outlined in Part IV make plain. The neo-liberal measures outlined in Part III are therefore much more than mere articles in a treaty: they become rights granted to corporations, guaranteed by a constitution designed to remain in place indefinitely (IV-446), with no revision possible unless all 25 member states vote unanimously to do so.

Not only does the constitution retain all the existing undemocratic features of the EU, it makes it virtually impossible to overturn them. The only EU body elected by universal suffrage, the parliament, would have no right to introduce legislation, this power remaining with the Commission, while the direction of policy would in any case be severely restricted by the provisions laid out in Part III of the treaty. The development of EU policy in a neo-liberal direction is itself a testimony to the influence brought to bear on EU decision-making by powerful lobbies of major European corporations. Privileged access to the European Council, the Council of Ministers and the European Commission by groups like the European Roundtable of Industrialists has long been a defining feature of the EU.[12] The opaque nature of negotiation between member states and the

Commission, and the complex and undemocratic web of overlapping interests between EU institutions and corporate lobby groups is kept intact by the constitution, which does nothing to overcome what is quaintly referred to as the Union's 'democratic deficit'. The constitution does grant the right to propose legislation by petition, however, on condition that a million signatures be submitted to the Commission. Yet there is no obligation on the Commission to act on any petition it receives. As the campaign drew to a close François Hollande claimed that if the Yes camp emerged victorious the Socialists' first act would be to submit a petition requesting legislation on public services. If the constitution represented a compromise between neo-liberalism and social democracy, as the Socialists claimed, there could be no better indication of who benefited most from it than Hollande's belated and abject promise.

Winning is just the beginning

The referendum dramatically exposed the faultline running through European politics: millions of people reject the neo-liberal consensus shared by mainstream parties of left and right alike. The victory of the No vote is the most significant blow dealt against this consensus to date. During the campaign between 60 percent and 70 percent of television coverage was given over to representatives of the Yes camp.[13] Chirac was given prime live television airtime on four separate occasions to plead the case for the constitution. But rather than mount a coherent defence of their neo-liberal agenda, establishment politicians of left and right endlessly repeated the same message: a No vote represented a nationalist, xenophobic, populist rejection of Europe. The No campaign's victory was a vigorous and glorious slap in the face for the mainstream's arrogance and dishonesty. It was the left's victory. Of those who voted No, 55 percent were supporters of left wing parties (19.5 percent were supporters of the FN), while 73 percent of the mainstream right's electorate voted Yes.[14] Most of the left's electorate voted No (58 percent of Socialists, 95 percent of Communists, 64 percent of Greens), as did most young people and 81 percent of workers.[15] The vast majority of No voters remained favourable to European integration. Their overwhelming motivation in voting No was the social and economic situation in France (52 percent), closely followed by the belief that the project outlined in the constitution was too neo-liberal (40 percent).[16] The exit polls, then, confirmed what the campaign itself had revealed to anyone who cared to see: the dynamic which propelled the No vote to victory was generated by the left.

The No campaign can be seen as the political expression of the ongoing struggles first opened up by the December 1995 strikes. In their aftermath Jospin's 'plural left' had prevented the emergence of a broad anti-neoliberal front by wedding elements of the radical left to his governmental coalition. The break-up of the 'plural left', and the subsequent failure of the Socialist leadership to hold the line on the constitution, are indications that the scope for such intermediary solutions to the crisis of French politics is narrowing. The centre cannot hold. The scale of the crisis facing France's rulers, the political elite's lack of solutions and the depth of opposition to neo-liberalism, mean that this will continue to be the case.

The defeat of the Yes camp was of course a defeat for Chirac, whose presidency was severely weakened, and his prime minister, Raffarin, who resigned soon afterwards. But it also dealt a major blow to the 'social liberalism' of the French Socialist Party, its compromises with the market. The campaign clearly showed that for now the principal dividing line in French politics is that which separates the neo-liberal mainstream from the rest of the population. Some failed to see this. Toni Negri cut a sorry figure in the company of former left-wingers Julien Dray and Dany Cohn-Bendit at a pro-constitution meeting in May, as he tried to convince a largely bemused audience that global capital could be defeated if workers made an alliance with the European ruling class and backed the constitution.[17] Lutte Ouvrière decided to oppose the constitution (having abstained in the 1992 referendum), but took no significant steps to convince anyone else to do so. The campaign as a whole, however, gave a powerful demonstration of the possibilities opened up by the unity in action of an anti-neoliberal alliance stretching from Attac to the revolutionary left.

After the referendum, media speculation centred on various possible combinations between the left of the PS and the Greens, the PCF and the Trotskyist left. Much of this speculation focused on the role of Fabius, once an architect of compromise with the market, now a prospective presidential candidate on a more radical platform. One of the most important elements in the campaign, however, was the way it developed into a movement in its own right. During the fortnight that preceded the poll some of the biggest rallies held on the left for a generation were organised by the No campaign. Over 5,000 people met in Toulouse, 1,200 in Dijon, 3,000 in Rouen, 5,000 in Martigues and 15,000 in Paris. These meetings, along with hundreds of others organized throughout France during the campaign, were combative and angry but also hopeful, even joyful (as so many of the speakers noted). The defiant, optimistic mood of the campaign, articulated through the hundreds of unity committees that formed its organisational core, reflected a movement that was finding its voice, and the measure of its potential. Over the coming months, amid the clamour of those seeking to stifle the radicalism of the campaign, this voice is sure to be heard.

NOTES

1: *Le Canard enchaîné*, 21 January 2005.

2: *Politis*, 24 March 2005.

3: *Newsweek International*, 27 March 2005.

4: *Libération*, 11 March 2005.

5: *L'Humanité*, 12 May 2005.

6: *Socialist Review*, February 2005.

7: Murray Smith, 'A New Wave of Struggles', *International Viewpoint*, March 2005.

8: See, for example, Yves Salesse, *Manifeste pour une autre Europe* (Paris, 2004) ; Fondation Copernic, 'Dire non à la "constitution" européenne pour construire l'Europe', September 2004; Fondation Copernic, 'Contre la "constitution", nous proposons une autre Europe', January 2005; Attac, *Cette 'constitution' qui piège l'Europe* (Paris, 2005); Attac, *Ils se sont dit Oui: Attac leur répond* (Paris, 2005).

9: *Journal du Dimanche*, 15 May 2005.

10: R M Jennar, *Europe, la trahison des Èlites* (Paris, 2004), p93.

11: Paul Alliès, *Une Constitution contre la démocratie?* (Paris, 2005).

12: G Carchedi, *For Another Europe: A Class Analysis of European Economic Integration* (London, 2001), B Balanyá et al, *Europe Inc: Regional and Global Restructuring and the Rise of Corporate Power* (London, 2003).

13: S Halimi, 'Médias en tenu de campagne', *Le Monde diplomatique*, May 2005; *Le Monde*, 29/30 May 2005.

14: http://www.ipsos.fr/CanalIpsos/articles/1608

15: *Le Monde*, 31 May 2005.

16: http://www.ipsos.fr/CanalIpsos/poll/8074

17: Another philosopher, Jürgen Habermas, made an equally embarrassing intervention, signing a patronising pro-constitution open letter in *Le Monde (2 May 2005)*, which revealed that his desire to see a European citizenship develop on the basis of 'constitutional patriotism' had degenerated into 'My constitution right or wrong'.

Stop the War

The story of Britain's biggest mass movement

Lindsey German and Andrew Murray
Foreword by Tony Benn
£12.99 from Bookmarks (normally £15.99)

The anti-war movement's leading lights, Andrew Murray and Lindsey German, tell in a new book, Stop the War, how they took on the government. People power forcefully made its point, and in its way this book is as important in understanding what happened as the Hutton and Butler reports.
Kevin Maguire Daily Mirror

This is a remarkable historical document, but it is not a wistful look back at something past and gone: it is the taking stock of a vital work in progress.
Derek Kotz RMTnews

I read Stop the War whilst I was campaigning in Sedgefield and thought it was a good account of people power and how a common voice can make a difference. It is an enlightening read about the 'real' story of Iraq, not the propaganda put out by the British and American government. It will galvanise others into action.
Reg Keys father of Lance Corporal Thomas Keys, killed in Iraq

The definitive story of the stop the war movement by those who made it happen. 288 pages packed with the memories, opinions and reflections of anti-war campaigners, from school students and trade unionists to artists, journalists, authors and celebrities.

Contributors include **George Galloway**, **David Shayler**, **Bruce Kent**, **Ken Loach**, **Denis Halliday**, **Yvonne Ridley**, **Benjamin Zephaniah**, **Harold Pinter**, **Adrian Mitchell**, **Michael Rosen**, **Pete Doherty**, **Ron Kovic**, **Military families Against the War**, **Billy Hayes**, **Tony Woodley**, **Jeremy Dear**, **Jeremy Corbyn**. Plus full colour section packed with photographs and art by **Banksy**, **Steve Bell**, **Martin Rowson**, **Simon Norfolk**, **David Gentleman** and **Leon Kuhn** including original and controversial works by **Ralph Steadman** and **Peter Kennard**.

OUT NOW
Published by Bookmarks Publications
Available from Bookmarks, the socialist bookshop
1 Bloomsbury Street, London, WC1B 3QE
Order it by credit card on 020 7637 1848 or mailorder@bookmarks.uk.com

Manufactured revolutions?

Dragan Plavsic

When is a revolution not a revolution? That is the question commentators have been asking following a wave of regime changes that has zigzagged its way progressively eastwards over the last five years. After Slobodan Milosevic's overthrow in Serbia in 2000 came the downfall of Edward Shevardnadze in Georgia in 2003, then Viktor Yushchenko's successful defeat of his presidential rival in Ukraine in 2004, and earlier this year the sudden fall from power of Kyrgyzstan's Askar Akayev.

For some commentators, analysis of these events is unproblematic. They argue that what we have been witnessing is a spontaneous resurgence of people power, necessitated by unfinished business from 1989. As Timothy Garton-Ash, the indefatigable doyen of velvet revolution, has put it, these events are 'the latest in a long series of velvet revolutions which have helped spread democracy around the world over the last 30 years'.[1]

Other commentators have seen matters quite differently. Instead of people power spontaneously reborn, they argue that thinly disguised pro-western coups have been taking place funded by a United States determined to manipulate elections to its imperial advantage. These are not popular revolutions at all but street scenes orchestrated by powerful external forces. One leading exponent of this view, John Laughland, has ridiculed what he describes as 'the mythology of people power' based on 'the same fairy tale about how youthful demonstrators manage to bring down an authoritarian regime, simply by attending a rock concert in a central square'.[2]

There are real problems, however, with both views. In Laughland's case, it is his implicit portrayal of the US as a near-omnipotent puppet-master successfully pulling all the key strings behind the scenes. This view reduces people power to little more than the pliant tool of the US. By contrast, Garton-Ash's argument remains locked within the mindset of 1989, steadfastly refusing to acknowledge the extent to which today's velvet revolutions have fallen increasingly prey to manipulation by ruling class and imperialist interests.

These events certainly involve a confusing mix of US imperial manipulation, internal opposition and popular revolt. In each case, the relative weight of these factors varies. An assessment of these events must therefore be concrete enough to cater for this.

The Serbian Revolution 2000

The overthrow of Slobodan Milosevic in October 2000 was a revolution caught between two epochs. On the one hand, its euphoric mass insurrectionary character harked back to the heady days of 1989 when revolutions were powered by revolt from below; on the other hand, the concerted operation by the Clinton administration to trigger Milosevic's removal by means of 'velvet revolution' served as a prototype for subsequent revolutions in the East.

Before 2000, Serbia's opposition had twice come close to toppling Milosevic. In 1991, he deployed tanks on the streets of Belgrade against mass demonstrations, and during the winter of 1996-1997 three months of mass demonstrations almost felled him over his refusal to accept that the opposition had won the local elections. The subsequent failings of the opposition, split and outmanoeuvred by Milosevic, led to the formation of the student-led organisation Otpor! in autumn 1998 by young activists first bloodied in the mass demonstrations of 1996-1997. It was the leadership of this mass opposition movement and its student activists that the US sought to co-opt in the aftermath of its failure to remove Milosevic during the war against Serbia in 1999.

There were three basic elements to US strategy in the year prior to the September 2000 presidential election. Firstly, the US Congress approved $10 million and $31 million in 1999 and 2000 respectively to support the opposition. Via a number of US foundations, notably the National Endowment for Democracy (NED) and its affiliates, this money found its way to pro-western opposition parties, such as Zoran Djindjic's

Democratic Party. Otpor! too received funds, helping it to produce thousands of posters and stickers emblazoned with its clenched fist symbol. Secondly, again using NED and its affiliates operating in Budapest and Szeged in Hungary, the US trained two dozen Otpor! activists in the techniques of non-violent struggle and 400 Serbian election monitors to spot electoral fraud. During the presidential election these monitors provided evidence of fraud, and organised parallel exit polls which, by predicting defeat for Milosevic, had an important galvanising effect on Serbs.[3]

Thirdly, the US pressured Djindjic into stepping down as the opposition's presidential candidate in favour of the conservative nationalist, Vojislav Kostunica. An opinion poll of 840 Serbian voters by a US polling firm had shown that only Kostunica could defeat Milosevic. Unlike other opposition leaders, Kostunica had been as consistently anti-US as he had been anti-Milosevic. This was critical in Serbia where sanctions and the bombing of the country in 1999 had turned the population bitterly against the US. Kostunica always rejected US money, famously describing Washington's support as 'the kiss of death' for his campaign.[4] But US strategy was simple: Kostunica would be the front man, and Djindjic, backed by the US, would be the power behind the throne and the nucleus of a Serbian capitalist class loyal to the US.

The character of the Serbian revolution was not, however, to be defined by these imperial machinations; rather, its character was ultimately and conclusively stamped by the depth, intensity and nationwide scale of an uprising powered from below by years of accumulated disgust with Milosevic. As two Serbian chroniclers of the revolution, Dragan Bujosevic and Ivan Radovanovic, have observed of the opposition's assessment of the driving forces of the revolution:

> The euphoric wave of popular rebellion against the Milosevic…regime was swelling, and even DOS [the Democratic Opposition of Serbia] was afraid of it. Some leaders of DOS were convinced that Milosevic was heading for defeat at the elections, that he would falsify the results, and that the opposition would then be lynched by the people unless it took a direct stand against the usurper of popular choice.[5]

The depth and intensity of this euphoric wave found its sharpest expression in the working class base of the revolutionary uprising against

Milosevic, spearheaded by 7,000 striking miners from the Kolubara strip mine, just south of Belgrade. For the first time in a decade, the opposition's call for a general strike had found a resounding echo. Kostunica's two visits to Kolubara and the constant presence there of opposition figures reflected what everyone in Serbia recognised: that the engine of the revolution had shifted perceptibly from the leaders of the opposition to the miners at Kolubara. Indeed, Milosevic's fate was irretrievably to be sealed by his failure to break the Kolubara miners. This is why his downfall was a victory for the Serbian working class, bristling with revolutionary potential. In subsequent weeks, workers across Serbia struck demanding the removal of company directors tainted by their ties to Milosevic; others struck for higher wages; and riots swept prisons as inmates demanded the removal of hated wardens.

At the same time, however, Milosevic's downfall was also a victory for the US, even if Kostunica has emerged as the dominant force in Serbian politics at the head of governments that remain stubbornly recalcitrant on important issues. Washington's strategy of 'electoral interventionism',[6] exploiting rigged elections in order to precipitate regime change, had worked; it could now serve as a template for future interventions elsewhere.

Georgia's Rose Revolution 2003

Georgia today plays a central role in US strategic thinking. One reason for this is the $3 billion oil pipeline under construction across Georgia from neighbouring Azerbaijan, thereby avoiding both Russia and Iran on its route to Turkey. But a pro-US Georgia is also in any event a valuable obstacle to Putin's more assertive Russia. Edward Shevardnadze, once Gorbachev's foreign minister, became Washington's man in Georgia in 1992. A supporter of NATO membership who welcomed a symbolic contingent of US troops onto Georgian soil, Shevardnadze also sent troops to Kosovo and Iraq. Under him, Georgia became the largest per capita recipient of US foreign aid after Israel.

Nevertheless, the Bush administration became increasingly disenchanted with Shevardnadze for two reasons. Firstly, his regime was visibly losing support amid a growing tide of popular anger at poverty, unemployment and crony privatisation. Secondly, as he sensed growing US disillusionment, Shevardnadze began to tilt his sails towards Moscow.

In Serbia, US strategy had been simple: to remove Milosevic. In Georgia, the strategy was twin-tracked: to maintain official support for

Shevardnadze, but also to cultivate those pro-US Georgian oppositionists skilled enough to voice popular anger without jeopardising US hegemony. Three leading figures were cultivated: Mikhail Saakashvili, a 35 year old lawyer and graduate of Columbia University Law School in New York, who had been Shevardnadze's minister of justice, Nino Burdzhanadze, the speaker of the parliament, and Zurab Zhvania, a former speaker. All were one-time Shevardnadze supporters. As the *Wall Street Journal* put it,

> The[se] three politicians are backed by a raft of non-governmental organizations that have sprung up since the fall of the Soviet Union. Many of the NGOs have been supported by American and other Western foundations, spawning a class of young, English-speaking intellectuals hungry for pro-Western reforms.[7]

The original purpose of this strategy was to oversee an orderly transition from Shevardnadze, due to leave office in 2005 having served two full terms as president, to the Saakashvili generation. But the US was also prepared to contemplate a Serbian-style solution if Shevardnadze outstayed his welcome or sought Russian help. It was not for nothing that Saakashvili visited Serbia, and veteran Otpor! activists, by now pale, degenerate shadows of their former selves, were hired to train members of Kmara, Otpor!'s Georgian counterpart.

Washington's initial reaction, therefore, when OSCE election monitors issued a statement pointing to 'serious irregularities' with Georgia's parliamentary elections in November 2003, was to call allegations of fraud an 'overstatement'. As the *Financial Times* reported, 'Observers believe the US had hoped to keep Mr Shevardnadze, its old favourite, in office until the scheduled 2005 presidential election.' Three weeks later, on 21 November, the US changed tack, declaring that it was 'deeply disappointed' with the way the elections had been run.[8]

By then, Washington was faced with mounting popular revolt. The opposition, led by Saakashvili, had embarked upon a campaign of demonstrations against electoral fraud that was soon being driven by popular anger at poverty and unemployment. After three weeks, Shevardnadze's authority had all but evaporated and a reported compromise the US tried to broker was abandoned in favour of unqualified support for Saakashvili. This Georgian scenario has recently been very well summarised by Russian socialist, Boris Kagarlitsky:

> As soon as Washington realises that popular dissent is rising in a country and that regime change is imminent, it immediately begins to seek out new partners among the opposition... The money invested in the opposition by various [non-governmental organisations] is a sort of insurance policy, ensuring that regime change will not result in a change of course, and that if change is inevitable, it will not be radical.[9]

Ukraine's Orange Revolution 2004

The 'multi-vector' foreign policy of outgoing Ukrainian president, Leonid Kuchma, shorthand for an unpredictable balancing act between Washington and Moscow, had always irritated the US. Typically, Kuchma despatched troops to Iraq while also leaning towards Russia. This policy reflected the split in Ukraine's ruling class between pro-US and pro-Russian wings, a split over which Kuchma had presided as ultimate arbiter. His departure from the political scene meant that the presidential election of November 2004 would be dominated by two presidential candidates who embodied Ukraine's ruling class divide.

The November election therefore resulted in a tense and potentially explosive ruling class and imperialist stand-off. On the one hand, Viktor Yushchenko, once Kuchma's prime minister, represented the oligarchic clans—closely knit capitalist groups—of the Ukrainian-speaking western Ukraine. Backed by the US, their principal object was to forge closer economic and political links with the West. On the other hand, Viktor Yanukovych, Kuchma's last prime minister, stood for the oligarchic clans of the largely Russian-speaking western Ukraine. Backed by Russia, their aim was to maintain their hegemony in Ukraine and to sustain, if not deepen, links with Russia.

Anticipating electoral fraud by Yanukovych, US strategy prior to the election closely followed the Serbian prototype of direct regime change. Via a number of US foundations and other Ukrainian NGOs, the US State Department channelled $65 million to Yushchenko in the two years prior to the election to fund his campaign, train election monitors and organise exit polls. According to one report as many as 150,000 people were trained to spot electoral fraud. Some 10,000 cameras were distributed to election monitors to record fraud. And Yanukovych's victory was instantly challenged by exit polls that gave Yushchenko an 11 point lead. Indeed, the aura of meticulous, well-funded planning pervaded the Ukrainian election. Symptomatic was the level of organisation in Kiev's Independence Square where Yushchenko's supporters were encamped. Multiple soup kitchens were organised and large supplies of tents arrived; 10,000 loaves of bread and 5,000 tonnes of porridge were provided every day; 300 toilets were set up and a fleet of doctors fielded 5,000 calls a day while in the background ten-hour daily rock concerts played on.[10]

This is not to deny the real enthusiasm of the Independence Square crowds who supported the campaign to overturn Yanukovych's initial victory. But it is to recognise that here was a 'revolution' whose popular forces were, from the very outset, carefully controlled and manipulated by Yushchenko. Unlike in Serbia, where the engine of the revolution shifted perceptibly to the miners at Kolubara, it is striking that in Ukraine no such shift to the crowds assembled in Independence Square ever took place. And by contrast with Serbia, where revolt bristled with revolutionary potential, events in Ukraine bristled instead with the threat of civil war. 'People power' in Ukraine never appeared as a force in its own right but was cynically wielded by Yushchenko's camp as a weapon in its constitutional struggle to have Yanukovych's victory overturned by the Supreme Court. The tense, Cold War-style character of this electoral stand-off certainly helped both camps control their supporters; squeezed between two sharply opposed ruling class blocs, each with their own imperialist allies, there was much less scope for discontent from below to find expression.

Ukraine in 2004 represents the low-point of the 'democratic' wave that swept all before it in 1989. This is because it also represents the high-point of ruling class and imperialist manipulation of 'people power'. What was once an inspiring expression of mass popular discontent had now transparently degenerated into a cynical and dangerous game of power politics.

Kyrgyzstan's Tulip Revolution 2005

Ukraine was a well-planned and controlled affair. Kyrgyzstan in March 2005 was not. Here two rounds of rigged parliamentary elections in February and March led to mounting protests against President Askar Akayev. The fractious nature of the Kyrgyz opposition, some of whose leaders languished in prison, meant that the scope for expressing popular discontent from below was significantly greater than in Ukraine.

The revolution was initially centred on an uprising in two southern towns, Osh and Jalalabad. Here, shortly after close of voting on 13 March, government buildings, police stations and airports were seized by opposition supporters. In Jalalabad a mass opposition congress, or kurultai, attended by thousands, passed a resolution demanding Akayev's removal, and was followed shortly afterwards by another in Osh. One leading opposition figure, Ishengul Boljurova, described the situation in Osh and Kyrgyzstan in these terms: 'The governor has fled. The authorities are afraid of the ordinary people. There is now dual power in the country. Popular rule is on its way'.[11] Eventually, on 24 March, the protests spread to the capital, Bishkek, where a mass demonstration, swelling to some 50,000, stormed the presidential palace, forcing Akayev from power. Widespread looting and arson then followed. Something of the flavour of these events was captured by *Times* reporter Jeremy Page when he visited the presidential palace:

> In Mr Akayev's personal quarters I found a protester in a general's hat raiding the fridge. Another was having a go on the president's exercise bike and a third was trying on his multicoloured ceremonial felt robes. The president himself had fled.[12]

These events demonstrate that, to use Page's phrase, 'geopolitics was not the driving force behind the Kyrgyz revolution'.[13] Although Kyrgyzstan has the rare pleasure of hosting both US and Russian air bases that are no more than 20 miles apart, the revolution caught everyone by surprise, even opposition leaders. What drove it forward was mass popular anger at poverty and unemployment and the Akayev family's corrupt monopoly of power and wealth.

Nevertheless, many of the opposition leaders who came to the fore during the revolution, such as Roza Otunbaeva, a former ambassador to Washington, had links with the US. This is not surprising. As in Georgia, the US followed a dual strategy in Kyrgyzstan; while supporting Akayev, it also financed an entire 'democratic' infrastructure capable of sustaining a network of opposition parties. *Asia Times Online* may not have been exaggerating when it noted that 'practically everything that passes for civil society in Kyrgyzstan is financed by US foundations, or by the US Agency for International Development (USAID). At least 170 non-governmental organisations charged with development or promotion of democracy have been created or sponsored by the Americans'.[14] In November 2003, US assistant secretary of state Lorne Craner officially opened a publishing house in Bishkek with the capacity to produce 18,000 newspapers per hour. Funded by the US state department and the US foundation, Freedom House, it published some 60 titles, including opposition newspapers the state publishing house refused to print.

This infrastructure also served as an important pole of attraction for disillusioned former Akayev loyalists turned oppositionists. What is striking about the Kyrgyz revolution is how many leading ex-loyalists have returned to the posts they once held under Akayev. Kurmanbek Bakiyev, a former prime minister is now acting president and prime minister; Felix Kulov, a former interior minister, is again in charge of security; and Roza Otunbaeva, a former foreign minister is once more foreign minister. These are people Washington can trust to ensure that very little will change. Indeed, when Donald Rumsfeld, the US defence secretary, visited Kyrgyzstan in April, Bakiyev promptly assured him that the US airbase in Bishkek could remain.

However, those who actually made the revolution may have other ideas. As Rumsfeld was visiting, several thousand landless squatters were seizing land they say should have been distributed to them after collective farms were disbanded in the early 1990s. As one report noted, 'Many of the new squatters say it was their revolution and insist that they have every right to take land after years of requests went unanswered'.[15]

Conclusion

In recent years, the US has worked hard to instrumentalise the velvet revolution, to exploit it for its own ends. With massive funds, it has used rigged elections to help trigger regime change, as in Serbia and Ukraine. It has anticipated revolt by cultivating oppositionists to lead it, as in Georgia. It has established and maintained a 'democratic' infrastructure of NGOs, media outlets and publishing houses that has spawned a host of intellectuals and activists for whom the most viable economic and political model is still the one offered by the victor of the Cold War. This infrastructure sustains US-friendly opposition groups who can emerge to lead sudden revolts, as in Kyrgyzstan. For all these reasons, US imperial manipulation today is qualitatively greater than it was in 1989. Now it has largely unfettered access to societies closed to it before the fall of the Soviet Union. And there it can freely target established opposition groups instead of secretly infiltrating the twilight world of the lonely dissident. This is why it is justified to talk of the degeneration of the 'velvet revolution'.

Nevertheless, there is another side to this story. If US strategy is indeed to work, it has ultimately to rely on popular forces to push change through. And this carries real dangers. Above all, there is the danger that the popular forces the US seeks to manipulate will sooner or later strike out in an uncontrollable direction of their own, well beyond the remit of the bourgeois oppositions the US would have them follow. Indeed, from the miners at Kolubara to the landless squatters of Kyrgyzstan, the potential of these revolutions has been palpable. This is the core contradiction at the heart of US strategy. And this is why every crisis the US seeks to manipulate is also an opportunity for socialists to voice independent demands that can help to push the revolution to altogether greater democratic heights.

NOTES

1: 'First Know Your Donkey', *The Guardian*, 27 January 2005.

2: 'The Revolution Televised' and 'The Mythology of People Power', *The Guardian*, 27 November 2004 and 1 April 2005.

3: See for this information R Cohen, 'Who Really Brought Down Milosevic?', *The New York Time Magazine*, 20 November 2004 and Michael Dobbs, 'US Advice Guided Milosevic Opposition', *Washington Post*, 11 December 2000.

4: P Watson, 'US Aid to Milosevic's Foes Is Criticized as "Kiss of Death"', *Los Angeles Times*, 28 August 2000.

5: D Bujosevic and I Radovanovic, *The Fall of Milosevic: The October 5th Revolution* (Palgrave, 2003), p4.

6: Jonathan Steele's phrase in his 'Ukraine's Untold Story', *The Nation*, 20 December 2004.

7: H Pope, 'Pro-West Leaders in Georgia Push Shevardnadze Out', *Wall Street Journal*, 24 November 2003.

8: G Dinmore, 'The Americas & Europe: Flaws Exposed in Strategy of 'Realpolitik''', *Financial Times*, 27 November 2003.

9: Quoted in P Escobar, 'What Kind of Revolution is This?', *Asia Times Online*, 2 April 2005.

10: See for this information D Wolf, 'A 21st Century Revolt', *The Guardian*, 13 May 2005 (based on his BBC4 documentary, 'Inside the Orange Revolution' shown on 15 May 2005).

11: Institute for War and Peace Reporting, *Reporting Central Asia* no 358, 18 March 2005.

12: 'President Ousted as Kyrgyzstan Revels in its Spring Revolution', *The Times*, 25 March 2005.

13: As above.

14: P Escobar, 'The Tulip Revolution Takes Root', *Asia Times Online*, 26 March 2005.

15: Institute for War and Peace Reporting, *Reporting Central Asia* no 367, 12 April 2005.

The strangling of Africa

The resources exist worldwide easily to wipe out Third World poverty and the G8 are guilty of not providing them. That was the message motivating very large numbers of people to demonstrate as we went to press. But there was also a conscious attempt by Britain's Tony Blair and Gordon Brown to divert the feeling over poverty into a neo-liberal agenda that will leave the system creating it untouched.

This agenda is embodied in the much hyped Commission for Africa. Run by Tony Blair, Gordon Brown and Britain's overseas aid minister Hilary Benn, this brings together those who have pushed the International Monetary Fund orthodoxy on Third World countries for the last two decades (like former IMF director Camdessus) and a handpicked selection of African capitalists, financiers and government ministers.

The two popstars who provide the most public face to the poverty campaign have thrown their weight behind its ideas, with Bob Geldof chairing the Commission for Africa. Their commitment to fighting poverty is genuine. But the measures recommended by the Commission would prove disastrous for Africa's workers, peasants and urban poor.

Its underlying assumptions are:
● The West's impact on Africa has been generally benign. In some 460 pages only a couple of paragraphs mention 'exploitation by the colonial powers', and it ignores completely the ongoing military interventions of the last half century.

● International Financial Institutions like the IMF 'can play an invaluable role' and clear the way 'for private sector investors' (p148).

● The key to poverty lies in the advance of private profit making. 'Successful growth will be led by the private sector' (p86).

● Africa's people can work their way out of poverty by exporting to the rest of the world if only free trade does away with barriers to them doing so.

How has this thoroughly neo-liberal approach managed to have an appeal for anti-poverty campaigners like Geldof, Bono and the leaders of some major NGOs? The appeal lies in a utopian vision of what capitalism can achieve in Africa if only certain obstacles are cleared away. It focuses on four things:

● Governance—the corruption and lack of commitment to free markets seen as cramping 'entrepreneurship' and foreign investment.

● Aid as the seedcorn that has to be provided from outside if the shoots of capitalist development are to take off.

● Debt relief for the poorest countries which cannot ever pay off existing debt (but only for such countries, for any other would hurt banks' profits) in return for working within the IMF and the World Bank

● Rapid moves to free trade, which it says would be fair trade with the removal of European Union and US farm subsidies.

This agenda has been the one promoted running up to the G8 by the virtually official campaign on the BBC.

Yet, as we show in the following pages, it is a disastrous agenda for the mass of people in Africa and elsewhere in the Global South.

Gavin Capps looks at how talk of relieving Africa's debt covers up for the continuing flows of wealth out of Africa into the pockets of western capitalists. Charlie Kimber analyses aid and governance, and shows how the new Commission for Africa orthodoxy would tie the mass of Africans into the system which bleeds them dry. Jacob Middleton extends the analysis to trade. And Pete Dwyer provides a brief survey of African protest movements.

They all point to a simple conclusion. There are ways to end world poverty very quickly. Cancel all Third World debt without any strings. Use the thousand billion dollars spent worldwide on arms on real, unconditional aid to the world's poor. End the exploitation of Third World wealth by Western multinationals. Support the demonstrations, riots and strikes by which the people of Africa and elsewhere challenge exploitation and oppression by their own rulers, the multinationals and the IMF.

Redesigning the debt trap
Gavin Capps

Gordon Brown has trumpeted loudest about his initiatives to reduce Africa's debt. If we are to believe the newspaper headlines and even the hype of some NGOs, the chancellor has not only led the way in tackling the debt of the world's poorest countries, but is now proposing to wipe it out altogether. All of this is a pack of lies. But Brown and his cheerleaders are able to get away with it because the issues around the debt are usually presented as too complex for ordinary people to grasp. Once we penetrate behind the deliberately mystifying terminology, however, the immense scandal of the debt and Brown's part in perpetuating is clear for all to see.

The new slavery: Africa's debt burden

The first feature of the African debt is the remarkable extent to which it has contributed to the continent's immiserisation. Its size does not appear particularly onerous at first sight. In 2003 the total external debt of sub-Saharan Africa stood at $213.4 billion, as compared to Brazil's $235.4 billion, the total for Latin America and the Caribbean of $779.6 billion, and of the South as a whole of $2,500 billion—a record high.[1] Meanwhile, the accumulated debt of the world's richest country, the US, had reached $2,300 billion.[2] Against this backdrop of rising global indebtedness, daily foreign exchange transactions accelerated from $800 billion in 1992, to $1.2 trillion in 1995 and nearly $1.6 trillion in 1998.[3] Africa's debt is thus a tiny drop in the ocean of international finance.

But African debt has distinctive features which have arguably made it the worst in the Third World. The debt is massive compared to the size and repayment capacity of the African economies sucking a proportionally greater volume of scarce resources out and directly impoverishing the region. Already marginal to the global system, sub-Saharan Africa plummeted faster and further than any other Third World region since the debt crisis of the early 1980s struck. By 1987 only 12 out of 44 African countries were able to regularly service their debts without debt relief.[4] The remainder were locked into an infernal cycle of further borrowing, compounding interest and accumulating debt stock and arrears [see Table 1]. A good indicator of a country or region's real debt burden is the relationship between the size of its debt and the size of its economy as indicated by gross national income (GNI) or gross national product (GNP). The true picture of Africa's multiplying debt burden was captured by the American NGO Africa Action in 2001:

> The ratios of foreign debt to the continent's gross national product (GNP) rose from 51 percent in 1982 to 100 percent in 1992, and its debt grew to four times its export income in the early 1990s. In 1998, sub-Saharan Africa's debt stock was estimated at $236 billion, and that of the whole continent was over $300 billion. Africa's debt burden is twice that of any other region in the world—it carries 11 percent of the developing countries' debt, with only 5 percent of its income. GNP in sub-Saharan Africa is $308 per capita, while its external debt stands at $355 per capita.[5]

As Chart 1 shows, Africa's debt-GNI ratio had not only overtaken that of Latin America by the 1980s, but continued to sharply rise through the 1990s while Latin America's fell.

The huge increase in Africa's debt burden was accompanied by a massive outflow of resources to foreign creditors. sub-Saharan Africa's annual debt service payments—ie the money spent paying back the debt and the interest on it—expanded from an average of $1.7 billion in 1970-1979 to $14.6 billion in 1997-1999.[6] The huge outflows were not matched by the inflow of new loans. Africa received total loans of $540 billion and paid back $550 billion during the three decades between 1970 and 2002, while retaining a total debt of $295 billion[7] [see Chart 2]. In 1990 African countries paid out $60 billion more than they received in new loans and by

1997 this had increased to £162 billion.[8] The 1990s were a period of worsening resource transfers—a trend which continued into the new millennium. In 2001 sub-Saharan Africa borrowed $11.4 billion, but paid back $14.5 billion—a net transfer of $3.1 billion.[9]

The social and economic cost of servicing Africa's debt has been immense. Year on year greater proportions of shrinking national budgets were diverted to repaying Western creditors at the expense of welfare or productive investment. During the 1980s debt service payments averaged 16 percent of African government expenditure compared to 12 percent on education, 10 percent on defence and 4 percent on health.[10]

The prioritisation of interest payments over human need was no less appalling a decade on. In 1999 creditor pressure forced the Zambian government to spend $14 million more in debt service than on its collapsing healthcare system as the AIDS pandemic reached new heights.[11] The same year 33 percent of Angola's GDP was sucked into debt repayments compared to 4.9 percent and 1.4 percent of GNP invested in education and health.[12] In 2001 debt service in sub-Saharan Africa as a whole amounted to 3.8 percent of GDP, compared to the 2.4 percent of GDP spent on health.[13]

Chart 3 clearly shows the obscene impact on social welfare of debt service expenditure. Little wonder then that the all-Africa Conference of Churches has called Africa's debt burden 'a new form of slavery, as vicious as the slave trade'.[14]

Debt and capital flight

Africa's ruling classes have also played a part in the outflow of resources by engaging in massive 'capital flight'. This is the transfer of locally owned capital to the advanced economies where it is typically invested in property and financial assets. A recent study of 30 sub-Saharan African countries by James Boyce and Léonce Ndikumana has estimated that total capital flight for the period 1970-1996 stood at $187 billion in 1996 dollars.[15] The authors argue that this was inextricably bound up with the accumulation of Africa's debt:

> External borrowing was the single most important determinant of both the timing and magnitude of capital flight from sub-Saharan Africa. Over the 1970-1996 period, roughly 80 cents on every dollar borrowed by sub-Saharan African countries flowed out as capital flight in the same year. This suggests

Table 1: Sub-Saharan Africa's External Debt, 1970-2002 [Source: UNCTAD, *Debt Sustainability: Oasis or Mirage?* (2004), p6]

	1970-79	1980-89	1990-99	1990-96	1997-99	2000-02
Total debt (US$ millions)	21,859	104,676	208,436	202,821	221,539	208,334
Arrears (US$ millions)	602	5,988	33,539	30,743	40,064	25,600
Debt service paid (US$ millions)	1,667	8,823	12,415	11,463	14,637	12,872
Total debt /exports (%)	66.0	159.0	237.5	243.2	226.3	184.2
Debt service paid /exports (%)	5.0	13.4	14.1	13.7	15.0	11.4

Chart 1: Debt Burdens of Sub-Saharan Africa and Latin America, 1970-2001 [Source: World Bank, Global Development Finance Tables]

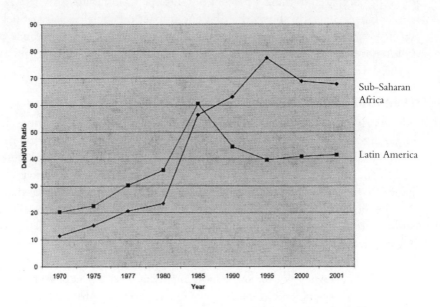

that external borrowing directly financed capital flight… Capital flight was also a response to the deteriorating economic environment associated with rising debt burdens. The mechanisms by which national resources are channelled abroad as capital flight include embezzlement of borrowed funds, kickbacks on government contracts, trade misinvoicing, misappropriation of revenues from state-owned enterprises, and smuggling of natural resources.[16]

When interest is added, the stock of capital flight in the sample stands at $274 billion, equivalent to 145 percent of the total debt owed by the same group of countries in 1996. 'In other words', conclude Boyce and Ndikumana, 'we find that sub-Saharan Africa is a net creditor to the rest of the world in the sense that external assets, measured by the stock of capital flight, exceeded external liabilities, as measured by the stock of external debt.' The difference, however, 'is that while the assets are in private hands, the liabilities are the public debts of African governments'.[17]

All of this would seem to support the claim of Blair's Commission for Africa that corruption is the single biggest problem facing the continent. Certainly, the private appropriation and reinvestment of loan funds by senior state officials and politicians reached extraordinary heights. Best known is Mobutu Seso Seko, the then dictator of Zaire (now Democratic Republic of Congo), whose personal assets reportedly peaked at $4 billion in the mid-1980s.[18] But simply attributing capital flight to the greed of African politicians hides more than it reveals.

It was, of course, the great powers who propped up African dictators like Mobutu because they guaranteed Western strategic interests during the Cold War. Mobutu was installed in mineral-rich Zaire following the CIA-backed assassination of the popular radical nationalist leader, Patrice Lumumba, and feted by Western governments, corporations and banks for much of his 32-year reign.[19] He and others like him were the creatures of exactly the same people who now cry foul about the endemic corruption of Africa's 'political class'.

What is more, the 'corruption argument' badly misunderstands the nature of the state in general, and that of Africa in particular. In all post-independence African countries, the state quickly emerged as a site, if not *the* site, of capital accumulation. Those groups in charge of the state were thus not simply 'politicians' and 'bureaucrats', but also capitalists. In other

Chart 2: The Worsening Resource Transfers of 41 Sub-Saharan African Countries, 1971-2000 [Source: J Boyce and L Ndikumana, 'Africa's Debt: Who Owes Whom?', PERI Working Paper 44 (2002), p10]

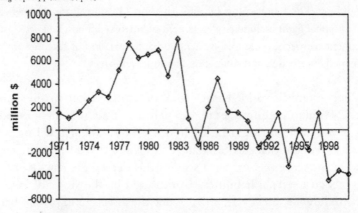

Chart 3: The Differences Between Public Expenditure on Debt Service and Health and Education in 11 Sub-Saharan African Countries, 1999
[Source: K Osuwu et al, *Through the Eye of a Needle* (Jubilee 2000 Coalition, 2000)]

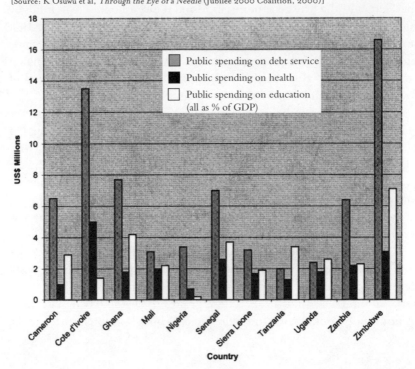

words, they were also an economic class and, ultimately, one subject to the exactly same logics and forces as capitalists located in the private sector.

This point is well illustrated by the case of apartheid South Africa. While the likes of Mobutu were shifting capital North in the early 1980s, so too was big South African business. Ben Fine and Zav Rustomjee have estimated that on average as much as 7 percent of GDP per annum left South Africa as capital flight between 1970 and 1988, an equivalent of 25 percent of non-gold imports.[20] This was entirely due to the transfer activities of the major corporations like Anglo-American and the Rembrandt Group. And their behaviour was no less illicit than that of the dictators. Shifting private funds out of South Africa in the 1980s not only defied local capital controls, but broke the international sanctions regime on apartheid. As such, the neo-liberal pathologisation of the corrupt black African state simply does not hold. The private 'white' capitalists of South Africa were busy engaging in capital flight as well.

Finally, the 'corruption argument' tells us nothing about the wider processes that were driving African capital flight. Fine and Rustomjee argue that the South African corporations shifted their resources in response to a combination of declining opportunities for local investment, particularly following the domestic economy's descent into crisis, and the new opportunities for financial and other investment opening up in the North.[21] This captures the greater truth. Whether Africa's capital exporters were located in the public or private sectors, they were doing no more than chasing profits—the essence of the entire capitalist system.

The overall situation is thus well summarised by Damien Millet and Eric Toussaint when they write that 'debt is a powerful mechanism for the transfer of wealth from small producers in the South to the capital-holders of the North, with the dominant classes of the developing countries skimming off their commission along the way'.[22]

Africa's debt profile and the neo-liberal offensive

The second distinctive feature of Africa's debt is the colossal leverage that it has given the Western powers over economies and states. The reason is to be found in the dominant sources of the African debt.

The external debts of Third World countries are usually from a combination of three different types of lending:[23] private or commercial lending by private banks and financial institutions; bilateral inter-government lending by other, mainly Western, states; and multilateral lending by the International Financial Institutions (the International Monetary Fund, the World Bank and its local affiliates like the African Development Bank). Bilateral and multilateral loans are often grouped together and described as 'public' or 'official' debt.

The vast bulk of Latin America's debt was derived from financial markets and in particular US and European banks. As such, Latin America's is overwhelmingly a private debt. In contrast, an increasing majority of African borrowing has come from public sources, rising from 61 percent in the 1980s to 80 percent by 2003.[24] The public-private composition of a country's or region's debt is significant because it subjects borrowers to different repayment conditions, and also different types of 'debt relief' scheme.

Private debt: In the 1970s the Western banks responded to the growth of highly liberalised financial markets, the lack of investment opportunities in the depressed advanced economies, and the oversupply of capital (idle Western funds having been boosted by an influx of oil revenues from the OPEC states), by massively increasing their lending to the Third World.[25] The bulk of this credit flowed towards the Newly Industrialised Countries (NICs) of Latin America, Eastern Europe and East Asia where it fuelled a spectacular burst of growth. A far smaller proportion of the new commercial loans also found their way into Africa. Most went to a handful of countries that possessed the strategic raw materials (particularly oil) or existing levels of industrialisation to generate sufficient export revenues to repay the debt. Angola, Nigeria, Congo-Brazzaville, Côte d'Ivoire, South Africa and Zaire were the main destinations.[26] The vast majority of the poorer African states were excluded from this source of credit, although a few of them managed to accumulate relatively small private debts in the 1970s.

This situation was effectively institutionalised after the official debt crisis broke in 1982. A combination of record high interest rates, oil price rises and a new world recession meant that borrowers could no longer generate the export revenues to service their rapidly escalating debts. The London Club—an organisation representing the interests of the private creditors—facilitated the commercial banks' withdrawal from the Third World debt market in general and sub-Saharan Africa in particular. With the exception of the strategic mineral economies, the banks barely lent to the continent again. Accordingly, private loans only account for around 2 percent of the region's total debt.[27]

Bilateral debt: The inter-state lending of Western governments was particularly significant in the build-up of Africa's debt and is the subject of the current Highly Indebted Poor Countries (HIPC) debt relief initiative championed by Brown. What Brown rarely mentions, however, is why the advanced capitalist economies lent so much money to the world's poorest countries in the first place. The reason is simple: profit.

The Western powers responded to the world recession of 1974-75 with a scheme which tried to boost demand for their home industries by underwriting the export of arms and machinery to the Third World. The liability for this 'export Keynesianism' lay with the Third World states themselves. The 'export credits' were in reality tied loans that could only be used for the purchase of specified imports. If the Third World country could not cover the costs, the export contract would be honoured by the Western government and converted into a bilateral loan which would either be charged at market interest rates or at (marginally lower) concessional rates and recorded as Overseas Development Assistance (ODA), ie aid.

The British, American and other Export Credit Agencies were, like the commercial banks, gambling on the Third World's future ability to repay. Between 1976 and 1980 the Third World's total debt grew at an annual average rate of 20 percent through such schemes.[28] In the end, the gamble failed and the outstanding bilateral loans accounted for at least a third of the poorest African countries' total debt.[29] But this did not stop the Western states continuing to subsidise their arms and other export industries. The Export Credit Agencies increased their commitments from $26 billion in 1988 to $105 billion eight years later. In 1996 they consequently held 56 percent of developing countries' official debt.[30] Bilateral debt has in effect really been killing Africans twice—by underwriting the export of arms to fuel its many wars, and then by sucking out desperately scarce resources to ensure that British and other firms can keep up their lively trade in death.

Multilateral debt: The final portion of Africa's debt is increasingly owed to the IMF, the World Bank and its affiliates. As a rule, the poorer an African country is, the more likely that these institutions will hold its debt. For example, in 2002 they held 79 percent of Burkina Faso's debt; 79 percent of

Burundi's; 78 percent of Chad's; 78 percent of Malawi's; 81 of Rwanda's and 77 percent of Uganda's.[31] These debts built up in one of three ways.

The World Bank increasingly lent money to fund 'development projects' in the Global South from the 1950s on. A new arm of the bank, the International Development Agency, was established to provide 'soft' or 'concessional' (ie cheap) loans to the poorest developing countries, 32 of which fell under the rubric of ODA aid, even though the money had to be paid back. All other project loans were charged at market interest rates. The bulk of the bank's lending went to major infrastructural projects like power stations or dams. These relied on Western construction companies, consultants and imports, and so they generated a healthy 'flowback'—the excess of the profits generated for a member state's firms over its contributions.[33] There was a particular orientation on financing extractive, export-orientated industries, such as mining, in partnership with private Western banks and multinationals. This was directly tied to the International Financial Institutions' wider goal of establishing new avenues of accumulation for Western capital in all corners of the globe.[34] Because the World Bank operated like a commercial bank, it was compelled to recover all its debts while continually expanding the number of new project loans, particularly from the late 1960s on.[35] The bank thus emerged as the pre-eminent multilateral institution for facilitating the flow of resources from the South to the North.

The IMF also began to specialise in lending to the Third World, providing short term loans to poor countries in Africa and elsewhere that were experiencing trade deficits (ie an excess of imports over exports) and balance of payments crises in the wake of the 1974–75 world recession.

The majority of sub-Saharan African countries were particularly vulnerable to downturns in the world economy because of their reliance on a narrow range of price sensitive primary commodity exports (like cocoa, coffee or copper)—a legacy of colonial rule. The slump of the 1970s saw most raw material prices collapse at a time when the cost of oil imports was shooting up. The IMF began to offer short term loans to 'stabilise' these countries' balance of payments. But harsh 'conditionalities' forced borrowers to implement an 'austerity programme' of slashing imports, reducing public expenditure and cutting wages in order to reduce their trade deficits and promptly repay the IMF. A second round of oil price rises and even deeper recession deepened the IMF's hold over the poorest African states. The nominal price of primary commodities fell a staggering 30 percent between 1980 and 1982; in real terms, allowing for inflation, they hit their lowest level since the end of the Second World War.[36] As one African economy after another effectively collapsed, the fund devoted more of its financing facilities to the region. In 1970-78 only 3 percent of the IMF's new conditional credit went to Africa, but by 1979-80 this figure had shot up to 30 percent.[37]

Both the IMF and the World Bank were able to consolidate their hold over Africa as a direct consequence of the debt crisis. They now assumed a dual role. They ensured that the commercial banks were repaid by lending African states more money to service their private debts. And they acted as debt collection agencies for the Western powers and themselves, working with the creditor governments through the Paris Club. This is an informal grouping of 19 states (Western Europe, Canada, the US, Japan, Australia, Russia) that aims to squeeze the maximum repayments out of the Third World debtors and ensure they don't default. It divides and rules by insisting all bilateral debts are rescheduled on an individual basis and will only agree to negotiate with a country if it has already signed a debt management agreement with the IMF.

The International Financial Institutions also insisted on the repayment of their own multilateral loans on even harsher terms. The charters of the IMF and World Bank specifically forbid debts that they hold to be rescheduled or written off. Moreover, most of this debt is charged at market rates.[38] This is one of the main reasons why Africa's total debt has continued to grow while an ever greater volume of resources has flowed out of the continent.

The net effect of the high public composition of Africa's debt was to overwhelming strengthen the International Financial Institutions' power.

When the Latin American states came to the brink of default in the early 1980s, the concentration of private bank loans in just three countries threatened to destabilise the entire international financial system by wiping out some of the world's largest banks. The major powers had no choice but to rush in and attempt to rescue the banks through massive bailouts and schemes designed to shift the burden of repayment onto the shoulders of the workers, peasants and poor.

The African debt was quite different. Not only was it small to the point of insignificance in world terms, but it was also spread over a large number of poor countries which had become increasingly dependent on Western aid as well as loans. As such, individual defaults did not present much of a threat to the system.[39] This gave the International Financial Institutions extraordinary leverage over sub-Saharan Africa and, through this, unparalleled capacity to launch the neo-liberal assault.

Debt and structural adjustment

The principal levers of the neo-liberal offensive were the new Structural Adjustment Loans of the World Bank and the IMF. Their overarching aim was, in the words of then US Secretary of State, James Baker, 'encouraging the private sector and allowing market forces a larger role in the allocation of resources'.[40] This would be achieved through a radical programme of privatisation, liberalisation and reduced public spending that would 'roll back' the state and subject the indebted economies to the full rigours of global competition. Structural Adjustment Programmes (SAPs) had effects in Africa over the course of the 1980s and 1990s which significantly shaped the form and content of the debt relief schemes that followed.

● They systematically undermined the formal independence of the African states. The new and powerful conditions attached to the loans enabled the International Financial Institutions to dictate the economic policy of almost the entire continent.[41] Regardless of whether an African country carried the trappings of formal democracy or was the most authoritarian of states, its key ministries were now answerable to the IMF and the World Bank. Their remit was further extended in the 1990s when the World Bank adopted its 'good governance' agenda. Now African states would themselves be re-engineered to complement the market economies forcibly constructed by the earlier wave of reforms.

● They significantly boosted the power and profits of the Western multinational corporations operating in Africa. Successive rounds of deregulation stripped the African states of what little control they had previously exercised over the activities of foreign firms. The wholesale privatisation of state-owned industries and utilities simultaneously provided the multinationals with 'public goods' in the form of bargain basement assets that could be stripped, squeezed and sold on. Between 1985 and 1995 the profits repatriated by the multinationals from sub-Saharan Africa rose from $4 billion to

$4.5 billion; and by 1997 the rates of return on US direct investments in the continent were, at 25.3 percent, the highest of any region in the world.[42]

● They spectacularly failed in their own terms. The stated aim of 'macro-economic shock treatment', as the World Bank called it, was to jumpstart growth and get Africa back on its feet. The indebted economies would be reoriented on the world market by shifting them away from industrial-isation strategies of the early decades after independence from colonialism. They were to be (re-)specialised in a narrow range of raw material and cash-crop exports. As a consequence, sub-Saharan Africa was effectively deindustrialised.[43] But the new surge in primary com-modity exports only flooded already saturated markets and forced world prices further down.[44]

Africa's fragile and marginalised economies went deeper into crisis. Annual average growth rates fell from a respectable 4 percent in 1970-79 to 1.7 percent in 1980-89 and 0.4 percent in 1990-94. Even the World Bank was forced to admit in 1989 that 'overall Africans are as poor today as they were 30 years ago',[45] and per capita income in sub-Saharan Africa in 2000 was 10 percent below the level reached in 1980.[46]

● They relentlessly assaulted the livelihoods and welfare of Africa's workers, peasants and poor. To take the example of Zambia, there were 140 textile manufacturers employing 34,000 people in 1991; just eight remained by 2000. Formal manufacturing employment fell from 75,400 to 43,320 between 1991 and 1998; and paid employment in agriculture from 78,000 to 50,000 in that decade.[47] Real wages in nearly every African country were estimated to have fallen between 50 and 60 percent since the imposition of the Structural Adjustment Programmes.[48] Food prices rocketed following the removal of subsidies on staples like maize, while the collapsing health and education sectors fell out of reach of most people thanks to the impo-sition of user fees.[49]

But there was immense resistance to the SAPs. Anti-IMF strikes and riots broke out across the continent in the 1980s and gathered momentum towards the end of the decade. Protests against the SAPs turned into strug-gles against the states that were implementing them. Between 1989 and 1992 some 20 African countries were rocked by mass democratisation movements which brought down one government after another.[50] It is against this background that the debt relief schemes now hailed by Brown began to emerge.

The big lie: debt relief from Lawson to Brown

Gordon Brown's latest plan for debt reduction slightly modifies the current Highly Indebted Poor Country (HIPC) initiative, which began in 1996. As with so much else New Labour holds dear, the foundations of this scheme were laid by the Tories.

In 1987, the same year that anti–IMF riots swept through Zambia, the then Conservative chancellor Nigel Lawson made a modest proposal to the Paris Club of creditor governments.[51] Loans in bilateral aid programmes should be converted into grants; outstanding bilateral debts should be rescheduled; and the rates of interest on some of these loans should be slightly lowered. This was not an act of philanthropy. Lawson was acting on what had become increasingly obvious to the Western powers. The African debt burden had to be reduced so that debt service payments could be maintained to the private banks. In addition to this logic, Lawson's proposals set out fundamental principles which would be enshrined in all further debt relief schemes. First, only the poorest and most heavily indebted countries would be allowed to qualify; second, all would-be participants would have to adopt and stick to Structural Adjustment Programmes to qualify; and finally, a 'ring fence' would be placed round the scheme. On no account were other debtors to be offered any debt relief and, even within the scheme, no debts would be written off.

There was strong resistance to Lawson's proposals within the Paris Club despite the pragmatism and timidity of the scheme. The US, IMF and World Bank in particular were worried that it would set a precedent and spread from bilateral to multilateral debt. As one US official put it at an IMF meeting, this 'would completely undermine efforts to persuade debtor nations that major economic adjustment programmes were the key to the eventual resolution of their problems'.[52]

By 1996, however, the World Bank and the IMF were under increasing pressure to shift their position. Mounting resistance to structural adjustment in Africa was combining with an increasingly vociferous campaign by the NGOs to implement full-scale debt relief. At the same time, more African states had failed to meet their debt service obligations, forcing the Paris Club to offer a series of piecemeal concessions which still proved inadequate to keep the payments flowing in. The IMF and the World Bank responded by jointly proposing the Highly Indebted Poor Country scheme which was adopted at the Lyon G7 Summit that year. It marginally reduced the public debt, including the multilateral portion, of the most desperate countries, and it refined the Structural Adjustment Programmes, which, in a typically Orwellian move, were now renamed Poverty Reduction Strategies. All of this was designed to show that the IMF and the World Bank were reforming.

The original Highly Indebted Poor Country scheme proved woefully inadequate and was further 'enhanced' in the wake of the massive anti-debt protests led by Jubilee 2000 at the 1998 G7 summit in Birmingham. Gordon Brown and Clare Short declared the enhanced scheme a triumph for New Labour's policy of working for the world's poor. But, in reality, both versions of scheme were designed to further the neo-liberal agenda.

The stated aim is to reduce the debt of the world's poorest states to 'sustainable levels'. This does not mean that it is writing off all their debt. Rather the International Financial Institutions attempt to reduce a debt to the point where a country is out of arrears and is able to sustain its debt service without recourse to further rescheduling. The scheme is based on three testing and time consuming stages through which a country must successfully pass before it is granted any debt relief. Each is policed by the IMF and the World Bank.

Stage 1: Qualification: To qualify for HIPC, a country must be indebted to an 'intolerable degree' and have an established track record of following SAPs. The IMF and the World Bank have determined that only 42 out of 165 developing countries are eligible for the scheme. Thirty four come from sub-Saharan Africa, but a number of heavily indebted African countries are excluded. For example, Africa's most populous country, Nigeria, has been kept out because, as an oil producer, it is not considered poor enough. This is clearly ludicrous as 70 percent of Nigerians live on below $1 a day.[53]

Each of the 42 countries deemed eligible have had to draw up a Poverty Reduction Strategy Paper with the IMF, containing on average over 100 conditions which are to be strictly followed for three years. These include privatisation and deregulation measures which will hypothetically generate resources to repay the debt, and commitments to use the funds released by debt reduction to reduce poverty. The strategy paper is meant to be drawn up democratically in 'partnership with civil society', ie local NGOs. But, as a growing amount of research has shown, this is just a rubber-stamping exercise. Throughout the process, power remains with the

International Financial Institutions, which hold the veto.[54] It is a continuation of 'conditionality' in anything but name.

The IMF and theWorld Bank use a market-based criterion at the end of the three-year period to calculate whether the 'economic reforms' adopted by the country are sufficient to sustain repayment of the debt. The ratio between the present value of debt and projected export revenues has to exceed 150 percent for it to be adjudicated unsustainable. Only then does the country reach the next stage, 'decision point'.

The criterion used is deeply revealing. The International Financial Institutions clearly believe that the retention of a large and costly debt after 'relief' is entirely legitimate. Their calculation takes no account of the level of poverty in a country, only its ability to pay. And their projections of future export earnings are invariably over-optimistic, so significantly reducing the value of the relief given and forcing the recipients to renegotiate their debts.[55] It is estimated that eight of the 15 Highly Indebted Poor Countries still at the qualifying stage—among them Angola, Kenya, Somalia and Sudan—will not be 'sufficiently indebted' to reach the next stage at all.[56]

Stage 2: Decision point: A certain amount of interest is reduced but none of the actual debt is written off for a country that reaches this stage. It must then pursue implementation of the Poverty Reduction Strategy Paper in full, which can take a further one to three years. Mozambique was one of the first to reach this stage. According to Patrick Bond, its conditions included the privatisation of municipal water; the quintupling of patient fees for public health services over a five-year period; and the privatisation and simultaneous liberalisation of the cashew-nut processing industry at the cost of some 10,000 jobs.[57] There are currently 18 countries at the decision point stage.

Stage 3: Completion point: Countries that successfully complete their Poverty Reduction Strategy Paper stage are judged to be ready to have their debt stock reduced. But even this is an illusion. Only the non-ODA (ie concessional) proportion of the bilateral debt is reduced. The rest of the bilateral debt stays in place along with the entire multilateral and private debt stocks. Interest payments on the multilateral debt are reduced, but this is only for a fixed period. Some $93 billion of the country's multilateral debt remains ineligible for cancellation.[58] As such, the nine countries that have reached completion point have remained locked in debt. The G7 promised to write off $100 billion in debt through the HIPC initiative. But since 1996 only

$46 billion has been cancelled and this was debt that was never going to be repaid. On average, the initiative will only cut the Highly Indebted Poor Countries' expenditure on debt servicing by a third. CAFOD have spelt out what this really means for some of Africa's poorest states:

> Mozambique was paying about US$120 billion a year in interest in principal. After debt reduction, the country will continue to spend more than US$70 billion a year in debt service. The reduction in Tanzania's annual debt service will only be about 10 percent. Cameroon and Zambia, where one in every five children does not live to see their fifth birthday and their parents earn less than 60 cents a day, will be left with a combined debt stock of nearly US$5 billion.[59]

The Brown plan to further indebtedness

So where do Brown's new proposals fit in with this massive con? The Brown initiative has generally been headlined as '100 percent debt cancellation for the world's poorest countries'. This is well off the mark.

● The Brown plan proposes to reduce the multilateral debts of a small and select group of countries, those which have already passed through the Highly Indebted Poor Country scheme, and thereby disqualifies most of the indebted South. The outstanding private and bilateral debts of the chosen few will remain untouched, while the HIPC approach will be strengthened.

● The multilateral debt relief is to be conditional on further structural adjustment/poverty reduction overseen by the IMF and the World Bank. Brown is thus once again using the debt as a means of furthering the neo-liberal agenda. This will mean yet more privatisation and misery in the Global South.

● A time limit has been set on the entire exercise. Brown is proposing a moratorium on debt service payments until 2015. As the World Development Movement puts it, the new 'debt relief commitment only covers the UK paying debt interest for selected poor countries for a period of time and not cancelling any of their debt stock'.[60]

● The IMF and the World Bank are not being asked to write off any of the debts. On the contrary, Brown has concocted an elaborate scheme to preserve their 'preferred creditor' status. This has been the most controversial area of the entire plan. It has two parts.

Multilateral debts held by the World Bank: Brown hopes to persuade the other G8 states to donate additional funds to cover the World Bank's lost debt service revenues from the eligible countries. In Britain's case, a pledge has been made to cover 10 percent of the bank's loss. Yet this money will also count towards Brown's much vaunted increase in Britain's aid budget.[61] As such, it is taking away resources that would otherwise have flowed into the South as aid. The US has tabled a counter-proposal that the World Bank cancels 100 percent of the debts owed by all 42 HIPC countries, but recovers the lost debt service revenues by taking the money out of their aid allocations. This, as NGOs have pointed out, 'effectively involves making poor countries pay for their own debt relief'.[62] Whatever their differences, then, it is clear that both Britain and the US are determined that under no circumstances will multilateral debt relief come for free.

Multilateral debts held by the IMF: Brown has proposed that the IMF sells off part of its huge gold reserves to cover the reduction in debt service payments it receives. But there would be strong opposition in the US Congress to the cost of such a move[63] and the powerful Gold Council has vigorously lobbied the US Treasury against it, fearing it will flood the market and lead to a fall in the world gold price. For the same reason, there are also reported splits at the cabinet level in South Africa, one of the largest gold producers in the world.[64]

In a sense, the intense speculation over which is the better of the rival debt relief schemes is superfluous. If the G8 were serious about writing off Africa's debt they could do it at a stroke. There was, for example, no problem cancelling Iraq's $120 billion debt when it suited their interests after the invasion in 2003. At the time, Bush argued that Iraq's liabilities endangered its 'long-term prospects for political health and economic prosperity'.[65] This is true of Africa's debt a thousand times over.

As the Senegalese activist Debar Moussa Dembele makes clear, the African debt has a purpose: 'It is an instrument of domination, control and plunder, used to promote Western countries' economic, political and strategic interests'.[66]

There is only one way to show real solidarity with Africa and the Global South. Demand that the entire Third World debt—multilateral, bilateral and private—is dropped, with no strings attached. This directly challenges the power of the exploiters, crooks and killers gathering at the G8 Summit to plan their next phase of global impoverishment and war.

NOTES

1: The terms Third World, Global South and South are used interchangeably in this article.

1: World Bank, Global Development Finance, 2005.

2: R Greenhill and A Pettifor, 'The United States as a HIPC—How the Poor are Financing the Rich', Jubilee Research and New Economics Foundation Report (2002), p3.

3: A Callinicos, *An Anti-Capitalist Manifesto* (London, 2003), p28.

4: S Riley, 'Debt, Democracy and the Environment in Africa', in S Riley (ed) *The Politics of Global Debt* (Basingstoke, 1993), p114.

5: Ann-Louise Colgan, Africa Action Position Paper: Africa's Debt (July 2001), p1.

6: United Nations Conference on Trade and Development (UNCTAD), 'Debt Sustainability: Oasis or Mirage?', Economic Development in Africa Series, (2004), p6.

7: As above, p5.

8: P Bond, *Against Global Apartheid: South Africa Meets the World Bank, IMF and International Finance* (Cape Town, 2001), p21.

9: J Boyce and L Ndikumana, 'Africa's Debt: Who Owes Whom?', Political Economy Research Institute Working Paper Series, 48 (2002), p1.

10: P Bond, as above, p22.

11: A Pettifor, 'Debt', in E Bircham and J Charlton (eds), *Anti-Capitalism: A Guide to the Movement* (London, 2001), p48.

12: K Owusu et al, 'Through the Eye of a Needle: The Africa Debt Report', Jubilee 2000 Coalition Reports, (London, 2000), p6.

13: J K Boyce and L Ndikumana, 'Africa's Debt: Who Owes Whom?' (2002), p1.

14: Cited in Ann-Louise Colgan, as above, p1.

15: J Boyce and L Ndikumana, as above, p2.

16: As above, p3.

17: As above, pp2-3.

18: As above, p3.

19: For a brief account of the relationship between Mobutu, the banks and Zaire's debt, see S George, *A Fate Worse than Debt* (London, 1990), pp106-118.

20: B Fine and Z Rustomjee, *The Political Economy of South Africa: From Minerals-Energy Complex to Industrialisation* (London, 1996), p177.

21: As above, p247.

22: D Millet and E Toussaint, *Who Owes Who? Fifty Questions About World Debt* (London, 2004), p87.

23: 'Debt' here denotes the external public debt of the developing countries. That is, the debt which is owed or guaranteed by Third World governments, as opposed to that owed by private enterprises in the Third World, which is termed the external private debt.

24: UNCTAD, as above, p3.

25: A Callinicos, 'Imperialism Today', in A Callincos et al, *Marxism and the New Imperialism* (London, 1994), p35.

26: Until 2004 just two countries, Angola and Nigeria, accounted for 53 percent of all FDI in sub-Saharan Africa (now down to 36 percent) with the rest concentrated on South Africa. World Bank, 'Sub-Sahara Africa Summary', Global Development Finance 2005, p4.

27: E Toussaint, *Your Money or Your Life! The Tyranny of Global Finance* (London, 1999), p198.

28: As above, p84.

29: Jubilee Research, 'Debt by Donor in Nominal Values (2002)', http://www.jubileeresearch.org

30: According to the international ECA Reform Campaign. Cited in S Bracking, 'Regulating Capital in Accumulation: Negotiating the Imperial Frontier', *Review of African Political Economy* 95 (2003), p21.

31: Jubilee Research, 'Debt by Donor...', as above.

32: The real impetus for the IDA was the need to outflank a rival initiative proposed by Third World states via the UN. Although the World Bank had little time for soft loans, the IDA would ensure that multilateral development lending remained under the North's control. W Bello, *Deglobalization: Ideas for a New World Economy* (London, 2004), p37.

33: 'Flowback' is the bank's own term. To give an idea of its magnitude, Eric Toussaint cites a speech by Belgium's executive director at the World Bank and the IMF to the Belgium employers' federation in 1986: 'Flowback...has risen seven to ten for all industrialised countries taken together. Which means for every dollar put into the system, industrialised countries got back seven in 1980 and 10.5 now'. E Toussaint, *Your Money or Your Life!*, as above, p131. The ghastly history of the World Bank's project lending has been well documented. Susan George and Fabrizio Sabelli provide a good overview—*Faith and Credit: The World Bank's Secular Empire* (London, 1994)—while Patrick Bond catalogues pertinent Southern Africa examples old and new—*Against Global Apartheid*, as above, pp61-67; and *Unsustainable South Africa: Environment, Development and Social Protest* (London, 2002).

34: A good example of this process was the World Bank's part-funding of infrastructure to support the development of the Selebi-Phikwe copper/nickel mine in Botswana in the 1960s. J Parson, *Botswana: Liberal Democracy and the Labour Reserve in Southern Africa* (London, 1984), pp75-76.

35: According to Eric Toussaintm, 'During the first 22 years of its existence, the World Bank provided loan financing for only 708 projects, to the tune of $10.7 billion. From 1968 onwards, however, loan totals skyrocketed. Between 1968 and 1973, the World Bank loaned $13.4 billion for 760 projects.' E Toussaint, *Your Money or Your Life*, as above, p82.

36: P Green, 'Debt, the Banks...',p27.

37: L Harris, 'The Bretton Woods System and Africa', in B Onimode (ed), *The IMF, the World Bank and the African Debt: The Economic Impact* (London, 19889), p19.

38: According to the World Bank in 1989, around 70 percent of Africa's total debt, including short term credits and drawings from the IMF, was set at commercial rates. World Bank, *sub-Saharan Africa: From Crisis to Sustainable Growth* (Washington, 1989), p21.

39: This point is made by no less a party than the World Bank, in *sub-Saharan Africa*, as above, p22; and echoed by Colin Leys, 'Confronting the Africa Tragedy', *New Left Review* 204 (1994), p36.

40: Cited M Hall, 'The International Debt Crisis: Recent Developments', *Capital and Class* 35 (1988), p8.

41: By 1990, 30 out of the 45 states in sub-Saharan Africa had some form of SAP in place. S Riley, 'Debt, Democracy and...', as above, p117.

42: The first figure is taken from E Toussaint, *Your Money or...*, as above, p197; and the second from J Saul and C Leys, 'sub-Saharan Africa in Global Capitalism', *Monthly Review* 51:3 (1999), http://www.monthlyreview.org/779saul.htm

43: According to Patrick Bond, 'sub-Saharan African manufactured products fell steadily from 18 percent of GDP in 1970 to 15 percent by 2000, while gross capital formation crashed from a peak of 25 percent of GDP in 1980 to just 15 to 18 percent during the subsequent decade (compared to China's steady 35 to 40 percent over the same period)'. P Bond, 'Bankrupt Politics: Imperialism, Sub-Imperialism and the Politics of Finance', *Historical Materialism* 12:4 (2004), p159.

44: Bond continues, 'From 1980 to 2000, cotton prices fell by 47 percent, coffee by 64 percent, cocoa by 71 percent and sugar by 77 percent. Africa's agricultural exports were down from US$15 billion in 1987 to US$13 billion in 2000.' As above, pp158-159.

45: World Bank, *sub-Saharan Africa...*, as above, p1.

46: UNCTAD, 'Economic Development in Africa: Performance, Prospects and Policy Issues', Economic Development in Africa Series (2001), p5&7.

47: World Development Movement (WDM), 'Zambia: Condemned to Debt— How the World Bank and IMF have Undermined Development', WDM Parliamentary Briefing (May 2000), p1.

48: See, for instance, the figures for real wages in Africa Unemployment Report 1990 (Addis Ababa, 1991), pp35-39.

49: See for example M Mackintosh, 'Questioning the State' in M Wuyts et al (eds), *Development Policy and Public Action* (Oxford, 1992).

50: For useful overviews, see C Allen et al, 'Surviving Democracy?', *Review of African Political Economy* 54 (1992); and L Zelig and D Seddon, 'Marxism, Class and Resistance in Africa', in L Zelig (ed), *Class Struggle and Resistance in Africa* (Cheltenham, 2002).

51: M Hall, 'The International Debt Crisis: Recent Developments', *Capital and Class* 35 (1988), pp14-15.

52: Cited in M Hall, as above, p8.

53: World Development Movement, 'The Non-HIPCs: Indebted, Excluded and Poor', WDM Debt Resources (2000), p2.

54: For revealing accounts of what NGO 'participation' really means, see P Bond, *Talk Left, Walk Right: South Africa's Frustrated Global Reforms* (London, 2004), pp80-85.

55: CAFOD, 'The Rough Guide to Debt', A CAFOD Briefing (nd), p4.

56: Jubilee Debt Campaign, What's Wrong with HIPC?, www.jubileedebtcampaign.org.uk /?lid=97

57: P Bond, *Against Global...*, as above, p74.

58: Jubilee Debt Campaign, Facts and Figures, www.jubileedebtcampaign.org.uk/ ?lid=247

59: CAFOD, 'The Rough Guide...', as above, p4.

60: World Development Movement, 'Africa Set to Gain Little from UK in 2005', WDM Press Release, 30 December 2004.

61: World Development Movement, 'Short Measures: Why the UK Government Proposals won't End the Third World Debt Crisis', WDM Media Briefing, 16 May 2005.

62: Jubilee Debt Campaign, Action Aid and Christian Aid, 'In the Balance: Why Debts Must be Cancelled Now to Meet the Millennium Development Goals', Joint NGO Media Briefing Paper for World Debt Day, 16 May 2005.

63: A Balls et al, 'IMF Weighs Gold Sales Options', *Financial Times*, 7 February 2005.

64: J Fraser, 'Worried SA to Speak to IMF about Gold Sales', *Business Day*, 10 February 2005.

65: Cited in M Engler, 'Debt Cancellation: Historic Victories, New Challenges', Foreign Policy in Focus Special Report, May 2005, www.fpif.org/papers/ 0505debt_body.html

66: D Moussa Dembele, 'Toronto, Naples, Lyon, Cologne and London: G7 Leaders and the Debt Trip to Nowhere', *Pambazuka News*, 10 March 2005, www.pambazuka.org/index.php?id=27188

Aid, governance and exploitation

Charlie Kimber

In the era where there is unlimited money for the war against Iraq, there is not enough money to save millions of lives in the Third World. The richer the rulers of most powerful countries have become, the less they have given in aid. Tony Blair and Gordon Brown's promise to seek a doubling of aid—even if it happens—comes after decades of decline. The G8 countries give half as much, as a proportion of the incomes, as they did in the 1960s. From 0.48 percent of their combined national incomes of the richest countries in 1960-65, aid had fallen to just 0.34 percent in 1980-85 and 0.24 percent in 2003 (see Charts 1 and 2).[1]

This has to be set against the target of 0.7 percent of gross national income (GNI) that all these countries signed up to when they adopted the Pearson Report and passed United Nations resolution 1522 in 1970. Having failed to achieve that, these same countries again voted at the Rio UN conference on the environment in 1992 to achieve 0.7 percent 'as soon as possible'. Ten years later the Monterrey conference reiterated the call for countries to 'make concrete efforts towards the target of 0.7 percent'.

The history of failed aid initiatives reads very much like the history of failed debt plans. And equally the reason has never been a lack of finance but a lack of political will. Today none of the G7 countries reach the 0.7 percent target. The US is the least generous in terms of aid, contributing just 0.14 percent of its GNI. Bush has already spent three times as much on the war in Iraq as it would cost to increase the aid budget to 0.7 percent.

Britain, despite the rhetoric from Tony Blair and Gordon Brown, is only about half way to the 0.7 percent target. New Labour has pledged that the target will finally be reached by 2013—but next year's planned expenditure is £700 million short of what was needed to move towards that target.[2] Most countries, including the US, Japan, Germany and Canada, have not even set a date.

An Action Aid survey in May 2005 suggested that declared aid figures are bogus. It found that 61 percent of aid flows were phantom, and that Britain, the US, Germany, Italy, France, Canada and Japan spend 0.07 percent of GNI on genuine aid.[3] The failure to meet declared aid targets means, according to Oxfam, that 45 million more children will die between now and 2015, and nearly 250 million more people in sub-Saharan Africa will be living on less than $1 a day.

Instead of massive inputs of resources and people—the sort of mobilisation that would be hurled into a war—the G8 leaders come up with ever more tortuous plans. One—the only one mentioned in the Commission for Africa's book for schools[4]—is a *voluntary* tax on air travel. Then there is Gordon Brown's International Finance Facility (IFF). He claims this will allow vast new funds to be released for crucial projects. In truth, much like the Private Finance Initiative (PFI) and other projects, it is a sleight of hand which will be disastrous in the longer term and it will undermine the pressure on the G8 to reach the 0.7 percent target and see aid levels plummet after 2015.[5] British Treasury figures show that the IFF will result in a net *reduction* of aid to poorer countries of $108bn over the lifespan of the scheme. There will be some extra money up front, but only by cutting back severely on aid in the future.

Meanwhile, 'World military spending in 2003 increased by about 11 percent in real terms. This is a remarkable rate of increase, even more so given that it was preceded by an increase of 6.5 percent in 2002. Over two years world military spending increased by 18 percent in real terms, to reach $956 billion (in current dollars) in 2003'.[6]

Aid and the medicine that kills

The basic lack of funding for aid is only the beginning of the debate, since aid does not mean the rich handing over the wealth they have looted for use as the people of the poorer countries democratically decide. It has always been used by the world's great powers as a political weapon, a method of

Chart 1: Gross national income and net official development assistance per capita 1960-2003, OECD countries [Source: Oxfam, *Paying the Price* (2003)]

Chart 2: Net official development assistance as percentage of gross national income 1960-2003, OECD countries [Source: Oxfam, *Paying the Price* (2005)]

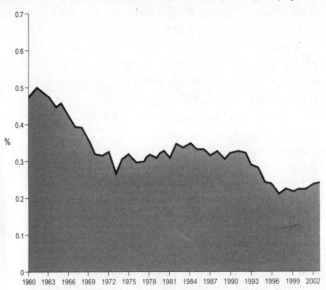

rewarding useful allies and of punishing those who dare to question the global order. It has been, and still is, linked to the interests of the donors.

It is limited in two ways. First by being tied to purchases from the donor country's firms. Almost a third of aid from the G7 countries is tied, it includes an obligation on the recipients to buy goods or services from the donor countries. The declared proportions range from the extraordinary 92 percent of Italian aid in 2004 to virtually nil for Britain—at least officially. The reality is much worse. An Action Aid study demonstrated that the top ten recipients of British technical assistance contracts offered to poorer countries were all British, US or Canadian multinationals.[7] Given that 'consultancy spending' now accounts for nearly 40 percent of aid expenditure, this is an increasingly significant factor. The World Bank has now admitted that $20 billion of the $50 billion global aid budget goes to 'consultants'.[8] Aid lines the pockets of private firms and is used to impose disastrous neo-liberal policies on poor countries.

One example of such spending was the privatisation of electricity in Andhra Pradesh in India. In 1995 the Indian government decided to reform the state electricity board (APSEB). Britain's Department for International Development (DFID) united with the World Bank to propose handing over the entire operation to the private sector, totally eliminating subsidies to farmers, and with annual price rises of some 15 percent. New Labour continued pushing this scheme through with, for example, £1.5 million given to consultants to advise the Indian government on privatisation and then over £100 million in grants and other transfers to smooth the way to sell-off. The plan eventually came into effect in 1999—and it almost immediately detonated a series of protests and strikes as farmers fought back against the huge price rises. Soaring power costs were one of the factors that indebted farmers and helped to turn Andhra Pradesh into fields of despair, a place where thousands of farmers have killed themselves because of the agricultural crisis.[9] The British government followed this up by supplying a grant of £1.65 million for a body called the Implementation Secretariat. Its task was to assess the state's assets, decide which were worth keeping, and either sell, close down or restructure the rest. The DFID did not operate this body itself, but gave the contract to what Christian Aid describes as 'the right wing, free market fundamentalists from the British-based Adam Smith Institute'.[10] By the end of their orgy of privatisation, the Adam Smith Institute advisers had helped sell-off, restructure or close 43 state bodies, with the loss of 45,000 jobs.

If this is aid, the poor should be grateful that the G8 countries are failing to meet their targets!

Such consultancy companies are part of a new industry—advising on privatisation—in which Britain is a world leader. Expertise gained from domestic privatisations and PFIs is now being put to work on the international stage. For example, in August 2003 the Government of Tanzania awarded the contract to run the water supply to Dar es Salaam (population 3.5 million) to City Water, a joint venture of Britain's Biwater International, Germany's Gauff Ingenieure and a local investor, Superdoll Trailer Manufacturers Limited. Privatisation of Dar es Salaam's water was a condition of the IMF's Enhanced Structural Adjustment Facility 1996 to 1999 and its Poverty Reduction and Growth Facility from 2000 to 2003, while continued restructuring and privatisation of public utilities was part of Tanazania's conditions for getting debt relief under the Heavily Indebted Poor Countries initiative. The British taxpayer, through the DFID, funded the pro-privatisation advertising campaign. A hostile Tanzanian public was subjected to a media campaign promoting the sell off at a cost of £430,000. The British gift to Tanzania's people, channelled through the Adam Smith Institute, included backing for a pop song whose lyrics included the words, 'Young plants need rain, businesses need investment. Our old industries are like dry crops and privatisation brings the rain.'

In fact, privatisation increased water prices and made poor populations more vulnerable to water-borne diseases like cholera. In May 2005 the Tanzanian government decided to cancel the contract because of the poor performance of City Water. As this article was written, the company was considering whether to take the Tanzanian government to court.

But aid is restricted, in a more general sense, even when it is not tied to particular deals. It is made conditional on certain economic or political behaviour.[11] It is instructive to look at who received aid from the G8 countries in 2004. The three biggest recipients of US aid were Egypt, Russia and Israel. The French government's favoured trio were Ivory Coast, French Polynesia and New Caledonia. Japan's money went to China, India and Thailand. Clearly such priorities were not about channelling cash to the poorest. The aim was to buttress strategic or trade interests.

Aid is used to shape the countries which receive it. In 1980 the World Bank began 'adjustment lending'—loans with strings. 'From that moment the Bank and the IMF cracked the whip. With adjustment lending came the stark choice: transform your economy or there will be no more foreign aid. It was a threat the poorest countries found hard to resist'.[12] Conditionality, as adjustment lending became known, grew rapidly. Between 1980 and 1998 the IMF and World Bank made 958 adjustment loans. Much has been written on the disaster caused by the neo-liberal policies demanded as the price of aid. The indictment is so overwhelming that I will not repeat it here. But again, don't believe that the great powers have learnt any lessons. Or rather, don't think they give a damn if, in order to maintain their system, millions are hurled into poverty, famine and ignorance or sentenced to agonising deaths. Aid is at least as ideological today as it was 20 years ago.

The World Development Movement has done a great service in exposing the way that British aid money goes to smooth the path of privatisation across the world:

The UK Government is ploughing millions of pounds of international aid money into:
● Expensive advice on water restructuring with a massive bias towards privatisation as the only solution.
● Public relations offensives designed to convince objecting communities that privatisation is in their best interests.
● Funding for privatisation, either by subsidising private water suppliers and the privatisation process, or by tying aid payments to privatisation, so the only way becomes the private way.
As part of this hijacked aid, the government's Department for International Development has paid enormous sums of aid money to wealthy consultancy companies, like Pricewaterhouse Coopers, Halcrow and Adam Smith International. These 'privatisation consultants' offer a comprehensive pro-privatisation service: from producing 'master plans' on how privatisation can be achieved, to running public relations campaigns showing sceptical communities that privatisation is what they want, even if they didn't think so. With these companies on the scene the outcome is guaranteed—ambitious programmes to involve the private sector with no consideration of alternatives or discussion of what is best on the ground. And when the dust

settles and people start protesting about the failure of those programmes, the privatisation consultants are long gone. But their bills are being paid with money supposedly earmarked to fight poverty.[13]

The governance agenda

There has been a shift in the ideology of conditionality in the last 15 years. Poor countries are somewhat less likely to be told simply that 'private is good, public bad'. Instead they will be lectured about the need for 'good governance', and the requirement to 'root out corruption'. This has been used as an excuse to explain the failure of neo-liberal policies, and as a stick with which to impose further neo-liberal measures.

New Labour's thinking has shifted in this direction, as reflected in the Africa Commission. The DFID released a policy paper in February this year, stating, 'We will not make our aid conditional on specific policy decisions by partner governments, or attempt to impose policy choices on them (including sensitive areas such as privatisation or trade liberalisation). The Africa Commission's report says that liberalisation should not be forced on African countries'.[14] But the question of 'governance' is at the top of its agenda. And the aim of 'change in governance' is 'to make the investment climate stronger'.[15]

The British government still bases many of its aid decisions on whether or not a country has received a positive assessment from the World Bank and the IMF. These assessments are dependent on neo-liberal 'reform'. The rulers of many poor countries are so desperate for aid and debt relief that they are prepared to take the measures necessary to get this money. They know, for instance, that unless they present a full menu of liberalising and privatising policies, no donor will visit the table. The IMF acts as final arbitrator for creditors: what it says—and believes—is what goes.

Poor countries have been so well schooled in the language of liberalisation that they can safely be left on their own to repeat the old Washington Consensus catechisms that they know are expected of them.[16]

As Kavaljit Singh writes:

> The good governance agenda is deeply rooted in the neo-liberal Washington consensus. Instead of accepting the failure of neo-liberal policies, the international financial institutions shifted the blame on the tardy application of

policies in the borrowing countries… The governance agenda reinforces the Washington consensus through institutional and political conditionalities. Governance reforms, as promoted by these institutions, are actually oriented towards strengthening market reforms instead of genuine democratisation and human rights. Consequently, promotion of good governance has become an integral part of the emergent global economic order.[17]

From the early 1990s donors such as the US government increasingly stressed 'corruption' as a key impediment to Third World development. It was not zeroing in on the way that capitalism breeds a culture of profits by any means necessary. It was seeking to define corruption as a function of the power of state control and an inevitable result of the 'stifling' presence of government regulation. As the World Bank's 1997 Development Report put it:

> The state's monopoly on coercion, which gives it the power to intervene effectively in economic activity, also gives it the power to intervene arbitrarily. This power, coupled with access to information not available to the general public, creates opportunities for public officials to promote their own interests at the expense of the general interest.[18]

Such an approach fitted well with the unleashing of the wrecking ball of market mechanisms across the globe. It meant, 'Economic liberalisation and multi-party democracy were presented (by donors to African elites and by elites to voters) as the most effective means of combating corruption'.[19]

So long as the Cold War raged, the White House was quite happy with the undemocratic practices of such useful butchers as Joseph Mobutu in Zaire. Samuel Huntington (later to write the hymn of the neo-cons, *The Clash of Civilizations*) wrote in 1968 that corruption was sometimes a symbol of modernisation, of 'efforts made by enterprising strata to circumvent the stultifying deadweight of oppressive states, to cut "red tape".'[20] Other theorists in the 1960s suggested that if elites reinvested the proceeds of their corruption then they might generate beneficial private investment or 'open up' the state to previously excluded groups—such as businessmen and the local agents of multinational capital. Corruption was seen as an act of defiance by private interests against the overweening strength of collective regulation. Only later was corruption regarded as rooted in the state itself and therefore the 'war against corruption' could usefully be emblazoned on the banners of the privatisers and the pro-market militias.

Today governance-related conditionalities are central to aid packages. They made up 72 percent of the measures demanded from African countries during 1997-99, 58 percent for Asian countries and 53 percent in Latin America and the Caribbean. Demands for good governance have greatly increased the hoops through which countries must now jump to get their aid money. The average number of criteria has risen from six in the 1970s and ten in the 1980s to 26 in the late 1990s.

One of the earliest forays was the British government's imposition of an Anti-Corruption Commission in Zambia in 1991 as the price of continuing aid programmes. This was followed up by a call from a meeting of the Paris Club (where donors review the progress of those who owe them money and recommend future action) for the removal of three members of the government accused of drug trafficking. They may have been guilty, but there was deep resentment in Zambia that equally corrupt ministers, who happened to be friends of the West, were never investigated, still less removed and barred from office at the command of foreign powers. Anti-corruption measures were supposed to strengthen the democratic hold of the population over their politicians. In this case the Paris Club had further subverted the democratic process. And this was in a country where internal pressures had achieved significant democratic change, entirely without support from the West.

As Morris Szeftel points out, it is not surprising, 'given low salaries and rapid inflation, that petty corruption is widespread among rank and file civil servants, a problem worsened by continuing economic crisis'.[21] He gives the example of Zambia in 1997 where the monthly cost of food for a family of six (excluding rent, transport, clothes, etc) was more than the top of the General Professional Scale salary in the civil service. 'In such circumstances low level corruption should surprise no one, and whether there is a multi-party or a single-party state, a market or command economy, is not likely to make the slightest difference.'

It is true there are many repressive and unaccountable governments in poor countries although, for example, sub-Saharan Africa has seen multi-party elections in 44 out of 50 countries in the last decade. It is true that many elections are, at least to some extent, rigged. But this is not some

African peculiarity. What would we think of a country where son follows father into power on the basis of a fixed vote, a brother controls the key state where the fixing took place, the executive power has a thousand golden links with big business, money desperately needed for health and education is channelled into arms spending, elections are won only by candidates able to raise vast wads of money, people of one ethnic background are systematically discriminated against in the voting process, and hardly half of the population votes anyway? This of course, is the US, the country that is holding high the torch of freedom and prepared for global war in order to spread 'democracy'. And that great apostle of governance, Tony Blair, holds office after failing to win the votes of 78 percent of the total electorate.

Corruption is being raised by the very powers that have encouraged and supported tyranny in the past, and who continue to defend unconditionally the rights of business to act with no democratic regulation or control. As Szeftel also writes:

> The resilience of corruption owes something to the disruptive nature of the reforms being imposed on African countries. More importantly structural adjustment, liberalisation and even democratic reforms have played a significant part in weakening the regulatory capacity of the state.[22]

A state honeycombed with private consultants and in thrall to the power of the multinationals is less likely to root out corruption than one which has to at least make some concessions to public interest. And who is calling for an accountability audit of Shell or General Motors or Citicorp? In the contemporary world the revenues of the biggest multinational corporations far exceed the GDP of many countries. The multinationals often form trade cartels and indulge in manipulative pricing causing substantial loss of tax revenue to the poor. Corporate governance has never been on the agenda of international financial institutions, powerful states and corporate entities.[23]

Corruption, as defined by Washington or the World Bank, ignores the central role of companies in subverting laws, evading tax and fixing prices, as exemplified in scandals such as Enron, WorldCom, Xerox, Global Crossing and Tyco International. The scale of the theft involved dwarfed the greed of even the most rapacious Third World minister, and exceeded the revenues of many governments. Corruption is not simply a feature of the state in poor countries. It is very much a hallmark of the private sector in the richest parts of the world as well.

Some of the worst cases of corruption have occurred where the private sector and the state interact. The growth in corruption in the 1990s was accelerated by the close relationship between government and political leaders on the one hand and businessmen who engage in corruption on the other.[24]

A history of shattering states

Totally missing from the Commission for Africa discussion on governance is what happened to the continent in the 17th, 18th, 19th and most of the 20th centuries. Africa, for so long in the vanguard of civilisation, was hurled backwards by the capitalism that arose in western Europe and North America.[25]

Egypt, in Africa, was one of the foremost early civilisations. The great pyramid of Gizeh was built over 4,000 years ago. Aksum, in the highlands of northern Ethiopia, was a developed civilisation in Roman times. The Zanj culture on the east coast of Africa south of the 'horn' of Somalia developed in the 7th century. Beginning in the area around Mogadishu, a linked set of city states stretched as far south as Mozambique within 100 years. A developed culture grew up from early times in the Katanga area of what is now the Democratic Republic of Congo.

In 1510 Leo Africanus, an exiled Moor from Granada, travelled to Timbuktu (in modern Mali) and wrote:

Here are many shops and merchants, especially such as weave linen and cotton cloth. Corn, cattle, milk and butter this region yieldeth in great abundance. The rich king keeps a magnificent and well furnished court. Here are great stores of doctors, judges, priests and other learned men.

In 1600 a Dutch trader entering the city of Benin in west Africa wrote,

The city looks very big when you go into it. The houses in the town stand in good order as our Dutch houses are. These people are in no way inferior to the Dutch in cleanliness. They wash and scrub their houses so well that these are as polished as a looking glass.'

But at the beginning of the 18th century Africa was devastated by the slave trade and colonialism. Between 9 million and 13 million slaves were shipped across the Atlantic between 1451 and 1870. As capitalism developed in Western Europe, it shovelled more enslaved human beings into the plantations of America and the Caribbean to provide the wealth to ignite industrial growth. The historian Patrick Manning has calculated that the removal of 9 million slaves across the Atlantic required the capture of 21 million Africans. Millions of others fled their villages and went into hiding. This all occurred when the population of the entire continent was only around 50 million. The population of Africa south of the Sahara did not grow at all between 1750 and 1850. This was catastrophic for societies which were short of enough people to develop further. The slave trade also transformed African political life. It meant the development of militaristic regimes which could either hold out against the slavers or which would capture their neighbours and sell them. In the first great phase of the arms trade British traders alone shipped an average of 330,000 firearms a year to West Africa between 1750 and 1807.

As the slave trade began to wane, colonial invasion exploded. Before 1880 nearly all of Africa was ruled by Africans. Within a few years five European powers (and the king of the Belgians) had divided almost the entire continent between them. Previously Africans had fought Western invasions and often won—a sign that they were not 'primitive' societies. But by the 1880s the West had a significant lead in certain weapons, especially accurate rifles and efficient machine guns. These were used to destroy African states and rob their wealth. At the Congress of Berlin in 1884-85 the Great Powers carved up the African continent. Not a single African was invited to attend.

Once European powers seized these territories they were squeezed for profit, regardless of the cost in human suffering or economic devastation. One particularly well documented example is Congo, taken virtually as personal property by King Leopold II of the Belgians. In 1875 he caught the mood of other European powers and wrote, 'We must obtain a slice of the magnificent African cake.' Within ten years he had international rights to 2.5 million square kilometres of the Congo basin, with a wealth of natural resources and a population of up to 20 million. Leopold had posed as a great supporter of human rights, even sponsoring an anti-slavery conference. But in Congo there was soon clear evidence of a carnival of massacres behind the veneer of the king's civilising crusade. Leopold's companies used ruthless methods to force people to harvest rubber. Each district was assigned a quota of rubber to produce. Those who failed were beaten, whipped or butchered. The Belgian authorities sent out punitive expeditions to terrorise those who resisted. The killers would hack limbs off the dead, or sometimes off the living. A Baptist missionary described how the soldiers cut off the hands of people they had shot and took them to the authorities: 'These hands—the hands of men, woman and children—were placed in rows. This rubber traffic is steeped in blood.' Before the arrival of the rubber companies Congo's population was around 20 million. An official census taken in 1911 revealed only 8.5 million. Entire regions were wastelands.

Even where colonialism was not so instantly murderous, it pauperised Africa. Half of all the profits on the minerals of the Gold Coast (Ghana) made between 1920 and the end of colonialism were sent out of the country, mostly to Britain. There are those, Gordon Brown among them, who would now like to whitewash the reality of what happened under colonialism. He declared on a recent tour of Africa, 'The days of Britain having to apologise for its colonial history are over... We should be proud...of the empire'.[26]

It would be interesting to hear how Brown balances such grotesque claims with the latest research on the huge scale of atrocities committed by British forces during the Mau Mau rebellion in colonial Kenya in the 1950s: the 320,000 Kikuyu held in concentration camps, the 1,090 hangings, the terrorisation of villages, electric shocks, beatings and mass rape documented in Caroline Elkins's book *Britain's Gulag*—and well over 100,000 deaths. This was a time when British soldiers were paid five shillings (equal to $9 in today's money) for each Kikuyu male they killed, when they nailed the limbs of African guerrillas to crossroads posts. And when they were photographed holding severed heads of Malayan communist 'terrorists' in another war that cost over 10,000 lives.

The sense of continuity with today's Iraq could not be clearer.

Such evidence is a timely corrective to the comfortable British mythology that, in contrast to France and other European colonial powers, Britain decolonised in a peaceful and humane manner. It's not as if these end-of-empire episodes were isolated blemishes on a glorious record of freedom and good governance, as contemporary imperial torchbearers would have us believe. Britain's empire was in reality built on genocide, vast ethnic cleansing, slavery, rigorously enforced racial hierarchy and merciless exploitation. As the Cambridge historian Richard Drayton puts it: 'We hear a lot about the rule of law, incorruptible government and economic progress—the reality was tyranny, oppression, poverty and the unnecessary deaths of countless millions of human beings'.[27]

Africans fought colonialism, and won independence for most of the continent by 1965. But this did not mean economic freedom or an end to rule by the rich. Local elites replaced the imperialists, and the economies were still often dominated by the multinationals and big banks that had ruled before. Often the new rulers were people who had been trained by the West, such as Bokassa in Central African Republic, who had served in the French army, and Mobutu in Congo who was helped into power by the CIA. Nor was that all.

There were repeated armed interventions to prevent African governments carrying through policies that conflicted with the desires of western governments. These tore apart states and made 'governance' reflecting the will of the mass of people impossible.

French troops invaded one or other of their former colonies almost every year. De Gaulle sent in French troops to aid governments in Cameroon in 1960-1961, Mauritania in 1961, Gabon in 1962, Congo in 1960 and 1962, Chad between 1960 and 1963, Niger in 1963, Central African Republic in 1967 and Chad again in 1968. The interventions in the 1970s included Djibouti, Western Sahara, Central African Republic and Zaire. The 1980s saw forces intervene in Chad, Togo, Central African Republic and Ivory Coast. The next decade's low point was the forces sent to Rwanda—twice—to prop up the government that would encourage genocide in 1994. This century has already seen French troops deployed in Ivory Coast and Democratic Republic of Congo.

Yet in many ways these direct invasions were less deadly than the US support for murderous African forces that were deemed Cold War allies. During Angola's 27-year civil war, which claimed at least 350,000 lives, the US handed arms and money to Jonas Savimbi's right wing UNITA organisation. Savimbi—who led a brutal rebellion against the MPLA government, was hailed as a 'freedom fighter' by President Reagan and accorded a welcome befitting a head of state. Renamo, the right wing butchers in Mozambique, did not receive quite such overt backing. But there is no doubt that official and unofficial support from the US was crucial to keeping the civil, war going for two decades, with hundreds of thousands of victims. US and British support was also very important in maintaining the monstrous racist regime of apartheid South Africa.

Yet the only references to this barbarous record by the Africa Commission book for schools is to claim that 'previously the rest of the world has tried to help by intervening once war has broken out' and 'sometimes violence is also caused by acts by powerful foreign companies or by foreign policies'.

For it to say more would be to recognise that African state systems are a product of imperialism and the interests of the local rich, and that the G8 leaders are the last people who will genuinely fight corruption.

There is repression, lack of democracy and, yes, corruption in African countries. It is not going to be ended by the G8. What is required is democratic revolt, power to the poor, the tearing down of the one-party states and the rulers who maintain control through fear. And the people to do it are the very people who suffer from the neo-liberal policies associated with all the talk of governance—the workers, peasants and poor. The struggle against repressive states has to be linked to the struggle against neo-liberalism.

Aid and the 'war on terror'

The pure hypocrisy of the G8 when they say that aid to Africa depends on 'governance' is shown by the new form of 'conditionality' that goes with much aid today. In a return to the ethos of the 1960s, countries in many parts of the world are judged not so much on whether they hold any sort of democratic elections, or even if they allow markets to flourish, but on whether they are part of the 'coalition of the willing'. A 2004 report released by Christian Aid[28] said donors were now prioritising strategic interests rather than the needs of billions of poor and vulnerable people. An unpublished briefing document by another British agency, Action Aid,[29] also warned that development programmes were being subordinated to foreign policy: there was a 'rush to draw aid into the foreign policy sphere'. In addition some forms of military training and intelligence gathering were being considered as suitable for funding from aid budgets and some donors had cut spending elsewhere to meet their commitments for Iraq and Afghanistan.

The proposed European constitution sees not only development aid but also humanitarian assistance as subordinated to the overall common foreign and security policy. Within the European Union's structures themselves the development decisions now fall under the review of foreign ministers rather than of development ministers.

The decisions by the Bush administration on supplemental aid in March 2003 give a glimpse of what its new priorities are:

● For Turkey: $1 billion in economic aid, part of which may be used for up to $8.5 billion in loan guarantees, to be available through fiscal year 2005.

● For Jordan: $700 million in economic aid to 'help offset the economic dislocation and hardship brought on by a conflict with Iraq', and $406 million in military aid for border security, fighter aircraft, and airbases. Jordan will also receive part of a $1.4 billion defence department reimbursement to countries cooperating in the war on Iraq and the war on terror.

● For Israel: $1 billion in military aid, which reportedly may only be spent on the costs Israel has incurred preparing to defend itself from Iraqi attacks. Israel will also receive $9 billion in loan guarantees, to be available through fiscal year 2005.

● For Egypt: $300 million in economic aid to 'help offset the economic dislocation and hardship brought on by a conflict with Iraq'. Egypt may use part of this money for up to $2 billion in loan guarantees. The money will be available through fiscal year 2005.

● In addition, $308.1 million in military aid was directed to 15 countries. They include Bahrain and Oman, which are providing logistical support for the war, but also Poland, Hungary, the Czech Republic, Estonia, Latvia, Lithuania, Bulgaria, Romania, Slovakia, and Slovenia, whose main contribution to the war effort has been diplomatic support for the US (the prime minister of Slovenia later announced that his country had been listed erroneously as a member of the coalition, and said that Slovenia would not receive the $4.5 million in military aid that had been designated for it).

Similar bribery in the form of military aid had gone to ten countries of 'New Europe' which lined up behind the US during the crisis at the United Nations over a second resolution on war against Iraq.

There was also money for co-conspirators in the war on terror. This included:

● For Pakistan: $200 million in military and law enforcement aid, for border security and aircraft. A defence department official said that Pakistan was likely to get 'in the region of $1 billion' for costs it had incurred, specifically mentioning the costs of moving troops away from the border with India.

● Djibouti, the Philippines, and Colombia also shared the $308.1 million in military aid with the Gulf and Eastern European nations listed above. All are deemed to be participating in the war on terror.[30]

Clearly such packages (much of which comes from the aid budget) have nothing to do with poverty reduction and everything to do with military concerns. This is confirmed by other examples.

In the name of a 'whole-of-government' approach to global security, some donors are seeking to 'expand' the criteria for official development assistance. In Australia for example, NGOs are concerned about an overt shift to a new agenda that conflates the combating of terrorism and combating of poverty, as if they were the same thing. Australian aid now includes several initiatives for counter terrorism capacity building, including bilateral counter-terrorism programmes with Indonesia and the Philippines, a 'Peace and Security Fund' for the Pacific Island Countries, and a contribution to an Asia-Pacific Economic Cooperation (APEC) fund for counterterrorism capacity building.[31]

John Foster of the Canadian North-South Institute has shown that there are in fact two different movements over aid, with two quite different agendas: 'that devoted to the aggressive exercise of the power of the imperial superpower and its acolytes, and the rather phenomenal world-wide citizen response for peace and justice'.[32]

What is aid for?

The politics of aid require a much more sophisticated approach than simply saying 'give more'. Aid may be linked to pressure for neo-liberal change, it may be part of the 'war on terror', it may be part of a military alliance or a 'regime change' strategy. And some writers have argued that we need to look very critically at who gets the aid. Ales de Waal has written persuasively in this area. Looking at the Ethiopian crisis of 1984, he wrote:

> It is now no longer seriously disputed that the massive inflow of aid following Band Aid contributed more to the survival of the Ethiopian government, whose army was the main reason for the famine, than the famine-stricken peasantry. Large amounts of international food aid were diverted to the government militias. The flow of aid allowed the army to

maintain garrisons that would otherwise have surrendered and kept open roads that enabled the military to resupply its front line. Food aid distributions enticed young men forward who were forcibly conscripted. Perhaps most inside of relief aid into Africa for over a decade has contributed to the institutionalisation of violence.[33]

De Waal also showed a clear link between the aid-distributing agencies in Somalia in 1991 and the pressure for US military intervention there:

Somalia was a guinea-pig for post Cold War humanitarianism. It was the first time that the International Committee of the Red Cross hired armed guards. It was the first time that relief agencies such as the Save the Children Fund took such publicly outspoken positions criticising the absence of the United Nations. And finally, it was the first time that international agencies successfully called for Western military intervention.[34]

The false claim to be 'saving the starving' became a pretext for imperialist invasion.

The conditions attached to aid and the way it is structured into imperialism has led some activists, including some in Africa, to say that Africa is better off with no aid. Ghanaian activist Charles Abugre has said:

I'm simply making the point that the whole process of the aid system has created complete take-over that for me could not be anything other than imperialism. It leads me to the point to say that we are much better off with less aid than more. The only justification for international aid is that it acts as a compensatory measure for the net flow that happens from the continent. The resource transfer to outside the country is happening in many ways. Aid acts supposedly as a compensation for that, but it has become much worse—in fact aid is much more dangerous to our structures now.[35]

This is a potent argument. But although the slogan 'Africa does not need aid' rightly reflects the pride and self-belief of Africans, and their desire to be seen as fighters for justice rather than cases for charity, it misses out on an important element in the global struggle for change.

If all aid is, and will always be, a bad thing, then we cannot angrily counterpose the US arms budget, or world military spending [see Graph A] to the amounts provided for health and education in the poorer countries. If Gordon Brown refuses to increase the aid budget, then it is presumably a bonus. It is much more powerful to demand real distribution from rich to poor on an international and a national scale.

Clearly this would involve greatly increased aid, without strings. I agree with Eric Toussaint and Damien Millet when they write that after debt cancellation (for all developing countries, in full, without conditions) new sources of funding to improve the human condition should include, 'A tripling of Overseas Development Assistance to 0.7 percent of the GDP of the rich countries and paying it exclusively in the form of donations, as reparation for a historic, human, moral social, ecological and social debt, this time owed to the South'.[36] They estimate this would bring in $150 billion a year, enough to make a considerable difference to the lives of hundreds of millions of people—and we could fight for much more.

Make Poverty History calls for 'More Aid and Better Aid'. If that is to be meaningful it must mean transformed aid, real aid, more aid. It would not be a handout laced with poisonous additions, but a recompense for what capitalism has done to the Third World, and it will be won by a joint struggle of workers and peasants in the Global South and the North.

Graph A: World Military Expenditure, 1999-2003 [Source: SIPRI Yearbook 2004]

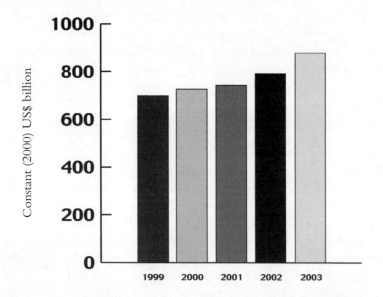

NOTES

1: Oxfam, *Paying the Price* (Oxfam, 2005), p6.

2: According to the The UN Millennium Project report. See Action Aid news release, 17 January 2005.

3: www.actionaidusa.org/ActionAidReal Aid.pdf

4: *Our Common Interest: What does the Africa Commission Say?*, available at www.commissionforafrica.org/english/schools/schools.html

5: A very good report by the World Development Movement on the IFF is available at http://www.wdm.org.uk/news/presrel/current/iff.htm

6: Sipri report, 2004.

7: Action Aid, 'Profile and Impact of DFID Technical Assistance', unpublished report, 2004.

8: 'Consultants Pocket $20 billion of Global Aid', *The Observer*, 29 May 2005.

9: For the full details see the excellent Christian Aid report, 'The Damage Done' (May 2005), pp 12-30.

10: As above, p23.

11: In 1991 a US aid shipment to Sudan was turned around a few miles from Port Sudan during a time of famine because the government had refused to back the US in the first Gulf War against Iraq. Not all 'conditionality' may be so obviously brutal, but it may be just as deadly.

12: Christian Aid, as above, p5.

13: World Development Movement, 'Dirty Aid, Dirty Water' (2005), http://www.wdm.org.uk/campaigns/aid/summary02.htm is a powerful resource.

14: Christian Aid, as above, p9.

15: Executive Summary, Report of the Africa Commission, p15.

16: Christian Aid, as above, pp10-11.

17: K Singh, 'Aid and Good Government' (January 2003), pp9-10.

18: The World Bank, *World Development Report 1997: The State in a Changing World* (Oxford University Press, 1997), p265.

19: M Szeftel, 'Misunderstanding African Politics: Corruption and the Governance Agenda', *Review of African Political Economy* no 76 (1998), p222.

20: Quoted in M Szeftel, as above, p227.

21: As above, p232.

22: As above, pp232-233.

23: K Singh, as above, p5.

24: J Warioba, 'Corruption and the State', *Soundings* 7, p198.

25: The only references to the European empires in the book for schools on the Africa Commission refers to the impact of the building of railways. Jeffrey Sachs' book, *The End of Poverty* (Penguin, 2005), is, in this respect, slightly more honest.

26: Quoted, for instance, by Seamus Milne in *Le Monde Diplomatique*, May 2005.

27: S Milne, 'Britain: Imperial Nostalgia', *Le Monde Diplomatique* (English edition), May 2005, http://mondediplo.com/2005/05/02empire

28: Christian Aid, 'The Politics of Poverty: Aid in the New Cold War' (May 2004).

29: 'Terror Puts the Freeze on Aid', *The Guardian*, 10 May 2004. Go to http://www.guardian.co.uk/comment/story/0,3604,1213622,00.html

30: Federation of American Scientists, 'Arms, Aid, and the War with Iraq, 2003', has all these figures. http://www.fas.org/gulfwar2/at/

31: Reality of Aid Report 2004, www.realityofaid.org , political overview, p5.

32: J Foster, 'Crisis Time, Repossessing Democratic Space' (2003), http://www.nsi-ins.ca/english/pdf/foster_reality_of_aid_paper.pdf

33: A de Waal, 'Humanitarianism Unbound: The Context of the Call for Military Intervention in Africa', *Trocaire Development Review* (1995), available at http://www.sas.upenn.edu/African_Studies/Hornet/milt_intv.html

34: As above.

35: 'Globalisation and Sub-Saharan Africa', international experts' meeting, European Parliament, Brussels, April 2004: www.tni.org/africa_docs/abugre.pdf

36: D Millet and E Toussaint, *Who Owes Who?* (Zed Books, 2005), pp154-155.

Africa: 'There is fire here'

Peter Dwyer

Towards the end of the 1980s and early 1990s strikes, riots and demonstrations forced 19 one-party states in Africa to institutionalise a democratic opposition. But the headlong rush into neo–liberalism and continued structural adjustment policies somewhat de–legitimised the 'birth of democracy' . The 2002 United Nations Development Report shows how between 1990 and 2001 living standards fell in Angola, Brunei, Burundi, Cameroon, Central African Republic, Chad, Congo, Djibouti, Gabon, Guinea-Bissau, Kenya, Madagascar, Niger, Nigeria, Rwanda, Sao Tome and Principe, Sierra Leone, Zambia and Zimbabwe.

This fuelled political instability and armed conflicts, but also gave rise to a new deepening and widening of popular struggle in the late 1990s. Workers and trade unions together with a variety of popular forces fought regimes hanging on to power in Burkina Faso, Burundi, Cameroon, Chad, Central African Republic, Comoros, Congo, Cote d'Ivoire, Gabon, Ghana,

Guinea, Kenya, Lesotho, Madagascar, Mali, Mauritania, Nigeria, Swaziland and Zaire. In 2001 alone there were popular and working class resistance (strikes, demonstrations, protests, walkouts, etc) in Benin, Cameroon, Central African Republic, Congo-Brazzaville, Congo, Cote d'Ivoire, Djibouti, Gambia, Kenya, Lesotho, Mozambique, Namibia, Niger, Sierra Leone, Swaziland, Zambia and Zimbabwe.

These were often what might be called working class struggles; but some grassroots movements, particularly those rooted in the rural areas, took on the dimensions of ethnic, tribal and religious struggles, albeit equally concerned to overthrow the existing regimes.

The most explicit 'anti-neoliberal' campaigns are in South Africa. Since the election in April 1994 (and subsequent re-elections in June 1999 and April 2004), the ANC's 'long walk to freedom' has metamorphosed into a quickstep to neo-liberalism with what is effectively a home-grown structural adjustment policy that has met with anti-privatisation strikes and protests. Organisations like the Anti-Privatisation Forum have emerged organically from a need to defend working class communities under attack from housing evictions and water and electricity cut-offs.

Explicit anti-capitalism is much less evident in the other major sub-Saharan economy and society, Nigeria. But traces of it can be found, particularly in the opposition to multinational corporations (MNCs) such as Shell International, and the struggle of the Ogoni people. Widespread demonstrations broke out as the price of fuel was doubled in December 1998 and January 1999 under pressure from the IMF. Nigeria's trade unions allied with Lagos residents in a mass strike aimed at reversing another IMF-mandated oil price increase, which led to the doubling of transport fares in June 2000. This last had the effect of cutting short a visit by US Treasury secretary Larry Summers. These were not simply 'bread-and-butter', economic strikes, but intensely political actions.

Strikes and protests took place in Mali in March 2001 in response to the IMF-inspired deregulation of petrol prices, and there were strikes in Mali and Cote D'Ivoire against the privatisation of Air Afrique at the behest of the World Bank.

Social forums in Africa

There exist a range of groups steadfastly campaigning, with few resources, against neo-liberalism. They include campaigns around HIV-AIDS by the

Treatment Action Campaign in South Africa, debt and social forum activists in Zimbabwe, ongoing campaigns against Shell in parts of the Nigerian Delta and campaigns aimed at World Bank projects including the Chad-Cameroon oil pipeline. In April 2005 a small but well organised Anti-Privatisation Forum based in Accra forced British multinational Biwater to pull out of the bidding for Ghanaian water. Jubilee South (debt) groups exist in Malawi, South Africa and Zambia.

Africa-wide social forums took place in Mali in 2001 and Ethiopia in 2002. They were the first substantial conferences since the era of liberation to combine progressive NGOs and social movements from all parts of the continent, and were followed by African Social Forum sessions in Johannesburg (August 2002) and Addis Ababa (January 2003). The first ever Southern Africa Social Forum (SASF) in Lusaka, Zambia, on 9-11 November 2003, brought together several hundred activists from social movements, trade unions, NGOs, churches, women's organisations and other groups. Most attendees were from Zambia and Zimbabwe, with a significant presence from South Africa and small numbers from Namibia, Botswana, the Democratic Republic of Congo, Angola, Malawi, Mauritius and Swaziland. The demonstration that launched the forum had the unifying global slogan of 'Now is our time' and a Zimbabwean song which says that 'the drum is beaten in the morning, at the start of the battle'—the battle against capitalism. There were differences between the more moderate NGOs who seek to lobby governments to lessen the impact of neo-liberalism and radical social movements that seek to challenge the structure of the global economy. But the forum was an important step forward for linking up Africa-wide resistance

The World Social Forum in Africa in 2007 offers the potential to consolidate these initiatives and to draw into them more radical activists from African social movements, so not allowing the priorities of more moderate NGOs to dominate.

Who are the Commission For Africa?

The commission was chaired by **Bob Geldof** and headed by prime minister **Tony Blair**, chancellor of the exchequer **Gordon Brown**, and minister for international development **Hilary Benn**.

It also included: **Michel Camdessus**, who as managing director of the IMF until February 2000 was behind scores of Structual Adjustment Programmes

Canadian finance minister **Ralph Goodale**, who represents Canada, Ireland and a group of Caribbean countries on the International Monetary and Financial Committee (IMFC);

Nancy Kassebaum Baker, former US Republican senator for Kansas, married to Howard Baker, Ronald Reagan's chief of staff, whose Baker Plan to save the US banks increased Third World debt by 20 percent in two years;

President **Benjamin Mkapa** of Tanzania, who has consistently steered Tanzania towards reconciliation with the IMF and the World Bank;

Prime minister **Meles Zenawi** of Ethiopia, who has driven Ethiopia towards the full adoption of World Bank and IMF programmes.

Trevor Manuel, architect of the neo-liberalisation of economic policy in South Africa since 1994, first as minister of trade and industry, then as minister of finance;

Linah Mohohlo, Botswana Central Bank governor, who has worked for the IMF, and serves on the boards of major corporations in Botswana and abroad;

Tidjiane Thiam, a senior executive of global insurance giant Aviva, which owns Norwich Union; a member of the World Bank Institute's External Advisory Committee, 1998 World Economic Forum (Davos) 'Global Leader for Tomorrow' and member of the 1999 Davos 'Dream Cabinet';

Kingsley Amoako, who went from the World Bank to the UN Economic Commission for Africa;

Dr Anna Kajumulo Tibaijuka, the convenor of Tanzania's Local Entrepreneurs Initiative (TALE), a voluntary group mobilising Tanzanians to form joint venture companies with overseas investors, and a director of a number of private companies dedicated to 'encouraging entrepreneurship in the marketing of agricultural commodities';

Mr Fola Adeola, a director of Guaranty Trust Bank Plc, and deputy general manager of the Continental Merchant Bank Limited (1986-1990);

Ji Peiding, NPC Standing Committee member and vice-chairman of the Foreign Affairs Committee, China;

Dr William S Kalema, 'leader of the Ugandan private sector', chairman of the Development Finance Company of Uganda and of its related financial institutions, including DFCU Bank, a commercial bank, and DFCU Leasing, the leading leasing company in Uganda;

The Director of Policy and Research and probably author of the Commission report is **Sir Nicholas Stern**. He was responsible for Russia and Eastern Europe at the European Bank for Reconstruction and Development in the 1990s, replaced the sacked Joseph Stiglitz as World Bank Chief Economist in 2001, and then became head of the British government's economic service.

Trading on poverty
Jacob Middleton

In 1980, median income of the richest 10 percent of countries was 77 times that of the poorest 10 percent. By 2002, this gap had increased to 122 times. The number of poor people rose between 1987 and 1998, and any gains in poverty reduction were 'relatively small and geographically isolated',[1] with the eastern seaboard of China accounting for the bulk of recent improvements.

The age of neo-liberalism, emerging in the 1970s from the wreckage of post-war 'Keynesianism', has been one of massively increased inequalities and staggering levels of deprivation alongside equally huge flows of global capital and the transfer of enormous wealth to a tiny minority.

This global economy is policed by a combination of international bodies, comprising the old Bretton Woods institutions, the World Bank group and the International Monetary Fund (IMF), and the newer World Trade Organisation (WTO), which work closely together to regulate and enforce the complex relationships between trade, investment, and economic growth. These have been increasingly drawn under a 'neo-liberal agenda', described by Robert Wade as 'deregulation, privatisation, flexibilisation—although not the elimination of agricultural subsidies or the lifting of restrictions on the cross-border movements of labour'.[2] The 'Washington Consensus', as this apparently inviolable set of policies became known, demanded strict fiscal orthodoxy (ie balanced budgets and low tax levels on the rich), and a thoroughgoing commitment to the free market from impoverished Southern economies. Often this was administered in the bluntest form through the now-notorious Structural Adjustment Programmes, imposed by the IMF on debt-ridden economies to meet the demands of Northern banks, eager to squeeze interest payments from the poorest people on earth.

The situation has hardly changed, even though a supposedly less rigorous approach is now claimed to be in operation, with talk of a 'multilateral' and 'consensus-based' approach to development. IMF conditions still hang over governments like those in Brazil, Ecuador and many others.

GATS and the WTO

The General Agreement on Trade in Services (GATS) has been in force since 1996, signed and sealed at the end of the 'Uruguay Round' of the General Agreement on Tariffs and Trade (GATT) talks that also created the WTO. GATS sits alongside two other major agreements: TRIPS on 'intellectual property' (patents and copyrights), and TRIMS, covering investment measures. Like them, it is explicit in its commitments to a neo-liberal economic order. It is designed to facilitate the opening of markets for services, with penalty clauses and sanctions potentially enabled against governments found breaching GATS regulations.

The rules of the agreement are little more than a list of ways in which signatory governments should not interfere with the market. Article XIX commits governments to 'achieving a progressively higher level of liberalisation…[and] increasing the general level of specific commitments undertaken by Members'.[3] This makes it unique among WTO treaties in expressly calling for a continual expansion of its powers.

The vision behind the document is that the large numbers of excluded services will be gradually reduced through negotiating rounds, bringing wider and wider zones of the economy into the free market. It is of particular concern for two reasons. First, because the adequate provision of services is essential for economic development—from necessities like electricity or clean water, to health and education. Insisting on the private provision of such vital services can be, and often has been, little more than a licence to extort for larger firms. Water companies have been particularly notorious with their attempts to significantly increase the bills paid by their often extremely poor customers in the developing world. Second, because the open-ended and expansionary nature of the GATS, combined with the sectors it covers, ensures it reaches far further into public life than conventional trade agreements. It necessarily dictates a future course of action for governments, severely restricting their decision-making powers, and so has serious consequences for democracy. Governments' abilities to regulate multinational corporations, in particular, are severely curtailed.

The WTO was established in January 1995 as a replacement for the earlier GATT negotiations. GATT talks had been taking place in a series of lengthy 'rounds' since 1947. These rounds of meetings were designed to enable countries to bargain over access to each others' markets; for relationships between the developed North and the developing South, it was envisioned that 'special and differential treatment' would apply, in which Southern economies were allowed preferential access to the North, without needing to reduce their own tariff barriers. This reflected a common view of economic development at the time, in which underdeveloped countries could build up their industries behind 'tariff walls', until they were able to compete with developed economies in the North.

The WTO significantly altered this situation. 'Special and differential treatment' was redefined as 'merely allowing developing countries longer adjustment periods in which to implement neo-liberal policies'.[4] The pressure from Northern multinationals, banks and governments has been to make these 'adjustment periods' as short as possible. The WTO has teeth: by imposing fines and other penalties on member countries, it attempts to enforce the rules it has devised. They bite, however, far more convincingly against smaller economies, less able to circumvent or ignore WTO rules if needed.

The WTO is theoretically a neutral, 'rules-based' and multilateral body at which trading partners collectively agree on the common good for the world economy. After all, the neo-liberal catechism tells us that freer trade benefits everyone: so who could possibly object? Clearly, many do. Aileen Kwa suggests that it is the WTO's *lack* of formal internal structures that most aid the interests of the powerful.[5] 'Consensus' is manufactured through an unseemly combination of arm-twisting, bribery and outright bullying. Negotiations at the WTO have until recently been dominated by the notorious 'Green Room' meetings. The larger member economies would meet in private—sometimes with carefully-selected smaller nations—agree policy among themselves, and then present these *faits accompli* to the rest of the membership.

Anger over this process was one of the major factors behind the developing countries' walk-out at the Seattle WTO meeting in autumn 1999. The walk-out, encouraged by the thousands of demonstrators outside the conference and divisions between the US and the European Union, brought about the collapse of the WTO's negotiations. The organisation has still not managed to recover, and the 2003 talks in Cancun were broken up by the G20 group of larger developing nations. They walked out after it became clear that the 'Quad' economies—the US, Japan, EU and Canada—would not budge on removing agricultural subsidies. The so called 'Doha Development Agenda', a face-saving exercised pushed through at the previous year's WTO meeting, seemed to be barely worth the paper it was written on.

Further talks are scheduled for December this year, in Hong Kong. NGOs are already criticising attempts by the EU and the US to repackage their agricultural subsidies so they appear legitimate under WTO rules. The possibility of a further stalemate for the Northern ruling classes is high; disguised behind the fanfare for Brown's plans for Africa is a frantic attempt to soft-soap recalcitrant Southern leaders into accepting neo-liberalism with a human face: slightly stronger words on poverty reduction, dubious commitments to increased aid, and, if all else fails, the hope of splitting and dividing the opposition within the WTO.

The emergence of a developing country bloc with sufficient power to disrupt the activities of the Quad has led some to believe that the G20 provides the key to ending the South's many woes. Combined with the turn towards bilateral trading agreements among the larger developing nations—such as those conducted between Venezuela and China—and the reappearance of nationalist leaders in the developing world, like Kirchner in Argentina, high hopes are being placed in the construction of an anti-neoliberal bloc, uniting Southern ruling classes, workers and peasants against the North's neo-liberal predations. In reality, the leading G20 powers operate in the interests of agrarian and industrial capitalists inside their countries (for example, the sugar, beef and soya beans barons of Brazil, Argentina's big agrarian capitalists, South Africa's white wine producers, the Birla and Tata family business empires in India, China's multimillion-aires). These want to advance their own positions within capitalism's international pecking order, which means pushing for rules that only allow them to break into advanced country markets. Success in building their exports will often be at the expense of the mass of people in their own countries—as when increased beef and soya exports from Brazil involve trying to take land off the country's indigenous people and peasant farmers. It can also mean trampling on the interests of countries that are poorer than them—as *The Observer* reported at the time of Cancun, 'Many African countries believe that the G23 is primarily concerned with access to western markets while small countries like Malawi, which has torn down all barriers to outside trade, are more preoccupied with protecting their own fragile businesses'.[6]

From this brief narrative, we can see at least three different solutions to the difficulties faced by developing countries: the one favoured by the neo-liberal hegemony, now given a fresh, new 'poverty-reducing' gloss by such figures as Jeffrey Sachs;[7] the beginnings of a turn towards what was once known as 'national development' among the South; and the very faintest glimmerings of a radical, anti-capitalist path. Each of these needs to be assessed against the development of global trade in recent years.

Trade in services and manufactured goods

Global trade expanded by about 6.5 percent a year over the 1990s, about twice as fast as the expansion in global output. In other words, the world economy was becoming increasingly biased towards international trade. Despite constant urgings by the WTO towards greater liberalisation, it is interesting to note that underdeveloped countries are among the most open to competition anywhere in the world. African economies are far more open to trade than developed. On average, exports account for 30 percent of African countries' GDP, compared to 20 percent across the developed OECD nations.[8]

Trade in commercial services expanded faster still over the decade, growing from a small fraction to about one-fifth of global trade in 2003. However, after allowing for a considerably slower growth in the value of transport traded, growth in total services trade has been similar to that in manufactures and primary commodities. Global trade remains strongly biased towards the 'tangible' goods produced by manufacturing, mining and agriculture. Great efforts by institutions like the WTO to all but compel trade in services have had little impact on this overall pattern. It is therefore unlikely, given only average growth in services trade generally, that developing countries will benefit from moves towards further liberalisation.[9]

Well-known successes, such as the expansion of India's business services industry through call centres and IT support, are not likely to be repeated in such global market conditions, since demand for services generally has not expanded by nearly as much. Encouraging developing countries to move into trading services, as is urged by the GATS treaty, is to encourage them into a zero-sum game, poorer nations being forced to compete against each other in low value-added service industries while leaving the fast-expanding sectors to richer, developed nations. For comparison, about half of world commercial services exports are accounted for by Western European nations. With the US and Japan, these countries entirely dominate the sector. China, the largest developing country services exporter, accounted for just 2.5 percent of the total trade.

Yet these developing countries are growing importers of commercial services. China recorded a deficit in commercial services trades in 2003, while even India managed only a tiny surplus over the year. The fastest growing imports are among those dominated by developed country multinationals: computer and information services, financial services, and insurance. Developing countries simply do not get a look in. The ongoing negotiations in GATS, where massive pressure is applied to Southern economies to deregulate and privatise, will simply create further opportunities for these multinationals in expanding markets, while exposing Southern economies to cut-throat competition in those growing less rapidly.

If we rule out a plausible, free-market path to development through services provision, we could turn instead towards the manufacturing sector. China is particularly heralded in this regard, manufacturing exports growing spectacularly over the last decade to make it the world's third biggest exporter in 2004.[10] This has not, however, been achieved by following the WTO's preferred route; indeed, China only became a full member of the WTO in 2002, still strictly controls capital flows, centrally-manages a large chunk of its external trade, and maintains a strong system of state-owned heavy manufacturing industry.[11] It is, additionally, impossible to separate China's current account surpluses from the US's burgeoning trade deficit: for as long as US consumers have access to easy credit, funded principally by East Asian investors, they can maintain high levels of domestic imports. The balance across the Pacific economy is precarious, however, and the weaknesses of the US economy are becoming increasingly apparent while there are many predictions that the Chinese economy is going to make a 'hard landing' from its runaway boom.

If we break down the growth of manufactured goods exports over the last decade, the biggest gains have been trade in office and telecoms equipment, which expanded at twice the average rate for manufactures. This industry now accounts for 12.1 percent of world merchandise exports. It is dominated by a few larger multinationals, overwhelmingly based in the North, and places high demands for capital and technological expertise on producers. Unprotected, and without substantial assistance, manufacturers in the great majority of Third World countries, especially in Africa, are ill-placed to compete. Areas where the less developed countries retain some comparative advantage—lower technology and labour-intensive sectors in the main—have expanded far less rapidly. Textiles and iron and steel products recorded below average trade growth in the 1990s, and showed a significant decline in their share of world trade over the decade.

For small economies facing a vast world market, it is the trends in growth elsewhere that dominate; they are, however, heavily biased against the less developed world. The neo-liberal strategy of removing barriers to trade and promoting exploitation of comparative advantages aims, at best, to promote the expansion of industries currently undergoing relative decline. At worst, the promotion of basic manufacturing locks less developed countries into intensively competitive, low value-added markets with the terms of trade shifting against them.

Agricultural trade

Agricultural trade, by value, grew globally on average by 2.4 percent each year between 1990 and 2002. This is somewhat faster than over the preceding 20 years, but is noticeably slower than growth in manufactures and services. For less developed economies, the prospects for continued growth through agriculture are not promising.

Most African countries are dependent on primary commodity exports, in some cases exceptionally so: 18 states were dependent on three or less primary produce exports for 70 percent or more of their export earnings throughout the 1990s.[12] With the share of agricultural goods in merchandise exports declining, economies heavily biased towards agricultural production become still more dependent on high and stable agricultural prices. In practice, primary commodities have experienced a long-term decline in their terms of trade relative to manufactured goods, extending over several decades [see Chart A]. This has discouraged investment while simultaneously exposing (especially smaller) producers to greater market risks.

More importantly, the structure of the agricultural trade itself is shifting over time. Exports of processed agricultural products grew significantly faster than other primary food exports, their share of agricultural trade rising from 42 percent in 1990 to 48 percent by 2002. For example, trade in beverages, which are considered to be 100 percent processed, recorded an above average expansion over 1990-2002, at 4.8 percent, while the trade in natural fibres, hides, and skins (considered to be entirely unprocessed) stagnated or even declined [see Chart B].

This pattern is almost certainly linked to the increased concentration of capital within agribusiness. Multinationals like Cargill and Monsanto have expanded horizontally by acquiring other businesses engaged in similar trades to themselves, and vertically by moving into different stages of the food manufacturing process. The attempt to patent crops, with which Monsanto is most closely associated, is one extreme end of this pattern, imposing direct control over the most elementary unit of production. Direct retail sales, at the other end of the agricultural business, remains largely in the hands of specialised retailers, themselves increasingly vast.

The further liberalisation of the agricultural export market is likely to benefit only the large agricultural multinationals able to exert increased control over almost the entirety of food production, distribution and marketing. They control the most lucrative, highest value-added stages of production, principally around canning and processing, and are steadily encroaching even on the activities of the direct producers. The capital and technological requirements for entering such production are prohibitive, especially if tariff liberalisation has removed an obvious source of revenues for less developed economies wishing to move into this industry. It is, in other words, a similar picture to that painted earlier for manufacturing and services industries, brightened only by a few highly exceptional relative successes,[13] feted beyond plausibility by the WTO.[14]

This strongly suggests that so called 'level playing fields' in international trade, and even attempts to smooth out the bumps, are of no help to developing countries. In the first case, many biases remain in the legal framework beneath apparent equality; as we have seen, the WTO functions as anything but a gathering of trading 'partners', more as an assembly of

Chart A: Decline in African Agricultural Commodities Terms of Trade, 1960-2000

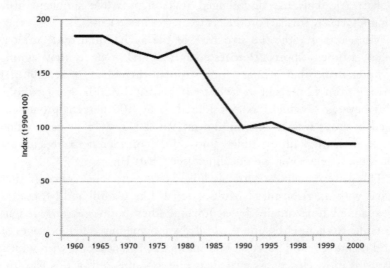

Source: UNCTAD

Chart B: World and African Exports 1948-2003

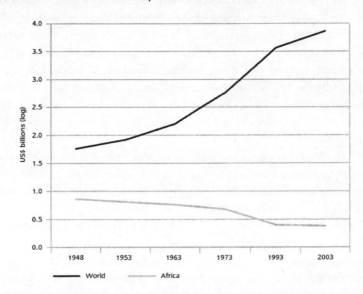

Source: WTO, 2003

Mafioso. Demands by the global justice movement to remove such overt biases, especially around subsidies for Northern agribusinesses, are wholly legitimate. But the problems for developing countries are far more pervasive than this.

As even Jeffrey Sachs has noted:

> If Europe cut back on its subsidies for staple crops (wheat, maize), the results for Africa could well be negative, not positive, since Africa is a food importing region... Africa will unambiguously benefit from liberalisation of trade in tropical products (for example, cotton, sugar, bananas), but subsidies for tropical products are only a small part of the reported $300 billion in artificial support for farmers in rich countries. In short, liberalise trade in agriculture but...the benefits will accrue overwhelmingly to the large food exporters: the United States, Canada, Argentina, Brazil and Australia.[15]

And, in a rare moment of honesty, the Commission for Africa recognises that freeing agricultural trade would probably lead to an increase in food prices—and hardship—in Africa in the short term, although insisting on long term benefits. 'If substantial progress is made with agricultural liberalisation in the Doha Round', it admits, 'world food prices may increase in the short-term, and some African food-importing countries could face a considerable adjustment challenge'.[16]

None of this, however, has stopped the apostles of free trade declaring it the solution to world poverty, with the BBC news, for instance, proclaiming every move to liberalise trade as a 'victory' for the anti-poverty movement.

The structure of world demand and the inability to acquire capital and technological resources to compete on even a level playing field cripple the countries of the global South. We may stop bribing the referee, but expecting a single developing economy to successfully take on the developed world is like expecting an under-12s' team to beat Arsenal.

The many 'achievements' of neo-liberalism

Oxfam has produced convincing evidence to demonstrate that movements towards greater liberalisation are correlated with lower growth.[17] Far from free trade and liberalisation automatically bringing economic growth, it is almost without exception the case that countries experiencing rapid growth and modernisation have done so under thoroughgoing protectionist systems: South Korea and Japan are good examples. The record left by three decades of continual appeals to liberalise and privatise, by contrast, is extraordinarily weak.

Meanwhile, the much-vaunted 'trickle-down' effect appears to be a 'trickle-up'. It is held that privatisation and liberalisation will unleash entrepreneurial talent, enriching a few massively but eventually benefiting all. The opposite has occurred: the rich became richer, as we have seen; but poverty also increased. The UN Commission on Trade and Development, in a recent report, summarise their figures as showing:

> Poverty is increasing unambiguously in those economies that have adopted the most open trade regime and in those that have continued with the most closed trade regime. But in between these extremes, there is a tendency for poverty to be declining in those countries that have liberalised their trade regime to a lesser extent, and for poverty to be increasing in those countries that have liberalised their trade regime more.[18]

We have already noted that the most liberalised region on earth is sub-Saharan Africa. The appalling record there speaks for itself.

New Labour, trade and development

The manifest failings of neo-liberalism have led some to extended soul-searching. In recent years, critics such as Joseph Stiglitz, former chief economist at the World Bank, have emerged from inside the great global institutions to condemn past failures, and demand a new course.[19] Yet what has emerged, among some of those most committed to the failed Washington Consensus, is a neo-liberalism, mark 2: plenty of breast-beating about the plight of the poor; targets and promises to end world poverty; but the same steadfast commitment to liberalisation and the tacit support for Northern multinationals. New Labour, as in so much else, has been a pioneer of the technique, developing its own international 'Third Way' very soon after arriving in office.

Margaret Beckett, the then trade secretary, made New Labour's ambitions for the global South quite plain within months of Blair's 1997 election victory. Writing in the *Financial Times*, she claimed New Labour would 'continue developing the conditions, at home and abroad, in which

British business can thrive... Britain's businesses need to be able to trade throughout the world's markets as easily as they can in home markets without facing high tariffs, discriminatory regulations or unnecessarily burdensome procedures'.[20]

Changes of ministerial personnel notwithstanding, New Labour's commitment to full trade liberalisation has remained constant. Their July 2004 White Paper on trade re-stated Beckett's ambitions, saying they would push 'at the international policy level to ensure any distortions created by other government interventions are minimised so that the UK can compete in global markets'.[21]

The link between this free-market programme and supposed 'development' was made explicit by Blair himself, speaking at the World Economic Forum in 2000. Defying overwhelming evidence to the contrary, Blair told this august gathering of the self-confessed 'global elite' that 'trade liberalisation is the only sure route' to economic growth for developing countries.[22]

Blair's brainchild, the Department for International Development (DFID), has adroitly promoted these interests, pushing further trade liberalisation under the guise of eradicating poverty. Clare Short made a now-notorious speech to business leaders, back in April 1999, bluntly stating the government's case:

> The assumption that our moral duties and business interests are in conflict is now demonstrably false... I am very keen that we maximise the impact of our shared interest in business and development by working together in partnership... We bring access to other governments and influence in the multilateral system—such as the World Bank and IMF... You are well aware of the constraints business faces in the regulatory environment for investment in any country... Your ideas on overcoming these constraints can be invaluable when we develop our country strategies. We can use this understanding to inform our dialogue with governments and the multilateral institutions on the reform agenda.[23]

The DFID's role in promoting a revised Washington Consensus could not be clearer. It has also acted as a support for Gordon Brown's rediscovered plans for Africa. After promising debt relief at the G8 summit 1999, with further promises on poverty reduction at subsequent G8 jamborees, Brown is claiming, once again, that he has only the very deepest concern for the underdeveloped world, and Africa in particular. He and the DFID have assiduously courted some of the larger NGOs in raising support for a package of initiatives to be presented at this year's G8 summit in Gleneagles. These include the International Finance Facility, the Commission for Africa and fresh attempts towards meeting the Millennium Development Goals target for aid and debt cancellation. The Make Poverty History campaign has been flattered with government time.

As Katharine Quarmby wrote in the *New Statesman*:

Both Blair and Brown have been keen to be associated with Make Poverty History, using political events as a forum. When Bono spoke at last year's Labour party conference, he congratulated the PM and Chancellor on their work for the campaign, dubbing them the 'Lennon and McCartney' of poverty reduction. Some groups involved in MPH were horrified. John Hilary, director of campaigns and policy at War on Want, was in the audience. 'When Bono said that, many NGO leaders who were there put their heads in their hands and groaned,' he recalls. 'It's just not useful, that kind of celebrity endorsement. In fact, it's a killer blow for us. To see the smiles on the faces of Gordon Brown and Tony Blair! This is exactly what they want— they want people to believe that this is their crusade, without actually changing their policy.' Oxfam's Adrian Lovett admits: 'It was a bit cheesy, but there were tough passages in the speech as well. You have to capture people's imaginations.'

Part of the closeness is in the exchange of personnel. This is not new. Frank Judd, a former director of Oxfam, became a Labour peer and spoke for the party on international development in the Lords in the 1990s. But the links have become more intimate under this government. Shriti Vadera, who advises Brown on international development, is an Oxfam trustee. Justin Forsyth was director of policy and campaigns at Oxfam before joining the Downing Street Policy Unit to advise Blair on the issue. When Oxfam recently advertised for Forsyth's successor, two of the four candidates called for vetting were either current or former special advisers. Vadera was on the interview panel. This process worries the likes of Mike Sansom, co-ordinator of the social justice organisation African Initiatives: 'NGOs have been rightly critical of the revolving door between business and government, but the same has now become true of NGOs and government.'

Links are similarly friendly on policy. On issues such as trade, Oxfam's position is much closer to the government's than other groups. When it published a report three years ago that advocated liberalisation of markets in wealthy nations and identified market access as a key mechanism for eradicating poverty, the line was strikingly similar to Gordon Brown's. Many NGOs were appalled, particularly as this was in the run-up to the crucial World Trade Organisation meeting in Cancun in 2003. Martin Drewery, head of campaigns at Christian Aid, explains: 'The reason Oxfam got a bad press in the NGO world was not because anyone disagreed that northern markets should be opened, but it was not the most important thing—and in practice the richest countries would not grant that access unilaterally and poor countries would pay a massive price for it'.[24]

Covered by the fetching new wrapping is much the same neo-liberal agenda New Labour has always pursued. The appeals to 'level playing fields' are particularly alarming: development in the South requires as a minimum precisely the opposite of a level playing field. While New Labour no longer uses formal tied aid—aid given on the condition it is used to buy specific goods from the purchaser—its use of 'globalised aid', aid tied to more general liberalisation, is increasing (as Charlie Kimber shows in his article). Debt relief itself has become another stick to beat the Southern economies into neo-liberal line: the promise of debt cancellation is held out, if an economy liberalises on demand. Campaigners should categorically reject such formulae.

'Fair trade' and national development

Two alternative strategies have become popular within the movement. Sales of Fairtrade labelled products rose 51 percent over 2004 to £140m.[25] The Fairtrade Foundation, responsible for administering the labelling system, aims to ensure a 'fair and stable price' paid to primary producers for their products as well as imposing strict environmental standards, and boasts of its success in promoting brand awareness and maximising revenues, while aiding poor farmers.

The scheme is becoming something of a victim of its own success, however. Multinationals like Nestlé, themselves responsible for the exceptionally poor conditions that rule Southern agriculture, are keen to move in on an expanding market. Those farmers taking part in a fairtrade marketing scheme may have some protection against the sudden fluctuations in price that mark the primary commodity markets. But the scheme offers little to the great majority who are excluded. The only hope for these is an expansion of the global market for the products they produce as result of rising living standards for the world's poor as a whole, not just for a few select groups lucky enough to be contacted by fair trade organisations. The poverty of millions of coffee farmers world-wide is the result of coffee output growing much more rapidly than the market for it ever since countries like Vietnam turned to coffee production. Yet there is no shortage of desire for people world wide to drink coffee. The trouble is that poverty in many countries in Latin America and the Middle East where coffee is the preferred hot drink are too poor to buy it at existing prices, let alone pay the higher price needed to overcome the poverty of the coffee farmers. Fair Trade, like charity, provides some relief for a few of the poor, but not any answer for the great majority. For that there has to be a transformation of the whole system in which the coffee producers live and work.

Gathering momentum is a distinctive shift towards a belief in what used to be known as 'national development'. Schemes for 'import substitution', replacing imported goods with the same domestic commodities, rigorous systems of tariffs and quotas, and plans for centralised, state-led mobilisations of investment capital were all once dominant in intellectual circles in developing nations. These fell away under the neo-liberal onslaught, but are currently enjoying something of a revival, in a new, 'globalised' form. The rise of the G20 especially, its cohesiveness in facing down the Quad nations and its use of bilateral trading agreements have all led to great enthusiasm for the creation of an alternative trading system among the developing world. Rather than national economic development, pursued through protectionism, this sees an internationalised version of the same as the route to economic growth and poverty reduction: larger developing countries are able to band together to exclude the developed, and so promote their own growth.

After nearly 30 years of neo-liberal hegemony, it is difficult not to see talk of protection and planned development as an advance. However, the weaknesses in this scheme reproduce those of its earlier incarnations, with some additional problems. The creation of stable and long-lasting trading blocs in the South is unlikely: not only are serious efforts being made to break up unity among Southern governments, with Brown's plans for Africa leading the way, the G20 ties together economies that are greatly dissimilar in terms of size, GDP per capita and so on, but rather too similar in competition over markets.[26] The bloc is fundamentally weak. Only the exceptional political conditions have made it sustainable at successive WTO meetings.

More importantly, national economic development fell apart when faced with the immense task of raising more than a handful of less developed countries to compete on the world stage in anything beyond crude manufactured goods and primary produce. The technological and capital 'bar' for entry into the world market was set so high as to all but exclude most developing countries. Import substitution, for its part, was fatally weakened by the huge gap between cheap, higher-quality Northern imports and expensive, poorer-quality Southern competitors, particularly with the spread of technologies too expensive to develop except by the biggest states and multinationals. The relics of state-led manufacturing schemes littered across the global South are tribute to this; though we should always note that the neo-liberal alternative has usually proved to be markedly worse for large sections of the population.

The gap between North and South in general is now extraordinarily large. For a brief period, a small group of economies concentrating on export-led growth, clustered around South East Asia, were able to exploit relatively cheap capital and relatively simple technology to gain a foothold in heavy industries and some light manufactures: the Japanese shipyards, for example, expanded hugely from the 1950s onwards, under the careful direction of the Ministry for Industry and Technology. These footholds enabled further economic development to be achieved, though with enormous upheavals and at enormous cost. Since the Asian financial crash in 1997, growth has resumed in most of the so called 'Tiger economies', many of which now resemble the developed economies of the North—whether measured in GDP per capita, the composition of employment, or access to education.

Elsewhere, economic development has proceeded, if at all, in fits and starts. There are areas of economies like Brazil and India that are relatively developed, maintaining a range of employment reliant on substantial, modern infrastructure and significant economic integration with the world economy. However, the inability of capitalism to deliver anything approaching balanced economic growth, and its combined tendencies to under-supply infrastructure while over-supplying capital in a few industries, leave these areas as islands in an ocean of underdevelopment. India maintains both highly sophisticated, internationally-competitive service sector industries in some of its cities alongside incredible rural deprivation, and—in recent years—deindustrialisation in 'rust belts' previously dependent on heavy manufacturing.

There is no returning to the era of state-led national capitalist development. Attempts by the state in such countries to even out the process of economic growth have ended in failure. Where development does occur today, as in eastern China, it is by an untrammelled turn to the world market, the other side of which is leaving vast sections of the population in unending poverty. There is economic growth and the sacking of up to half the workforce in the old industries. There is the expansion of the cities and the search each year by tens of millions of people from the countryside for jobs in the cities which do not exist. But for the poorest countries in Africa, as in most of Central America, the Andean region of South America and the vast agrarian inland regions of South Asia, even this option is not on offer. To claim that people can 'lift themselves' out of poverty through 'enterprise' and 'trade' if only a few hurdles are removed is to tell those who cannot afford shoes to pull themselves up by their own laces. It is asking Southern workers to sweat blood to compete, on under-capitalised machinery and limited technological resources, with workers in other Southern states as well as those in the North.

A systematic programme of planned, globalised economic development is achievable, but not under the competitive conditions imposed by the free market and regulated by the transnational institutions. It is necessary if we are not to abandon hundreds of millions of people to a grim economic fate, and if we are not to wreak immense environmental damage in doing so. The embrace of neo-liberalism by the elites of the South is an expression of the common interest they increasingly share with the ruling classes of the North in exploiting their own people, even while they argue over their small share of the spoils. By the same token workers and peasants in the South have a common interest with workers in the North in fighting this exploitation and breaking the system as a whole.

NOTES

1: C E Weller, R E Scott and A S Hersh, 'The Unremarkable Record of Liberalised Trade', *International Development Economics Associates*, February 2002.

2: R Wade, 'The Ringmaster of Doha', *New Left Review* 2:25 (Jan-Feb 2004).

3: WTO, General Agreement on Trade in Services, Article XIX.

4: R Wade, as above.

5: A Kwa, 'Power Politics in the WTO' (2002) at www.focusweb.org/publications/2002/power percent20politics_final.pdf

6: *The Observer*, 14 September 2003. A leader of the international organisation of peasants, Via Campesina, said at Cancun, 'Anyone who believes that the export of a ton more of soya from Argentina or Brazil saves a single child from death through starvation does not understand the dynamic of poverty'. Peter Rosset, *La Jornada*, 2 October 2004. This article contains a detailed analysis of the 'betrayal' of the poor countries by the 'leading countries in the G20', and especially by Brazil and Lula.

7: J Sachs, *The End of Poverty* (London 2005).

8: World Bank figures, quoted at http://www.wdm.org.uk/news/presrel/current/g8blairtrade.htm

9: Figures in this and following paragraphs taken from WTO, 'World Trade 2003'. See http://www.wto.org/english/news_e/pres04_e/pr373_e.htm for summary.

10: Exports at $583.1 billion moved just ahead of Japan for the first time, but remained below Germany's $893.3 and the US's $795 billion, as well as being only half the European Union's exports to non-EU countries of $1,109 billion. See www.cia.gov/cia/publications/factbook/fields/2078.html

11: Still more fanciful are those free-market apologists who presume a direct correlation between democracy and the free market. The Chinese Communist Party, after nearly 30 years of continual marketisation of its state-capitalist economy, shows no great inclination to abandon its grip on political power. Indeed, given the great social strains unleashed by marketisation and rapid, geographically unbalanced economic growth precisely the opposite could be argued: only under a rigid system of political control are elements of the free market able to be successfully introduced.

12: R Bush, 'Undermining Africa', *Historical Materialism* 12:4, p177.

13: Chile, an economy that has successfully expanded its agricultural outputs at every stage of food processing over 1990-2002, is often hailed in this regard.

14: Figures in this section are taken from the WTO report, 'World Trade 2003'.

15: J Sachs, as above, p282.

16: 'Commission for Africa Report', p284.

17: Oxfam, *Rigged Rules and Double Standards: Trade, Globalisation and the Fight Against Poverty* (London, 2002), figures 5.3, 5.4.

18: UNCTAD, 'Least Developed Countries Report 2002: Escaping the Poverty Trap', p115 at http://www.unctad.org/en/docs/ldc2002p2ch3_en.pdf

19: J Stiglitz, *Globalisation and Its Discontents* (Harmondsworth, 2002).

20: *Financial Times*, 'Towards Full Market Access', 10 July 1997.

21: DTI, Trade and Investment White Paper 2004: Making Globalisation a Force for Good, Cmnd. 6278, July 2004, p61.

22: Tony Blair, Speech to the World Economic Forum, 18 January 2000 http://www.pm.gov.uk

23: Quoted in M Curtis, *Web of Deceit* (London, 2002).

24: *New Statesman*, 30 May 2005.

25: *Financial Times*, 'Big Groups Profit from Fairtrade's Rising Sales', 28 February 2005.

26: A Narlikar and D Tussie, 'The G20 and the Cancun Ministerial: Developing Countries and their Evolving Coalitions in the WTO' (2004).

On the road to catastrophe: capitalism and climate change

Paul McGarr

Two terrible threats define the 21st century. One is imperialist war and all that follows in its bloody train. The other is the accelerating threat of catastrophic climate change.

Few people today doubt the scale of the climate change threat—though some of the tiny minority of deniers happen to head the world's most powerful government and the world's biggest oil corporation.[1] George W Bush and global oil giant Exxon notwithstanding, there is a remarkable consensus, at least in words, that stretches from political and environmental activists to heads of government, and even heads of (some) of the very corporations most responsible for global warming.

A useful summary of this consensus came in a speech made in September 2004:

> The emission of greenhouse gases [principally carbon dioxide]…is causing global warming at a rate that began as significant, has become alarming and is simply unsustainable in the long term. And by long term I do not mean centuries ahead. I mean within the lifetime of my children certainly; and possibly within my own. And by unsustainable, I do not mean a phenomenon causing problems of adjustment. I mean a challenge so far-reaching in its impact and irreversible in its destructive power, that it alters radically human existence…
>
> Let me summarise the evidence: the ten warmest years on record have all been since 1990. Over the last century average global temperatures have

risen by 0.6 degrees Celsius: the most drastic temperature rise for over 1,000 years in the northern hemisphere.

Extreme events are becoming more frequent. Glaciers are melting. Sea ice and snow cover is declining. Animals and plants are responding to an earlier spring. Sea levels are rising and are forecast to rise another 88cm by 2100 threatening 100 million people globally who currently live below this level.

The number of people affected by floods worldwide has already risen from 7 million in the 1960s to 150 million today... By the middle of this century, temperatures could have risen enough to trigger irreversible melting of the Greenland icecap—eventually increasing sea levels by around 7 metres.

The man delivering the speech was Britain's New Labour prime minister Tony Blair.[2] He is unquestionably right on the immense threat we face.

News headlines about severe storms, cold snaps, heatwaves, floods or hurricanes certainly focus debate and attention on climate change. It is impossible to link individual short term weather events with global warming. The earth's climate system is far too complicated for such a simple mode of causation and prediction. But when such events coalesce into a general pattern, as seems to be happening today, the causal link with global warming is much clearer.

Global warming is caused by the growing concentration in the atmosphere of a series of gases which act as a blanket, trapping the sun's heat. By far the most important of these greenhouse gases is carbon dioxide, and the main source of the extra carbon dioxide is the burning of fossil fuels such as coal, oil and gas in power stations and in internal combustion engines.

The concentration of greenhouse gas in the earth's atmosphere, especially carbon dioxide, has increased at an unprecedented rate as measured by air samples taken year on year in Hawaii over recent decades, and further back from ice core samples taken in polar regions.[3] This growing concentration of carbon dioxide is directly correlated with a systematic rise in global mean surface temperatures over the last century, and especially over the last few decades. Beyond question the general effect of heating up a system like the earth's climate will be an increase in extreme weather events across the globe.

Some global warming has already taken place and more is inevitable in the coming decades as the result of already emitted carbon dioxide. Even if all greenhouse gas emissions were halted tomorrow global temperatures are likely to rise by at least another half a degree Celsius and sea levels rise another 11 centimetres by the end of this century. As Gerald Meeh, a lead scientist on the definitive Intergovernmental Panel on Climate Change reports, argues, 'Many people don't realise that we are committed right now to a significant amount of global warming and sea level rise because of the greenhouse gases we have already put into the atmosphere'.[4] The result will be a major increase in storms, heatwaves, droughts, floods and hurricanes across the globe, with all the human and social consequences that brings. Dealing with this will be among the major challenges facing humanity in the coming decades.

But far from halting all carbon dioxide emissions, the world's major states and corporations are pumping out ever-increasing amounts with little sign of any meaningful cuts. The potential consequences are almost unthinkable—but all too real. Extra heat in the earth's atmosphere will melt glaciers and polar ice caps at some point (possibly rapidly, on a timescale of years and decades). Significantly raised sea levels could submerge whole areas that are now land, wiping out whole states from Bangladesh to the Netherlands, and destroying major world cities, including New York and London. One can only imagine the social and human impact of this kind of catastrophe.

Continued global warming will at some point have large-scale, relatively sudden and unpredictable impacts on global rainfall, wind and temperature patterns and on the related ocean water and heat circulation patterns. The details of these shifts are inherently unpredictable, but that they will occur with dramatic impact on global and local climate, agriculture and much else is beyond doubt. Changing climate will also see shifts in the global distribution of disease-carrying insects, with potentially huge impacts on human health. All of these effects would cause untold misery and immense social upheaval.

In a world already riven with imperialist war, and by economic and military tensions, the potential for such upheaval to spark armed conflict, including the ultimate spectre of nuclear annihilation, is not a morbid fantasy, but all too likely.

The history of human society shows that when environmental and climatic changes have meshed with social tension to produce immense upheaval the results have been often bloody, and sometimes even led to the utter collapse of the society involved.[5] Global warming has the ultimate potential to cause such a social collapse on a world scale, and to throw into question anything deserving the name human civilisation.

The Hollywood film *The Day After Tomorrow* had many, many faults, but its basic premise is entirely plausible—global warming could lead to the interruption of a key circulation of ocean waters and thereby plunge the world into huge and relatively sudden (if not quite as quick as Hollywood producers demanded) climatic shifts which no society could withstand. Such sudden and large-scale shifts in climate are built into the kind of physical system the earth's climate is. One way to picture it is to see the earth's current climate as a ball in a mountain valley which is being pushed up the sides of the surrounding hills by global warming. The valley represents the general type of global climate the earth has had in the recent past. If it is pushed too far, to the top of one of the surrounding hills, it may not come back to the valley at all, ever, but instead roll off down the other side of the hill into entirely different terrain, a new and very different global climate.

New Labour's record of failure

I quoted Tony Blair on the scale of the threat we face. He has not been shy of spelling out the action needed to tackle the threat. He concluded, 'The UK needs to reduce our carbon dioxide emissions by 60 percent by 2050. This implies a massive change in the way this country produces and uses energy. We are committed to this change.' He has repeatedly stressed making the war on global warming 'our top priority' and putting it to the top of the agenda at the G8. Never one to let his neighbour make all the running, New Labour chancellor, Gordon Brown, also weighed in with his own major climate change speech in March 2005.[6]

But what is the reality behind New Labour's rhetoric?

Quite incredibly, Britain's carbon dioxide emissions are actually rising—by 1.5 percent in 2004 and 2.2 percent in 2003. Overall emissions are 3 percent higher than when New Labour first came to office in 1997.[7]

The reality was that the Tories' massive onslaught on the coal industry in the 1980s and 1990s had led to a switch to gas-generated electricity. The Tories were not motivated by curbing climate change, but the policy had the unintended consequence of slashing carbon dioxide emissions. Blair seized on the fall to spin his way to the moral high ground on climate change, arguing that Britain was leading the world with carbon dioxide emissions 14 percent lower in 2002 than they had been in 1990. Blair, carried away by his own rhetoric, even pledged that Britain's carbon dioxide emissions would be 20 percent down on 1990 levels by 2010, and embraced the Royal Commission on Environmental Pollution's call for a 60 percent cut by 2050.[8]

But Blair's spin and rhetoric have evaporated in the face of today's growing carbon dioxide emissions. Why? The problem is that all New Labour's initiatives on climate change (and there have been many) share one fundamental characteristic—a reliance on business and market mechanisms.

New Labour ruled out renationalising the power generation industry and simply assumed that the energy market would continue more or less in its then current state of relatively low gas prices and higher coal prices. It did not even consider what could happen if gas prices for power generation rose and coal prices on the international market fell. Yet that is exactly what has now happened as North Sea gas supplies have started to dwindle while large sources of relatively cheap imported coal have become available. The British power generation energy market has done what any such market was bound to do faced with this new situation, and moved back to coal as the fuel for power generation over recent years. Between 2003 and 2004 this shift pushed Britain's overall emissions back on an upward course, and there is little sign as yet of anything which will change that upward trend.[9] As Friends of the Earth's detailed analysis concludes, 'The conditions that led to the carbon reductions in the 1990s are unlikely ever to be repeated'.[10]

Other government initiatives on climate change include the Climate Change Levy, introduced in April 2001.[11] This sounds like a good idea, a tax on the firms pumping out carbon dioxide and other greenhouse gases. But it has a series of fundamentally disabling flaws built into it, ones which prevent it having significant impact. Firstly, it is currently set at a very, very low level, following New Labour's general view that gentle persuasion of business is all that is now allowed from the state. Secondly, the levy is also what New Labour calls 'revenue neutral', in that any money it raises is given back to business through reduced employer national insurance contributions, so it is hardly a tax that is clobbering business at all.

More seriously, there are huge exemptions from paying the levy, exemptions which leave key areas involved in pumping out carbon dioxide outside its reach. So, for example, the Climate Change Levy does not apply at all to transport or electricity generation, yet these are the two largest sources of greenhouse gas emissions! It does not apply to oils at all (and so rules out a fossil fuel that is, to put it mildly, at the heart of the climate change crisis), nor does it apply to the important aluminum smelting industry. On top of all this some energy-intensive industries are also eligible for a discount of up to 80 percent on the levy as long as they sign an agreement which contains some ten-year energy use reduction targets. In short, what started as probably a good idea has been so watered down as a result of concessions to business as to become almost useless.[12]

The same picture is true of the government's 'renewables obligation', under which it hopes to gently cajole electricity suppliers to use a greater proportion of renewable energy sources, such as wind, wave, tidal and solar power. The government targets are for 5 percent of electricity to come from renewables by this year, 10 percent by 2010 and 20 percent by 2020. Even such modest targets are not being met, with the figure for renewables this year only 3.86 percent. The government this year also looked to be reneging on a commitment to help fund the development of solar energy, with the Department of Trade and Industry claiming 'the climate we have does not lend itself to solar energy'.[13] This claim is straightforward scientific nonsense: solar power is perfectly viable in Britain. Germany (not noted for its hot climate) has a significant 300 megawatts of solar-generated electricity capacity already, around 50 times more than Britain. New Labour has often talked up its commitment to wind power. So Blair announced £6 billion of investment in offshore wind farms. But this is not £6 billion of public investment (which would be an excellent first step). Instead it is money the government *hopes* to attract from private firms, making the expansion of renewables dependent on a dressed-up form of the Private Finance Initiative which has been such a resounding disaster throughout Britain's public services. It is hard to disagree with the Royal Commission on Environmental Pollution's seminal report[14] which argued that, 'Considering the enormous potential of UK renewable energy sources it has been slow to make progress.'

One of the biggest holes in New Labour's rhetoric on climate change centres on transport. No serious attempt to cut carbon dioxide emissions can work without a serious reduction in the amount of road traffic. Transport now accounts for around 26 percent of all Britain's carbon dioxide emissions, and between 1980 and 2002 carbon dioxide emissions from transport rose by 39 percent. Yet New Labour has performed a massive U-turn on transport that will make things worse, not better. As Transport 2000 points out, 'When Labour came to power in 1997 it promised a new direction on roads. It cancelled 42 road schemes [but]…in July 2000 £30 billion of road building was announced'.[15]

Instead of a move away from ever more cars and lorries towards public transport (by far the surest way of slashing carbon dioxide emissions from transport) New Labour is presiding over a drift in precisely the wrong direction. Since 1997 bus fares in Britain have risen by an average 16 percent, rail fares by 7 percent, while the cost of motoring has actually fallen by around 6 percent. On current plans heavy goods vehicle traffic on Britain's roads is predicted to rise by 25 percent in the next decade and van traffic by 44 percent. No wonder Transport 2000 concludes, 'The government leads the world in rhetoric on climate change, but cannot claim to be serious about tackling it'.[16]

One of the fastest growing sources of greenhouse gas emissions is aviation, which now accounts for around 10 percent of all greenhouse gas emissions globally and will on current trends account for about 25 percent of all Britain's emissions by the year 2030.[17] Yet the government seems obsessively committed to an insane expansion of airports and air travel. Incredibly, airlines currently pay no VAT or duty at all on aviation fuel, which in Britain amounts to a £9 billion a year tax break.[18] The plain fact is that any climate change policy that does not aim to curb air travel is simply not serious.

There was an international conference involving European governments and airlines earlier this year, but it ended with no agreement on doing anything to tackle rising emissions due to air travel.[19] Former British Airways boss Rod Eddington put the conference outcome, of doing nothing to limit the expansion of air traffic, down to a simple fact: 'Many European policy makers share business concerns that we will be put at a commercial disadvantage'.[20] Whatever the rhetoric on climate change nothing can be allowed to touch the profits of the airlines. Eddington has been appointed by New Labour's Gordon Brown as a government transport adviser.

We should not be conned by the fake populist argument that the explosion of budget air travel is a boon for ordinary people and that its continued expansion is something we should champion. Most air travel could and should be replaced by high-speed rail. In Europe for example half of all flights are for journeys of less than 500 kilometres. All could be done as quickly by rail as by air (allowing for city centre rail stations as opposed to out of town airports), if the investment was directed into building high-speed lines, and without the damaging effect on climate.

Whichever aspect of New Labour's climate change policy you look at, a picture emerges of a government habitually bowing to the demands of business. Under industry pressure the government has, for example, refused to tighten energy efficiency requirements for new buildings.[21] In opposition prior to 1997 Labour favoured statutory targets to cut domestic energy usage by 30 percent over ten years through better insulation and many other measures which would help the poor as well as curb greenhouse gas emissions. A Labour MP sponsored a private member's bill on this in 2002, backed by Age Concern, Friends of the Earth, Shelter and hundreds of MPs. But the government used a series of parliamentary wrecking amendments to destroy the bill.[22]

Many of those who had campaigned over climate change used to take New Labour rhetoric seriously. Greenpeace, hardly noted for being soft-headed on such issues, supported the government's climate change policy right up until last November. It now says, 'Recent retreats on emissions trading, fuel duty and domestic energy efficiency compound a record of failure which has seen carbon dioxide emissions actually rise since Labour came to power'.[23] And even the staid Environmental Audit Committee of the House of Commons has concluded that the government's whole climate change strategy is 'seriously off course'.[24]

No doubt in the run-up to the 2005 G8 summit in Scotland Blair and Brown will indulge in more rhetoric on climate change. But whatever their words, the record has shattered all of New Labour's claims to be champions of action on climate change.

Kyoto's false promise

Are things any better internationally than in Britain? After all, the keynote international deal on climate change, the Kyoto agreement (first reached in 1997), finally came into effect in February this year, becoming legally binding on all 141 signatory states.[25]

Kyoto is a complex deal, but its centrepiece is a general commitment by signatories to cut carbon dioxide emissions by 5.2 percent from their 1990 levels by 2012. As already noted some countries went further, with Britain for example pledging a 12.5 percent cut by 2012.

A major problem is that the state responsible for more carbon dioxide emissions than any other, the US, with a quarter of all global emissions, refuses to sign the Kyoto agreement or any other international agreement on climate change.

But that is not the only thing wrong with Kyoto. All the fanfare around the deal is reminiscent of Hans Christian Andersen's tale of the Emperor's New Clothes. It is utterly worthless. The cuts in carbon dioxide emissions envisaged under Kyoto will do nothing significant to halt global warming and climate change even if fully implemented. And there are no international plans whatever to set post-Kyoto targets for further cuts in carbon dioxide emissions after 2012. The European Union claims to be leading the rest of the world on climate change, yet when its governments met in February this year they too refused to set any post-2012 targets for emissions cuts at all.[26]

Business and many governments argue that there is nevertheless a key feature of Kyoto which will deliver real emissions cuts—'emissions trading', a market where companies and countries buy and sell the right to pump out quotas of carbon dioxide. And some NGOs which have a good record of campaigning on climate change have accepted this as part of the solution. It is not.

One of the most important emissions trading schemes was formally launched by the European Union in January of this year. The theory is that the market will set a price on the right to emit one tonne of carbon dioxide (or the equivalent amount of five other greenhouse gases). Companies will then have to buy a permit for the amount they pump out. The idea is that if the price is high enough market pressure will cause companies to find ways to cut emissions.

The idea at first glance can have an easy appeal, as is often the case with theories based on the market. You could imagine things working like that. A reality check, as usual with the market, quickly dispels such illusions. When the scheme was piloted in January 2004 the price of the right to emit one tonne of carbon dioxide was around 12 euros. By the time the scheme came into full operation in January 2005 it had fallen to around 7 euros. At this level there will be little market pressure to change behaviour at all. Even enthusiasts for the scheme acknowledge that the price needed to rise, not fall, to force any switch. The Green Alliance think-tank, in a study of the scheme, concludes bluntly, 'The first phase of emissions trading from 2005 to 2007 is not going to deliver emissions reduction'.[27]

The scheme only applies to a limited number of establishments. Some 12,000 are included in the scheme, accounting for less than half of the European Union's emissions.

It is also open to crude manipulation. For example, Britain's government this year tried to simply increase by 3 percent the baseline emissions for the 1,000 establishments big enough to be included in the trading scheme. It then claimed that under Kyoto targets its own quota should be set 5.2 percent below this increased baseline, in effect watering down the Kyoto cut from 5.2 percent to just 2.4 percent. Even the European Union thought this New Labour scam a little too blatant and blocked it. The British government, a supposed global champion of action on climate change, has now launched legal action against the European Union to win the right to fiddle its emissions figures.[28]

The global emissions trading scheme linked to the Kyoto protocol is similar to the European scheme, but with additional features which have generated a whole series of fancy-sounding names which pepper and confuse discussions. The most important go under the grand titles of the Clean Development Mechanism and the Joint Implementation Mechanism. In essence they are much the same, and amount to a multinational company earning credits by sponsoring in some country a scheme which supposedly reduces the amount of greenhouse gases. These credits can then be used to increase its own emissions elsewhere without facing a penalty.

So a transnational company could sponsor a plantation in a poor country, and claim that if this hadn't been done more carbon dioxide would have gone into the atmosphere, on the grounds that trees lock up carbon. (In passing it is worth noting that, however laudable the idea of planting trees may be for all sorts of reasons, the notion that trees are a solution to climate change is silly, as the carbon is released when the trees die. They are at best a temporary help in locking up some carbon and not a substitute for slashing carbon dioxide emissions.) Another example could be a corporation investing in some electricity generation project involving, say, hydroelectric power and dams, and claiming that otherwise fossil fuels would have been burned and put more carbon dioxide into the atmosphere. In such cases a carbon credit can be earned based on a calculation of the supposed difference between what has happened and what might otherwise have happened.

The whole scheme is open to abuse over who decides what would otherwise have happened, and who does the resulting calculation. Things get worse still when you find out that an absolutely central role in the emissions trading process will be played by an entity called the Prototype Carbon Fund—an arm of the World Bank. The Transnational Institute and Carbon Trade Watch argue in a definitive report on emissions trading:

> Trading programmes in effect privatise the problem of air-pollution. Government and communities lose control over environmental protections, placing it in the hands of the polluters. When the incentive to reduce emissions is profit and cost-effectiveness, there is incredible pressure to cheat by overestimating reductions, while underestimating emissions.[29]

The report is a devastating critique of emissions trading, based on schemes that are already under way. It concludes with justice that emissions trading schemes remove any credibility at all from the Kyoto protocol:

> A country will be able to meet 100 percent of its Kyoto reduction commitments through purchasing credits in the market rather than reducing climate change emissions at source... Unfortunately the protocol's market-based mechanisms such as emissions trading allow countries and companies to escape their responsibilities to reduce their own emissions. With the inclusion of these 'flexible mechanisms' this hard-fought agreement may actually be a first step backwards.

A scandal that erupted in April 2005 around one of the first schemes backed by the Prototype Carbon Fund shows how rotten the whole process is. A supposedly model project involved the Plantar corporation setting up a massive eucalyptus plantation in the state of Minas Gerais in Brazil to produce wood for making charcoal to be used in pig iron production. The corporation argues that otherwise it would have used coal, producing even more carbon dioxide, and is claiming a carbon credit under the Kyoto scheme with the backing of the World Bank. A whole series of Brazilian and international NGOs and social movement groups have united to slam the fraudulent scheme, which involves the forcible eviction of people from land in the area to establish a huge monocultural plantation. These organisations have signed an open letter calling for the Prototype Carbon Fund to be shut down. They draw out more general arguments about emissions trading which those climate change campaigners who have accepted emissions trading as part of the solution would do well to heed:

> The Prototype Carbon Fund was born out of the World Bank's efforts to promote neoliberalism. It is an instrument to commodify the atmosphere, promote privatisation and concentrate resources in the hands of a few, taking away the rights of the many to live with dignity. The PCF is not a mechanism for mitigating climate change.
>
> Having followed the PCF's activities and projects to date, we have learned by its doings that it does not avert dangerous climate change but instead increases hardship for local communities. This exposes inherent flaws not only in its own projects, but in project-based 'carbon trading' as a whole and the offset culture underpinning it. Any other similar fund or trading regime will systematically replicate these flaws.
>
> The PCF extends the World Bank's unacceptable political activities into a new sphere with its own special technical impossibilities. The PCF accordingly must be closed down as a first step in the right direction. It is neither 'carbon' nor pollution that is being traded, but people's lives and paper certificates claiming to be carbon credits. Offset culture and pollution trading must be rejected as false solutions to climate change.[30]

Emissions trading is not the only fashionable but false proposed mechanism for tackling climate change. In recent years many businesses and governments have latched on to what is dubbed 'carbon sequestration' as the answer. Oil companies, in particular Norway's Statoil and Britain's BP, have been particularly keen to push this idea, and both have major projects under way. In essence the idea is to capture some of the carbon emitted by burning fossil fuels and store or 'sequestrate' it in secure deep rock formations or in exhausted undersea oil reservoirs. Ron Gueterbock, one of Greenpeace's climate change experts, rightly argues, 'This whole approach is the wrong way to tackle climate change'.[31] It diverts resources away from measures to cut emissions and is an attempt by the giant fossil fuel corporations to say we can have business as usual while they come up with a technical fix which will get us off the hook of climate change.

Carbon sequestration is also inherently risky. Nick Riley of the British Geological Survey points out, 'If we put this stuff away for thousands of years then what happens if it leaks? Nobody understands fully what the implication would be of leakage into the marine environment'.[32] Roger Higman of Friends of the Earth says, 'We need to guarantee that this won't happen not just for ten years, not just for 100 years and not just for 1,000 years but for tens of thousands of years. It's an inherently risky project... Meanwhile it distracts from the fundamental issue which is that we need to cut back on our emissions'.[33] The reputable US Union of Concerned Scientists puts similar arguments.[34] A glimpse of some of the dangers sequestration could involve was given by an entirely natural disaster, when in 1986 a huge bubble of carbon dioxide escaped from rocks under the bed of Lake Nyos in Cameroon. As the gas is denser than air it hugged the ground as it emerged from the lake, killing 1,700 people living around the shores.

Stoking up the heat in the US

The US is responsible for the largest share of global greenhouse gas emissions and refuses to sign any international agreement on climate change. For many years US president George Bush and the oil companies behind him, especially the world's largest, Exxon, have denied the reality of climate change, with Exxon using its financial muscle to ensure US politicians echo its message and funding scores of 'scientists' prepared to play its tune.[35] Bush has changed tack a little in the last couple of years. His administration still questions the evidence of climate change. But they do now talk of greenhouse gas emissions probably leading to global warming and of the need for some action. The official 2002 US Climate Action Report concluded, 'Continuing growth in greenhouse gas emissions is likely to lead to annual average warming over the US,' and it lists a string of potentially dire consequences. As a result of this, Bush's 2002 Energy Plan claimed it would 'set America on a path to slow the growth of our greenhouse gas emissions'.[36]

But Bush's Energy Plan is in fact a giant con, and if fully implemented would allow the US to emit even more greenhouse gases than now. The whole plan is couched in terms of reducing *not* greenhouse gas emissions, but rather what it terms greenhouse gas 'intensity'. This is the amount of greenhouse gas emitted relative to the size of the economy. So if the economy grows and the amount of greenhouse gas emitted also grows, but at a slightly slower rate than the economy, Bush's plan would call this a 'cut'. This nonsense translates into a target which could allow the US to increase its greenhouse gas emissions by a huge 13 percent over the next ten years (a faster rate than the already worryingly large 4.9 percent rise in US emissions from 1997 to 2002).

As a devastating report by the US national wildlife federation argues, 'President Bush's global warming response is simply a smokescreen of accounting schemes that hide the increased pollution from the president's energy plan... The president's energy priorities such as promoting more coal fired power plants will increase the nation's dependence on fossil fuels'.[37] Another detailed analysis reveals that Bush's plan involves an increase in the burning of coal, oil and gas, alongside cuts of around one third in government funding for renewable energy and fuel efficiency measures.[38]

Yet there are some within the US state who are worried at where global warming could lead. The US Defense Department commissioned an October 2003 report on climate change which the US government first unsuccessfully tried to suppress. It concluded that there was now 'substantial evidence to indicate that...global warming will occur during the 21st century', and (in an echo of *The Day After Tomorrow*) argued, 'There is a possibility that this could lead to relatively abrupt slowing of the ocean's thermohaline conveyor... [The] result could be a systematic drop in the human carrying capacity of the earth's environment'.[39] Translated out of Pentagon-speak the report is arguing that climate change will lead to famine and death on a huge scale. It worries that this will cause immense global instability, with enormous refugee movements and political upheaval. Unfortunately while the analysis is refreshingly accurate, if grim, remember this is the Pentagon, which only knows one answer to all the world's problems—prepare to build the military capacity to deal with the resulting 'security threats'. Wage war against climate change. It would be funny if it weren't so tragic.

The only conclusion possible is that those at the head of the US state have no serious intention to take action to tackle climate change.

What are the solutions?

I have so far painted a bleak picture of the prospects for effective action to curb carbon dioxide emissions. What makes this dismal picture all the more frustrating is that the solutions to climate change, action which could dramatically slash carbon dioxide emissions, are simple and in principle relatively easy to achieve.

Power generation and renewable energy

The biggest single source of global carbon dioxide emissions is power stations. In the US around 33.2 percent of carbon dioxide emissions comes directly from power plants.[40] Similar figures apply to most other industrialised countries. One rare exception is Britain, where transport now accounts for a greater proportion of carbon dioxide than power generation—25 percent compared to 16 percent.[41]

The only realistic way to cut emissions from power generation is to stop burning fossil fuels (coal, oil and gas) and use modes of generating power that do not contribute to global warming. We need a major shift to what is called renewable energy—electricity generation driven by wind, wave, tidal and solar power. All of these technologies are already reasonably well developed, and could quickly (within a few decades) become the dominant form of electricity generation if the political will was there.

Those who say we cannot quickly shift to renewable energy often argue that it is unproven technology and that it is too expensive compared to fossil fuel electricity generation. This is false on both counts.

As one important study argues, 'According to the G8 Renewables Trade Forum the barriers to the deployment of renewable energy are not technological but financial and political'.[42] There is more development work needed on methods of storing electricity generated from intermittent energy sources. But these problems are already solved in principle. To give one example, you can use part of the energy when the wind is blowing to pump water up to a storage site, and then when the wind is slack, letting the water fall again so driving a turbine to generate electricity.

And the price differences with fossil fuel generated electricity are not that great now. The Royal Commission on Environmental Pollution looked in detail at the alternatives to fossil fuels in the British situation using a detailed technical assessment carried out by the Department for Trade and Industry's own Energy Technology Support Unit.[43] It found that wind-generated electricity cost between 2.9p for offshore wind and 3.5p for onshore wind farms per kilowatt hour (kWh) compared at that time with around 2p for gas-generated electricity and around 2.5p for coal. Wave power came in at around 4p per kWh and solar power at around 7p per kWh. Yes, renewables are currently a little more expensive, but only a little, and in the case of wind only a very little.

Yet fossil fuels have had decades of enormous subsidy, and investment on a vast scale. This is why they have appeared 'cheaper'. One serious study puts the subsidy figure at $235 billion a year globally,[44] another, more conservative one at around $244 billion between 1995 and 1998 for example;[45] in Britain one estimate puts it at £4.5 billion between 1990 and 1995.[46] If this money was switched instead to investment and subsidy for renewable energy very dramatic shifts in patterns of power generation would happen within just a few years. Even accepting the need for renewables to be 'competitive' with fossil fuels (which I do not—the future of the planet and the people who inhabit it ought to take priority), this could be achieved relatively rapidly.

Even the minimal level of investment in renewable energy that has taken place in recent years has already had a dramatic impact, cutting the cost of US wind-generated electricity from around 40 cents per kWh in 1980 to between 3 and 6 cents, and solar-generated power cost from 100 cents to around 10 cents now.[47] The British government's own review by its Performance and Innovation Unit in 2001 concluded that wind power would be significantly cheaper than fossil fuel alternatives by 2020 even without any radical step change in investment.[48] BP admits that 'within the next five to ten years PV [solar electricity] will become cost competitive with traditional power sources in countries with extensive electrical infrastructure'.[49]

There is not some limit on how much these renewable energies could be utilised, condemning them to a marginal role. A Department of Trade and Industry study found that offshore wind turbines alone could provide at least double, and possibly much, much, more, Britain's current peak electricity use.[50] A European Union report came to the conclusion that wind power and wave power could between them generate all Britain's current energy needs three times over.[51]

There has been a spate of recent cases of campaigns against wind power, with people arguing against building wind farms (groups of turbines) on the grounds that they visually ruin local environments and cause noise pollution.[52] We must robustly reject such arguments. Wind turbines are no more an eyesore than windmills were in the past, and certainly a lot more elegant than many other pieces of infrastructure—from railway lines to pylons and motorways. If the options are between having windmills around the countryside and continuing to burn fossil fuels leading to catastrophic climate change then there is no real choice at all. And by far the best sites for large-scale wind farms are not on land at all, but instead in shallow offshore waters—where winds are stronger and more constant. The key to making this offshore wind power generation possible is large-scale investment in providing the infrastructure to connect up the wind farms to local and national electricity grids (and with the necessary electricity storage schemes built into the plans).[53]

The same arguments apply in principle to other forms of renewable energy. Wave power technology is well developed; all that is needed is massive investment to make it more efficient and provide the infrastructure to build it into local and national grids. In the slightly longer run one of the best and biggest sources of energy is tides. Around Britain for example this includes both tidal bores, such as the one which runs up the Severn Estuary, but also tidal streams, such as that which flows through the Pentland Firth off the north coast of Scotland. These are truly enormous potential sources of power, and on a global scale the proper utilisation of tidal power could be key to a sustainable future. But once the initial capital investment has been made tidal power is probably the cheapest of all power sources. Though it is intermittent (with four tidal streams a day, as the tide comes in and out twice a day) it has the great advantage that it is absolutely predictable on a daily basis, which makes planning for and using storage technologies relatively simple. The DTI Energy Unit found that once the initial capital cost has been paid off tidal barrages were by far the cheapest of all forms of electricity generation it studied. A barrage across the Severn Estuary could generate up to one fifth of all UK current electricity demand at a running cost of just 0.05p per kWh.[54] The technology for such barrages is well established and proven. There are none in Britain, but just across the Channel between St Malo and Dinard a tidal barrage across the mouth of the River Rance has been running for decades and generating a huge amount of electricity. Only political will prevents such examples being rapidly multiplied in a matter of years.

Solar power is another renewable technology with a vast potential. Often people think it is only usable in hot sunny climates. This is simply false. In most climates, and certainly those prevailing in major industrialised countries from the US to Britain, from Germany to Japan, solar power is perfectly viable, especially in the form of water heating panels in buildings. But even the more complex photovoltaic cell (PV) generation of solar power will work in most climates.[55] Underinvestment means that at present solar-generated power is often more expensive than fossil fuels, but even here major investment could quickly slash costs.

In short, there are no fundamental technical or serious cost barriers which prevent a radical and quick shift in electricity generation, whether in Britain or on a global scale, away from fossil fuels to renewable energy. The only barrier is a lack of determination by governments to insist that this shift will happen, and compel it to happen through massive investment. Investment could be financed through, firstly, diverting the enormous subsidies that fossil fuels now get into renewables, secondly, through diverting the billions that goes into military spending and war into renewable energy and, thirdly, through a serious taxation of the profits of fossil fuel companies to fund expansion of renewables.

Nuclear power—no thanks

There is one form of energy that is no solution to global warming—nuclear power. Until recently it looked as though in many countries, including Britain, the argument about the utter insanity of nuclear power had been won and it was being phased out. Now it seems some in the industry who would benefit from the huge profits to be made in building new nuclear power stations have managed to convince at least some politicians that nuclear power could be sold as an answer to climate change.

Key figures within New Labour have been arguing for the building of a new generation of nuclear power stations. Their logic starts from Britain's failure to meet its international commitments on cutting carbon dioxide emissions on current trends. They argue that nuclear power does not produce carbon dioxide (true) and that therefore it is a form of energy which can save us from environmental disaster (totally false). Unfortunately some who call themselves environmentalists have fallen for this argument, for example James Lovelock, best known for his Gaia theory.[56]

Nuclear power is the most insane way to generate electricity ever invented. It amounts to basically using a controlled nuclear reaction to boil water so that the steam can then drive an electricity generating turbine. It is inherently dangerous and prone to huge disaster, as witnessed by the string of catastrophes from Three Mile Island to Chernobyl. The evidence that it creates immediate health problems, such as radioactive seas and clusters of cases of leukaemia, is well documented, for instance around Britain's Sellafield plant.

Nuclear power is fundamentally linked to nuclear weapons. In an age when western governments tell us we should oppose any new country wanting to acquire such weapons it seems a bit strange to then push nuclear power as a force for good. And in an age when those same governments constantly warn of the dangers of 'terrorists' getting hold of enough nuclear material to build a 'dirty bomb' it would by that logic be an act of wilful insanity to go on producing more and more such material in nuclear power stations.

Added to all these arguments is the simple fact that nuclear power is more expensive than any of the renewable energies even at current prices. A hugely detailed study by Greenpeace International ignored all the extra costs of decommissioning and dealing with waste and concluded, 'regardless of these additional costs and considering only the generating costs nuclear power remains uncompetitive', costing around double coal-generated power.[57]

The 'additional costs' cannot be ignored. There is the enormous and insoluble problem of the massive amounts of deadly radioactive waste generated by nuclear power stations, waste which will remain deadly for hundreds of thousands or even millions of years and which no one has any safe way to deal with. And the costs of dealing with this in Britain are put by most commentators at around £60 billion, and that is only from existing nuclear power stations—not any new ones that may be built. Nuclear power could not exist without enormous subsidies. In Britain the industry had to be bailed out from going bust by a £1 billion handout from New Labour, and that is on top of a £7.8 billion subsidy the industry got from taxpayers' money in the 1990s.[58]

There is not a single argument for nuclear power except the desire to produce material for use in a nuclear weapons programme, and the idea that it is part of the solution to environmental disaster is almost laughably insane—so mad you just couldn't make it up. Anyone serious about fighting to tackle the climate change crisis should reject the move to rehabilitate nuclear power and do everything in their power to mobilise to prevent New Labour covering up its failure to take real action on climate change with a new drive to nuclear power. We must say loud and clear, in the words of the old but still valid international slogan, 'Nuclear power—no thanks.'

A new direction on transport

After power stations, the second largest single source of global carbon dioxide emissions is transport (road and air in particular). A coalition of some of the world's largest and most powerful corporations—the oil companies, the car corporations, the tyre and rubber multinationals, the airlines and aviation firms—are all committed by their very nature to the single aim of selling more of what they depend on for their profits. They want to sell more cars, more petrol, more rubber for tyres, more tarmac for roads, they want more planes flying from more airports. They bend governments to policies which favour this.

The result has been the transport disaster we see in cities in the richer countries, one which has now been replicated in far worse form in the giant cities of the third world. And now the same coalition of profit chasers want this disaster to spread even further, with a relentless drive to recreate all its worst features right across hugely populated countries like India, China and Indonesia. This nightmarish prospect is one that if not tackled will plunge the climate more and more rapidly down the road to disaster. This is not any kind of argument against people in all these countries having the right to access the best in modern transport and the fruits of modern production, only that 'development' in these countries need not and should not replicate the worst features of what has happened elsewhere.

Tinkering with marginal adjustments to policies, messing about with small-scale schemes (however beneficial such schemes may be in other ways), or individuals exercising any degree of personal choice, is not going to wrench either British or global transport policy onto a new course. Nor are schemes like road pricing or congestion charges going to solve the problem. Such schemes may cut traffic levels on some roads and in some city centres, but do little to curb overall traffic levels and therefore are of little importance in an assault on global warming. They also depend on pricing the poorer off the charged roads or out of the charging zones while the rich can afford to pay. A much more serious assault on the issue is needed, one that inevitably means challenging head-on the logic of the network of fossil fuel corporations at the heart of the disaster.

There needs to be an end to the entire £30 billion road building programme, a total halt to all new airport schemes and an immediate ending of the £9 billion a year tax subsidy to the airlines.

Along with this has to go a huge investment in massively expanding rail and bus travel, and in the cities tram, light rail and underground networks. The aim should be to create public transport of sufficient quality, regularity, reach and reliability that in most circumstances no rational person would want to travel any other way.

This requires the renationalisation, without compensation, of the rail and bus industries and of the airports (along with air traffic control). Subsidies should also be poured in to slash fares on public transport in the cities, with the aim of moving as rapidly as possible to a free network. If you could travel free around London on a massively improved and expanded bus, tube and rail network, the impact on the city and traffic would be immense—and make the city a far better place for all.

Within cities too a major expansion of safe cycle routes (properly separated from traffic as they are in many European countries and not the death traps painted in green in many British cities today) is needed—along with measures to establish widespread and safe cycle storage facilities in city centres, workplaces and at tube and bus connections. While pushing policies to curb the number of cars, some measures could also be taken to limit the damage cars do. Banning all cars which do not meet minimum fuel consumption requirements would be a good start—and in this way also getting rid of the gas-guzzling and dangerous SUVs would be a good thing on lots of other grounds too.

Road freight must also be slashed, and driven back to rail and water. Simply banning all lorries above a certain size from the roads would be a good start (governments can do these kind of things, whatever New Labour may claim). Putting in place a system which punitively taxed firms which did not shift the majority of their freight to rail or water would be another great help. The vast bulk of goods could and should be moved between major centres this way, with lorries only used for local deliveries at the end of the chain.

While rail is clearly the key to such a strategy, water should not be forgotten especially for non-perishable bulk goods. Britain in particular has the potential for many goods to be moved by coastal freight ships, and also has a vast canal network which could and should be used to move goods. It is only the drive to cut costs by just-in-time production systems which puts pressure for quick deliveries that acts as a block to this form of transport. Then why not put a tax system in place which made it more expensive for firms to move goods by road than to accept a slightly slower movement by water-borne freight?

A systematic drive to replace flights in Britain and Europe with high-speed rail connections (with cheap fares) should also be planned and implemented. The widespread use of decent sleepercar facilities on trains could also make rail a far more attractive option for journeys that were slightly longer by rail than they might be by air. Strict overall limits on the number of flights should also be put in place, starting with slashing the number of quite unnecessary business flights, which are largely an excuse for rich men, and a few women, to jet around the world wining and dining in fancy restaurants and staying in fancy hotels, plotting how better to rob each other—and us.

Any jobs lost in the falling number of cars, planes and roads being built under such a radical shift in transport policy could be more than compensated for by these workers using their skills to build the new rail lines, trains, buses, tram and underground networks needed—and if that is not enough many could also be employed in building the wind turbines, or tidal barrages needed in the drive to shift power generation to renewable energy.

In the long run a further shift is needed in the way society is organised to demand ever more travelling in the course of daily life, to and from work and school—a trend which contributes massively to car journeys and so fuels global warming.

To take one example of what could be done, New Labour's sham of parental choice in schools should simply be abolished at a stroke. It is a sham, a right exercised by a privileged few and under which it is schools in a competitive market, not parents, who make the choices. All pupils should go to their local primary and secondary school, with all religious and suchlike schools abolished too. This would not only quickly improve education for all, but linked to the development of safe local walking and cycling routes and the use of walking trains for collecting younger pupils to take them to school, would make a significant contribution to curbing traffic.

Similarly, using planning and other government powers to insist jobs and other social facilities are sited where people live, or that affordable public homes are built where there are jobs, could both curb traffic, help end the housing crisis, and make people's daily lives more stress-free with more free time.

I do not pretend this is any kind of worked-out and costed programme, but I hope it gives at least an indication of the kind of measures that need to be driven through, and driven with speed and determination.

Energy efficiency

A third key area which could make a major contribution to tackling climate change is very simple—energy efficiency. Governments insisting (not persuading, or cajoling, or relying on some market mechanism, but insisting, backed up with severe penalties for those firms which do not comply) on proper insulation and better energy efficiency in every area of society could make a significant contribution to tackling climate change.

Among these measures are obvious things like proper insulation on all new buildings and bringing older buildings up to that standard too. As someone who lives in a 1960s tower block which was recently refurbished in this manner I can personally vouch for the effectiveness of such straightforward measures, with electricity and heating bills down by over 50 percent. Insisting on much more widespread use of fluorescent light bulbs might seem an unglamorous measure—but they use a quarter of the energy of the incandescent light bulbs which account for 80 percent of all lighting energy used in Britain. A shift would have an impact. Putting in solar water heating panels on all new, and over time older, buildings would also make a major contribution.

The Intergovernmental Panel on Climate Change estimates that if good design and insulation were extended globally greenhouse gas emissions could be cut by up to 40 percent. Britain's Royal Commission found that elementary energy efficiency measures such as high quality insulation of new buildings could cut energy use in the service sector by 18 percent within a few years, and that proper insulation, good design and using combined heat and power plants to provide local hot water and electricity could together slash energy use in homes by between 25 and 34 percent in a few years.[59]

Can the solutions be implemented?

If, as I argue, the solutions to the climate change crisis are relatively straightforward in principle, the real question is, can we ensure such measures are implemented before it is too late?

The evidence so far is that, left to their own devices, those who dominate society today, in government or at the head of the world's giant corporations, will not push through such changes. This is true even when they recognise the danger that faces the whole world. All the major oil companies, with the exception of Exxon, may now talk of the need to take action on climate change, as do the car, tyre, power and other corporations responsible for pumping out greenhouse gases,[60] and Shell and BP may have moved into renewable energy. But no one should be fooled into thinking this is a strategic shift away from fossil fuels. Behind the greenwash it is business as usual.

Whatever the views of those at the top, and however genuine their concern over climate change, they are prisoners of the remorseless logic of profit by which corporations live or die. On average all the oil companies still depend on fossil fuels for 95 percent of their revenues and profit. So renewables account for just 0.8 percent of Shell's global investment, and for just 1 percent of the $8 billion BP spends a year on fossil fuel exploration and production. It is the same story with the car firms. Ford, for example, makes lots of green noises about climate change. But it is utterly committed to selling more and more cars, expanding into newer markets like India and China, and so contributing even more to global warming.

It may be argued that the measures needed to tackle climate change are not somehow fundamentally incompatible with capitalist society. And it is quite easy to imagine a capitalism that lived off the profits based on the production and sale of renewable energy. There is indeed no reason in abstract why capitalism has to be dependent on fossil fuels and industries linked to them. Capitalism can profit from anything it can turn into a commodity—and the history of capitalism is one of showing a remarkable facility for turning just about anything imaginable into commodities.

The problem is not one of principle or logic, but rather, as someone once remarked, that we are where we are. For historical reasons we have a capitalist society where the fossil fuel corporations lie at the heart of the production for profit on which the whole system depends. This fact has shaped everything about the world we live in, including the very ideologies and policies of the political parties and politicians who run most of the world's governments and global institutions.

Capitalism has an immense inertia at its heart. Once patterns of production become established and with them great concentrations of wealth and power established, they are hugely resistant to change. The people who head the giant corporations, and who embody the logic they must follow to survive and expand as profit-seeking beasts, will resist with all their power anything which fundamentally threatens their current basis of profit and power—the fossil fuel based economy.

The record of human history is that those who control societies have often been prepared see the whole of society plunge into disastrous chaos and collapse rather than accept change which undermined their power. I see no reason to suppose the most powerful ruling class in human history, those who today head the giant global corporations at whose centre stand the fossil fuel corporations, will behave any differently to their predecessors whose societies' fate is witnessed only by ruined monuments.

It is just about imaginable that faced with an immense global crisis due to climate change, one which threatened upheaval and instability on a scale that questioned the very survival of key sections of global capitalism, some dramatic shift could happen. In such circumstances I can imagine a section of the global ruling class, and perhaps some governments linked to them, seeking a way out of the crisis by shifting away from fossil fuels in dramatic fashion, even if that involved serious conflict with other sections of the global ruling class who wanted to resist change. But I think it would be foolish to gamble the future of human civilisation on such imaginings or potentialities becoming realities.

A surer path to change is needed. A strategy to win real action on climate change starts with maintaining and intensifying popular mobilisation and pressure. A large part of the reason governments, business and most world leaders have today to at least talk about doing something over climate change is a result of such pressure. The rich tapestry of coalitions against climate change that have begun to emerge in Britain and elsewhere also need to be developed and broadened. The kind of alliances we have seen in recent years in the global anti-capitalist movement and anti-war movements need to be replicated within a real and growing movement over climate change. We need once more the trade unionists and environmental campaigners in the industrialised countries marching side by side with the small farmers and the social movements of the poorest countries. The international day of protests called for 3 December this year provides an important focus for all this.

In Britain, we need pressure and protest to tell the New Labour regime loud and clear that any attempt to build new nuclear power stations is unacceptable and will be met by determined and militant opposition. That opposition must instead demand real action from the government to meet the public commitments Blair has made on cutting carbon dioxide emissions.

Without such mobilisation and campaigning we have no hope of winning any effective action on climate change.

However, for such pressure to be really effective it needs to go further. The movements need a perspective of overturning governments whose commitment to the capitalist system means bowing down to the corporations that pump out greenhouse gases.

Only state action can fully implement a programme of changes such as I have sketched. But any government that tries to do so will face determined opposition from those with real power today—the corporations linked into the fossil fuel economy and from business and the rich more generally. They would fight with all means at their disposal to block the assault on their wealth and privilege which is needed to finance the necessary transformation of society. They could only be beaten by mobilising the power of millions of ordinary people, above all those workers who produce the wealth and profit on which the whole edifice of today's capitalist society sits. But that means connecting the struggle against those who create the greenhouse effect with struggles against poverty, poor housing, unemployment, war, racism and all the other issues that afflict the great mass of people and will get worse as the climatic changes take place.

In short, the struggle over climate change raises the question of wresting power and wealth out of the hands of those who have it now. It points to the desperate need for a society run in a fundamentally different and democratic way, one in which not profit but the needs of ordinary people and the future of the planet we live on are at the heart of all action and policy. Such a transformation is what I mean by a revolution, and is an aim I call socialism.

Of course such action needs to be international in scope, and ultimately involve the US, if it is to be successful in heading off climate disaster. But to wait on international agreement would be a recipe for no effective action at all. What is needed is for one or a group of countries to begin taking radical action and use that to mobilise social forces in other countries to demand, or enforce, similar action there.

Not everyone who wants to resist the threat to the world's climate sees the need to transform society from top to bottom. It would be absolutely mistaken to restrict mobilisations and campaigns to those who do. We have to mobilise as widely as possible for protest and action. But we also have to see that the fight to halt climate change also has an inherent logic that goes beyond mere reforms within the existing structures of economic and political power.

NOTES

1: I do not propose in this article to devote space to a detailed rebuttal of the arguments advanced by various 'climate change sceptics'. Most are the paid hirelings of the fossil fuel corporations or their front organisations. Others, including the media-lionised Danish 'sceptical environmentalist' Bjorn Ljumberg have been unmasked as scientifically 'dishonest' by scientific peers. Of course there are huge uncertainties in predicting how the earth's climate will be affected by rising greenhouse gas concentrations. But making the atmosphere warmer will undoubtedly lead to more severe weather conditions of all kinds, simply because it will put more energy into the overall climatic system. The overwhelming scientific consensus across the world is that climate change is happening, and is set to get rapidly worse. In the face of this consensus it is simply wrong-headed to the point of insanity to do anything other than base political policy on the need for immediate and large-scale action to slash greenhouse gas emissions. For full and detailed discussion of the science of global warming see the authoritative series of reports from the Intergovernmental Panel on Climate Change at www.ipcc.ch and the (invariably excellent on all aspects of the debate on climate change) US-based Union of Concerned Scientists website www.ucsusa.org. For specific details of the dodgy credentials of some of the most prominent 'climate change sceptics' see

New Internationalist 357 (June 2003) at www.newint.org

2: Full text of Blair's speech on 15 September 2004 available at www.guardian.co.uk. The demand for a British cut of 60 percent in carbon dioxide emissions by 2050 was the centrepiece of the generally useful and detailed report by the Royal Commission, Environmental Pollution Energy: The Changing Climate 2001, available at www.rcep.org.uk

3: For details on the evidence of global warming see the Intergovernmental Panel on Climate Change's definitive reports at www.ipcc.ch and the Union of Concerned Scientists, as above. For a useful directory with descriptions of the content of many global warming related websites also see the portal www.climateark.org

4: Quoted on Environmental News Service website, 18 March 2005, www.ens-newswire.com

5: P McGarr, 'Why Green is Red', in International Socialism 88 (Autumn 2000).

6: The Guardian, 15 March 2005.

7: Figures from the Department for Trade and Industry's official energy statistics published 31 March 2005 on www.gnn.gov.uk

8: See Royal Commission report at www.rcep.org.uk

9: For a full and detailed report on Britain's carbon dioxide emissions see the informative and well researched 'What Should the Government Do to Tackle Climate Change?', Friends of the Earth's response to the Climate Change Programme Review (March 2005), available at www.foe.co.uk

10: As above.

11: For details of the climate change levy see the government's own www.defra.gov.uk/environment/ccl

12: For useful discussion of the Climate Change Levy and other government policies see www.climate-change-uk.co.uk

13: *The Guardian*, 8 April 2005.

14: www.rcep.org.uk

15: See the transport campaign group Transport 2000 www.transport2000. org.uk, and the climate change campaign group Rising Tide, www.risingtide.org.uk for details and all figures quoted on transport.

16: www.transport2000.org.uk

17: *The Independent*, 21 March 2005.

18: www.risingtide.org.uk

19: *International Herald Tribune*, 19 March 2005.

20: As above.

21: *The Observer*, 6 March 2005.

22: See an account of this at www.greenparty.org.uk

23: www.greenpeace.org

24: Quoted on www.transport2000.org.uk

25: Global carbon dioxide emissions fell by around 5.6 percent between 1990 and 2000, but this was nothing to do with Kyoto or government action—it was entirely down to the economic collapse of the USSR and Eastern Europe, and emissions have started rising again now. See the UN's official Framework Convention on Climate Change website for figures http://unfccc.int

26: *The Guardian*, 10 February 2005.

27: Quoted on BBC news report, 16 February 2005. See www.bbc.co.uk

28: *The Guardian*, 12 March 2005.

29: See 'The Sky is Not the Limit' on www.tni.org/reports

30: Letter published in full on www.tni.org

31: *The Guardian*, 5 September 2003.

32: As above.

33: As above.

34: www.ucsusa.org

35: See the excellent www.exxonsecrets.org for details of these links.

36: See the devastating report on Bush's Energy Plan and climate change, 'Beneath Hot Air', by the US National Wildlife Federation on www.nwf.org

37: As above.

38: www.sierraclub.org

39: See reports on www.ems.org (Environmental Media Services) and *The Observer*, 22 April 2004.

40: www.ucsusa.org

41: See www.transport2000.org.uk and *The Times*, 24 October 2004.

42: 'Catalysing Commitment on Climate Change' by Simon Retallack and Tony Grayling on www.ippr.org.uk. Grayling used to be the environmental policy officer for the Labour Party.

43: www.rcep.org.uk

44: BBC report, 21 June 2004 and New Economics Foundation, *The Price of Power*, at www.neweconomics.org

45: S Retallack and T Grayling, as above.

46: *The Guardian*, 10 November 1999.

47: www.ucsusa.org

48: Quoted in a Reuters report on the portal www.climateark.org

49: www.bpsolarex.com

50: ETSU, *New and Renewable Energy: Prospects for the 21st Century* (DTI, 1999).

51: European Commission report 'Study of Offshore Wind Energy in the European Community' (EC, 1998).

52: See *The Guardian*, 19 April 2005, for the start of the inquiry into the Whinash wind farm in Cumbria, for example.

53: See 'Blowing Away the Myths', report by the British Wind Energy Association at www.bwea.com

54: ETSU, as above.

55: See www.ucsusa.org

56: *The Times*, 24 October 2004.

57: See 'The Real Costs of Nuclear Electricity Production' by Greenpeace International (March 2005), at www.greenpeace.org

58: See W Cavendish and R Gross, 'Nuclear Power: A Price Worth Paying for a Stable Climate?', www.iccept.ic.ac.uk

59: www.rcep.org.uk

60: See summary, for example, in *The Observer*, 20 February 2005.

Sartre's century

Ian Birchall

This year's centenary of the birth of Jean-Paul Sartre will be an ambiguous affair.[1] In France, and even in Britain, there will be academic conferences and articles in the more intellectually inclined papers and magazines. But enthusiasm will be distinctly restrained. As Lenin pointed out long ago, the bourgeoisie tries to convert dead revolutionaries into 'harmless icons'.[2] But Sartre—like Lenin himself—remains resistant to conversion. It is scarcely possible to deny that he was both a great writer and an important philosopher, but his political commitment still sticks in the throats of our rulers and their intellectual errand-boys.

His steadfast opposition to French colonialism in Algeria and American imperialism in Vietnam has all too many echoes for today's occupation of Iraq. His insistence on the unity of theory and practice is anathema to the postmodernists, for whom the rejection of the 'unitary subject' provides the ideal alibi for intellectual and political inconsistency. Even on the socialist left some will try to prove their political virility by stressing their differences with Sartre rather than what they have in common.[3] So we can expect tributes to Sartre to be qualified with quibbles about his role during the German Occupation,[4] and above all with the claim that he was a supporter of Russian Stalinism.

Back in the 1950s and 1960s things looked very different. For those of us who discovered Sartre in the aftermath of the political crises of 1956 (Suez and Hungary), his plays and novels reflected on the one hand alienation and the loneliness of individual freedom, on the other a demand for responsibility, commitment and action. It was a potent combination at a moment when the old certainties of Stalinist Marxism had crumbled forever, and a new left was still struggling to be born. In France Sartre's opposition to the Algerian War made him a hero for those campaigning against the war, many of whom went on to be leaders of the student revolt in 1968. In the 1960s Sartre and Bertrand Russell, the two most renowned living philosophers, albeit from very different traditions, came together to oppose the Vietnam War. They inspired many thousands of young people who joined the anti-war movement, and in May 1968 Sartre backed the insurgent French students from the very first day. In the aftermath of 1968, when he sold banned socialist newspapers on the streets to defy the state[5] and addressed a meeting outside the Renault car factory, he seemed to embody the hope that Marxist theory and revolutionary practice were coming together for the first time since the 1920s.

Sartre's century

Even the French so called 'new philosopher' Bernard-Henri Lévy, hostile to Sartre's politics, calls the 20th century Sartre's century.[6] He was born in the year of the Russian 'dress rehearsal' revolution of 1905 into a bourgeois family; one of his earliest political memories was of the Russian Revolution of 1917. He died just before the rise of Solidarnosc in Poland in 1980. His lifetime covers the historical epoch stretching from the birth of Leninism to the death of Stalinism. Sartre witnessed the great events of his lifetime, commented on most of them, and took part in a number of them. He lived through a period marked by violence and social upheaval.

He had a successful academic career in the inter-war years, studying in Berlin in 1933-1934, but scarcely seeming to notice the Nazi regime. He was then best known for his novel, *Nausea* (1938). In 1940 he was taken prisoner by the German army, and spent time in a prisoner of war camp, where he wrote his first play. Later he returned to France and briefly attempted to organise a resistance grouping, Socialism and Liberty. In 1943 he published his first major philosophical work, *Being and Nothingness*.

After the war he became famous with several plays and novels; he launched the monthly journal *Les Temps modernes*, which was intended to publish political and literary material from an independent left standpoint. He was involved in the launch of the RDR, a movement that stood for a socialism independent of both Washington and Moscow. When this collapsed, Sartre moved for a time very close to the French Communist Party (PCF), though he preserved his political independence. But in 1956 he violently denounced the Russian invasion of Hungary, and broke his links with the PCF. In 1964 he refused the Nobel Prize.

The years 1939-1962, in which most of Sartre's major work was produced, were a period of almost uninterrupted violent conflict for his native land. The German Occupation gave way almost immediately to national liberation struggles, first in Indochina, then in Algeria. The centrality of violence in Sartre's work cannot be detached from this context. The question of racism, a central issue in the politics of the 20th century, was of great importance to Sartre. His 1946 book *Anti-Semite and Jew* attempted to give a psychological and political explanation of anti-Semitism.

But if it is clear that Sartre's work is deeply rooted in the events of his own time, is he relevant to the 21st century? For most of his life Sartre believed that the solution to the problems of humanity must consist in some sort of socialist reorganisation of society. For those who believe that the very idea of socialism is obsolete, Sartre's work can have little value other than as purely aesthetic documents. Many would be only too glad to let Sartre's corpse fester under the ruins of the Berlin Wall. But for those of us who believe that socialism—stripped of the monstrous deformations of Stalinism—still offers hope to humanity, Sartre's work belongs not just to the 20th century, but also to the 21st.

Existentialism

Sartre first became famous—or notorious—as the representative of the philosophy of existentialism. He did not choose the label; it was imposed on him. He was often caricatured as being a pessimistic philosopher, a gloomy figure who dwelt on the most squalid and miserable aspects of human existence. And some of his statements seem to justify such criticism. His novel, *Nausea*, depicts a young writer confronted by the absurdity of existence, the realisation that in a godless universe nothing has any meaning. It contains the statement: 'Every existing thing is born without reason, prolongs itself out of weakness, and dies by chance'.[7]

Sartre's attack on conventional moral values and his defence of the oppressed made him a natural enemy for those on the political right. In the 1950s the young Jean-Marie Le Pen declared that 'France is ruled by homosexuals: Sartre, Camus, Mauriac'.[8] Sartre's main philosophical work, *Being and Nothingness*, is several hundred pages long and frequently obscure, and it is not altogether surprising that Sartre's philosophy was often misunderstood. However, some sections convey their message vividly, notably the section on what Sartre called 'bad faith' (the strategies we adopt to evade responsibility for our own freedom), with its portraits, almost like short stories, of the cafe waiter and the woman unsure how to respond to her lover's advances.

A closer study of Sartre's thought makes it clear that what characterises it above all is a vigorous and indeed scandalous optimism. Sartre acknowledged this in his 1945 lecture 'Existentialism and Humanism', saying of his critics:

Their excessive protests [against existentialism] make me suspect that what is annoying them is not so much our pessimism but, much more likely, our optimism... What is alarming in the doctrine...is...that it confronts man with a possibility of choice.[9]

The most fundamental assertion of Sartrean philosophy is that we are condemned to be free—free in all circumstances. Even with a gun held against my head, I can choose to resist—and die. Since we are free, we make the world—there are no external obstacles other than those we determine by the choice of our own projects. We are responsible for the world as it is—and free to make it other if we so choose. For Sartre there is no human nature: human society is something quite independent of the laws of nature. Hence society does not have to be as it is; it is possible to change the world. Each of us is free to accept or reject our condition in the world; even if we fail, we are always free to rebel. The laws of the economy are quite different from meteorological laws, since they result from human choice. There is no such thing as an 'economic climate'.

Thus in *Being and Nothingness* Sartre argues that 'destruction is an essentially human thing and...it is man who destroys his cities through the agency of earthquakes'.[10] Earthquakes are a human creation. If there were no human beings, an earthquake would be a purely meaningless movement of matter. It becomes a catastrophe only when it comes up against the human project of building a city. Sartre's point is very relevant to the recent tsunami. This was not a simple 'natural disaster' or an 'act of god'; the disaster was very largely the product of poverty, inadequate precautions and the fact that warning systems were too expensive.

The central theme of all Sartre's work is the question of the unity of theory and practice. Sartre's whole philosophy is geared to the fact of human action; it centres on the question of values, and hence is a highly moral philosophy, even though Sartre disavows any kind of conventional moralising. This sets him firmly in opposition to postmodernism, which is based on a quite willing disjunction of theory and practice, leading to a fatalistic attitude towards both knowledge and action.

This concern for the unity of theory and practice led Sartre to become less interested in pure philosophy or pure literature, and more directly interested in political questions. For Sartre writing was not an activity separate from other human practices that could be judged only by its own standards. In 1964 he caused great consternation when he stated in an interview that 'alongside a dying child, *Nausea* does not make the weight'.[11] That he should put Third World starvation and a novel in the same scales seemed outrageous to many people. But such a comparison is central to Sartre's whole worldview.

Sartre and Marxism

Sartre's concern with political action brought him into dialogue with Marxism. This was not only a dialogue with the intellectuals of the French Communist Party such as Roger Garaudy and Jean Kanapa, but also with a number of independent anti-Stalinist Marxists such as Pierre Naville, Claude Lefort and Daniel Guérin.[12]

In 1960 Sartre published the *Critique of Dialectical Reason*, in which he proposed to reconcile existentialism with Marxism. It is a very long and difficult work; perhaps if Sartre had been less famous, his publisher might have sent him away to cut it to half the length, which might have been a great improvement. He never completed the second volume, and he certainly failed to resolve all the theoretical questions he had posed. But it does contain some very illuminating passages, notably the section on the bus queue and the storming of the Bastille discussed below.

For me, the question of whether Sartre was a Marxist does not seem very important—indeed, such questions easily become almost theological. What is important are the questions that Sartre asks about Marxism, the challenges he puts to Marxists. (In general Sartre is more interesting for the questions he asks than for the answers he gives.) Certainly in the period after 1956, when many Communist intellectuals in France and elsewhere broke with Stalinism and started looking for ways to renew Marxism, Sartre made an important contribution to the rebirth of Marxism as a critical and radical method of thought rather than a sterile dogmatism.

For Sartre one of the most important questions was the place of the individual human being in the Marxist explanation of the historical process. This had long been a preoccupation of Sartre, but it acquired additional relevance in the crisis of Marxism after 1956. In 1956 the Russian leader Khrushchev had given his so called 'secret speech' in which he denounced the crimes of Stalin. But Khrushchev's account was very much a psychological account. It is undoubtedly true that Stalin was an extremely unpleasant and brutal person—what Khrushchev did not and could not explain was why such an unpleasant individual had become all-powerful in a so called workers' state.

In the introduction to the *Critique of Dialectical Reason* Sartre discussed Marxist literary criticism and the ways in which Marxist critics had analysed the French poet Valéry. As he put it, 'Valéry is a petty bourgeois intellectual, no doubt about it. But not every petty bourgeois intellectual is Valéry'.[13] It is important to point out that Sartre was not innovating here, but rather reviving a current in Marxism which had been suppressed by Stalinism. At the time of the rise of Hitler Leon Trotsky had written, 'Not every exasperated petty bourgeois could have become Hitler, but an article of Hitler is lodged in every exasperated petty bourgeois'.[14]

By raising the question of the role of the individual in Marxism, Sartre asked important questions for political practice which had been neglected in the classic Marxist tradition. Marx argued that class struggle was the motor of history; Lenin contended that a revolutionary party was necessary for the conquest of state power. But neither of them posed the existential question 'Why should *I* join, why should *I* get involved?'

Sartre thus came into conflict with the deterministic philosophy that was current in the French Communist Party. In a polemic against Sartre, Roger Garaudy wrote a passage in which he denied that he exercised any free choice, or that he had any responsibility for his own actions:

I AM A COMMUNIST WITHOUT ANGUISH. First of all because I didn't choose to be a Communist. I didn't choose it because it is not for me to deny the reality of the internal contradictions of capitalism, of its crises and of the class struggle which is the motor of its development. Since the day when the analyses of *Capital* taught me the dialectic of history, I have found myself faced by a compelling force. And at no moment have I the choice between Marxism and those who deny it. I should gladly say, as Luther did to his judges: 'Here I stand: I can do no other'.[15]

That Garaudy himself began as an orthodox Communist, became a dissident Communist, then a Christian and finally a Muslim shows that the explanation of individual conduct through historical laws is not so easy.

Here again Sartre was not saying anything new. Rather he was counterposing the genuine Marxist tradition to the crude determinism of the Stalinist tradition. He quoted with approval the position argued by Engels that 'men make their own history, but in a given environment by which they are conditioned'.[16]

Sartre developed his view that we are not the products of our circumstances, but that we choose ourselves within our given circumstances, in various biographical studies. Jean Genet was born illegitimate, abandoned at birth and farmed out to a peasant family; he soon found himself in a juvenile penal colony. He might have seemed condemned to a life of crime on the margins of society; instead he became one of the finest writers of his generation. Sartre attempted to resolve this enigma in his book *Saint Genet* (1952). Later he spent many years on a biographical study of the 19th century novelist Flaubert, designed to develop in concrete fashion the themes of the *Critique of Dialectical Reason*. Flaubert was born into the middle class, yet instead of becoming a doctor or lawyer like other members of his family he became a writer. Sartre traces this back to his childhood slowness in learning to read. Yet at the same time he analyses what it meant to choose to be a writer at this time, examining ideas of literature in the post-Romantic period. Sartre never completed the study, *The Family Idiot*, but he provided a fascinating example of what biographical writing involved. (He was, incidentally, strongly influenced by Isaac Deutscher's biography of Trotsky.)

Sartre's concern for the role of the individual led him to confront the question of morality. In 1947-1948 he wrote a manuscript of over 600 pages on the question. He never completed it to his satisfaction, and it was published only after his death. Here he argues that the question of morality cannot be evaded: if we attempt to exclude it from our analyses, it returns in one way or another. As Sartre points out, the PCF had a private and a public doctrine. In the manuals of Marxist theory capitalists acted according to immutable historical and economic laws, but in the pages of the party's daily newspaper, *L'Humanité*, employers were described as 'wicked'.[17] At the same time Sartre insists that morality is not autonomous, that it is impossible to impose universal moral standards in a world in which human beings live in a situation of gross inequality. It would only be possible to have a real morality in a world where all human beings found themselves in an equal situation; in the meantime the most important moral imperative is to change the world.

The question of morality is therefore tied up with the question of history. In his discussion of ends and means, Sartre rejected the idea, held by some Marxists, that history has a pre-given end, which it is possible to know, and towards which the historical process is making its way. For Sartre there is no pre-given end to history—how history develops will depend on human action and human choice. Thus he wrote during the Second World War, 'Tomorrow, after my death, some men may decide to establish fascism, and the others may be so cowardly or so slack as to let them do so. If so, fascism will then be the truth of man, and so much the worse for us. In reality, things will be such as men have decided they shall be'.[18]

Today it is very clear that not only can we not talk about an inevitable future, we do not have any certainty that, in human terms, there will be a future at all. In his last play, *Altona*, Sartre gave a vision of the world in the 30th century, when humanity had disappeared and the only beings able to judge the history of humanity were a court of crabs. Sartre was thinking of nuclear war, but the crabs could well be swimming in the waters that will have overwhelmed our cities after centuries of global warming.

Here again, Sartre stands in the classic Marxist tradition, the tradition of Karl Marx, who wrote that each stage of the class struggle leads either to a new and higher form of society, or to the 'common ruin of the contending classes'.[19] As Rosa Luxemburg put it, 'socialism or barbarism'.

Sartre was also very much concerned with the question of collective action. In his play *In Camera* three people are brought together in a hotel room—a Latin American radical journalist, a snooty upper class woman who has killed her baby and an aggressively working class lesbian (the true heroine of the play). Slowly they realise that they are all dead, and that they only have each other to give meaning to their past existence. The play contains what is perhaps the best known quotation from Sartre: 'Hell is other people'.[20] But Sartre does not argue that human beings are inevitably in conflict with each other and that collective action is impossible. He notes the fact that it is very difficult to achieve. This puts him in opposition to the rhetoric of the PCF in the 1940s and 1950s, which presented the working class as an already formed collective which could be counted on to act in a united and cohesive fashion, a collective generally seen as identical with the Communist Party or the trade unions under its control, a rhetoric which announced that, for example, 'the working class will not permit' certain policies.

In the *Critique of Dialectical Reason* Sartre argued that human groups could take two different forms. On the one hand there was seriality, of which he gave the example of the bus queue.[21] In the bus queue a number of human beings come together in the same physical space. They share the same objective—to get on the bus. But because of scarcity—there are not enough places—each of them opposes the interests of the others, each is an obstacle to the aims of the others. But sometimes seriality is replaced by the 'fused group'. Here the example is the crowd storming the Bastille.[22] Again human beings come together in the same physical space to pursue the same aim. But this time, rather than each being an obstacle to the other, nobody can achieve their aim without the assistance of the others. I cannot storm the Bastille on my own.

Sartre, Stalinism and political action

Sartre did not content himself with merely confronting Marxism on the theoretical level. From 1945 onwards he made a consistent effort to involve himself in political activity that was compatible with his principles.

Many of Sartre's critics have attempted to discredit him by claiming he was naive about Stalinism or even corrupted by it. The recent study of Sartre by the former Maoist Bernard-Henri Lévy is based on total rejection of Communism in its very essence—'it was revolution as such which was perverse and criminal'. For Lévy Communism is 'that Sartrean passion, the object of his desire for at least 30 years'.[23] The actual story of Sartre's relations with the USSR, the PCF and Communism is rather more complicated. He made mistakes, some of which deserve vigorous criticism.

But they were mistakes made amid the difficulties of a multifaceted historical period, and Sartre's motivation was rather more complex than is often suggested.

At the Liberation Sartre did not as yet see himself as a Marxist, but he certainly used many ideas borrowed from Marxism. In October 1945 he decided to launch *Les Temps modernes* as a journal of the independent left. Sartre was quite happy to co-operate with the PCF, while at the same time maintaining a dialogue with other Marxists and socialists. He recognised that the majority of French workers felt an allegiance to the Communist Party, and considered that the USSR, whatever its weaknesses, still at least aspired towards socialism.

The PCF, however, saw Sartre's popularity as a threat to its own hegemony, especially over intellectuals and students. A flood of books and articles were published to denounce Sartre and existentialism. Roger Garaudy wrote a book about Sartre and others entitled *Gravediggers of Literature* (1947). Sartre responded, 'Gravediggers are honest people, certainly unionised, perhaps Communists. I'd rather be a gravedigger than a lackey'.[24] He was attacked by name by Stalin's cultural policeman Zhdanov, and *Les Temps modernes* was condemned by the same figure for publishing the decadent work of Jean Genet. In 1952 complaints were made at a meeting of the PCF Political Bureau that factory libraries (run by factory committees controlled by the PCF-led CGT union federation) were ordering a book by Sartre.[25]

As the PCF attack got stronger Sartre began more and more to stress his independence of both Washington and Moscow. In 1948 he wrote:

> It would be strange if I were accused in New York of anti-Americanism at the very moment when in Moscow *Pravda* is denouncing me as an agent of American propaganda. If that did happen, however, it would show one of two things—either that I am indeed unhandy at my job, or that I am on the right track.[26]

In 1948, at the time of the Communist take-over in Czechoslovakia and the Berlin blockade, Sartre joined with the former Trotskyist David Rousset, and various other activists from the social democratic, non-Communist and Trotskyist left to form the Rassemblement démocratique révolutionnaire (Revolutionary Democratic Assembly) (RDR). Its founding statement in February 1948 stressed independence of both blocs:

> Between the rottenness of capitalist democracy, the weaknesses and defects of a certain social democracy and the limitation of Communism to its Stalinist form, we believe an assembly of free men for revolutionary democracy is capable of giving new life to the principles of freedom and human dignity by binding them to the struggle for social revolution.

As Sartre put it in December 1948, 'To refuse to choose between the USSR and the US does not mean yielding first to the one, then to the other, letting ourselves be tossed about between them. It means making a positive choice: that of Europe, socialism and ourselves'.[27]

Initially the RDR seemed to have great potential, with large meetings and many enthusiastic supporters.[28] But the bureaucracies of the Socialist Party and the PCF succeeded in preventing its further expansion. Then Rousset and other leaders moved more and more towards a pro-American position. By the autumn of 1949 it had collapsed.

Rousset then launched a campaign against the labour camps in the USSR. Sartre's position on this question is often misrepresented. Sartre did not deny the existence of the camps, as some PCF members did. *Les Temps Modernes* published several articles, including one by Victor Serge, about the Russian camps. In an editorial in January 1950 Sartre and his fellow editor Merleau-Ponty declared:

> There is no socialism when one out of every 20 citizens is in a camp... Two years ago one of us wrote here that Soviet society is ambiguous, and that both signs of progress and symptoms of retrogression are found in it. If there are 10 million concentration camp inmates—while at the other end of the Soviet hierarchy salaries and standard of living are 15 to 20 times higher than those of free workers—then quantity changes into quality. The whole system swerves and changes meaning; and in spite of nationalisation of the means of production, and even though private exploitation of man by man and unemployment are impossible in the USSR, we wonder what reasons we still have to speak of socialism in relation to it.[29]

However, Sartre refused to associate himself with Rousset's campaign because the latter had launched it in a right wing newspaper—*Le Figaro*

Littéraire—and refused to condemn repressive regimes in the Western bloc, such as Greece and Spain.

However, Sartre now seems to have despaired of the possibility of an independent left. He later claimed that before 1968 'there was *nothing* to the left of the PCF'.[30] In fact his own writings show that this was untrue. In the 1950s Sartre polemicised against Ernest Mandel, Claude Lefort and Pierre Naville;[31] he was certainly aware of the existence of the Fourth International and of the Socialisme ou barbarie grouping which argued that Russia was state capitalist.

In 1952, when the government was taking repressive measures against the PCF at the time of mass demonstrations against General Ridgway, the new head of NATO, Sartre announced his 'agreement with the Communists on certain precise and limited subjects, reasoning from *my* principles and not from *theirs*'.[32] For four years Sartre became—*almost*—the model fellow traveller. But his motivation was not the totalitarian mentality which Bernard-Henri Lévy attributes to him, but a much more complex set of tactical considerations.

Firstly, as he had put it in 1947, 'The majority of the proletariat, strait-jacketed by a single party, encircled by a propaganda which isolates it, forms a closed society without doors or windows. There is only one way of access, a very narrow one, the Communist Party'.[33] The crucial fact about the Communist Party for Sartre was not its doctrine nor its link to Russia, but the fact that it had the votes of some 5 million workers and, through the CGT union federation, led the best organised section of the working class. And secondly Sartre's alignment with the USSR was motivated by Karl Liebknecht's principle that for revolutionaries 'the main enemy is at home'. In a world divided into warring blocs, both of them guilty of aggression, brutality and repression, Sartre insisted that his first priority was to attack the crimes committed on his own side.

It is undoubtedly true that Sartre, especially between 1952 and 1956, defended the indefensible in Russian society. In particular he published five articles in *Libération* in which he took a naively uncritical view of Russian society and made some appallingly dishonest claims about the freedom of criticism permitted there.[34] However, it should be added that Sartre's concessions to Stalinism were relatively small in comparison to those of some of his contemporaries. He never wrote anything comparable to Brecht's defence of the Moscow Trials.[35] British writers like Raymond Williams,

Eric Hobsbawm[36] and Edward Thompson,[37] who made an enormous contribution to Marxist understanding were, before 1956, far more deeply implicated with Stalinism than Sartre ever was. In fact his alliance with the PCF was short-lived. In 1956 Sartre denounced the Russian intervention in Hungary, saying that socialism 'is not brought at bayonet point'.[38] But he denied the right of criticism to those who had backed US imperialism in Guatemala in 1954, or who supported the Franco-British invasion of Egypt taking place at that very moment.

But even before this break with the PCF Sartre's position had sharply diverged from that of the Communists over the war in Algeria. As early as 1955 *Les Temps modernes* committed itself to a course of opposition to the war that would soon run up against the limits of legality. In October of that year an editorial statement appeared under the title 'Refusal to Obey'. This described Algeria as a 'colony' (rejecting the official fiction that it was an integral part of France) subject to 'the most obvious exploitation'. It went on: 'A war is starting in North Africa; it is up to the government whether to stop it, or, on the contrary, to make it inevitable... To this war, we say no.' At this time almost the only active campaigning against the war was coming from a handful of anarchists and Trotskyists.[39] In 1956 the PCF voted in favour of 'special powers' for the government to deal with the situation in Algeria.

Over the next few years, Sartre's consistent anti-imperialism, and his courage and outspokenness in the service of Algerian independence, were an inspiration to a new generation who had been radicalised by Algeria, and who were repelled by the role played by the traditional left in the PCF and the SFIO. In September 1960 Sartre was one of the most prominent signatories of the celebrated Manifesto of the 121, drafted by Maurice Blanchot and Maurice Nadeau. (Nadeau had been a Trotskyist in the 1930s and 1940s and close to surrealist circles.) The statement declared:

> We respect and consider justified the refusal to take arms against the Algerian people. We respect and consider justified the actions of those French people who regard it as their duty to offer assistance and protection to Algerians oppressed in the name of the French people.

The PCF did not support the Manifesto. But it was signed by Alfred Rosmer, a veteran opponent of the First World War, the surrealist André

Breton, the historian and anti-imperialist campaigner Daniel Guérin and others from the non–Stalinist left.

In 1968 Sartre, siding with the students against the authorities from the very outset, denounced the PCF for its attitude, which he said was not revolutionary and not even reformist.[40] His position on Russia also became much firmer. After the Russian invasion of Czechoslovakia he spoke of 'Soviet imperialism',[41] while saying that it followed different laws to US imperialism. He argued that 'it is impossible to reach socialism by starting from Stalinism, for one will never reach anything except something whose instrument has been Stalinism'.[42] In 1973, Sartre developed the argument further by claiming that there was nothing specifically socialist about nationalisation. If an enterprise was nationalised while the capitalist struc- ture was preserved, then what resulted was 'state capitalism'.[43]

This was scarcely a man who worshipped Stalin or who was essen- tially a totalitarian.

Sartre, violence and resistance

One of Sartre's most important articles is called 'To Write for One's Own Age'.[44] The strength of Sartre's work is that it is rooted in the problems of his own age, and it is therefore dangerous to try and argue what Sartre would have thought of the very different world in which we live. Yet such speculation may have some value. Sartre lived through an age of violence, and much of his thought revolved around the question of violence. So it may be interesting to enquire what Sartre might have thought of the war against terrorism in our own day.

Sartre is often seen as an apologist for violence and terrorism. Many of his critics recall his visit to Andreas Baader of the armed German group, the Red Army Faction, in 1974. But Baader scarcely felt that Sartre was a supporter. He commented, 'I thought I was dealing with a friend but they sent me a judge'.[45]

Sartre observed that throughout the course of history the holders of power and privilege have not lightly abandoned their positions, and that it has almost invariably been the case that they had to be violently removed. Human history is, whether we like it or not, the history of violence, and our present ills and privileges are rooted in violence. Hence in Algeria, and later in Vietnam, he refused to equate the violence of the oppressed with that of the oppressors. As he wrote:

> During the Algerian war I always refused to make a parallel between the terrorist use of bombs, the only weapon available to the Algerians, and the actions and extortions of a rich army of half a million, which occupied the entire country. It's the same in Vietnam.[46]

The text often quoted to show Sartre's support for violence is his preface to Fanon's *The Wretched of the Earth*. The language is angry and at times provocative, but time and again Sartre repeats the point that the violence of the national liberation struggle is a product of, a response to, the existing violence of colonialism:

> For at first it is not *their* violence, it is ours, which turns back on itself and rends them... It is the moment of the boomerang, it is the third phase of violence; it comes back on us, it strikes us, and we do not realise any more than we did the other times that it's we that have launched it. We have sown the wind; he [the peasant fighter] is the whirlwind... If violence began this very evening and if exploitation and oppression had never existed on the earth, perhaps the slogans of non-violence might end the quarrel...[47]

Sartre was first practically confronted with the questions of violence and terrorism during the German occupation of France. The PCF, like the Iraqi resistance today, had a policy of killing as many occupying soldiers as possible. Often the PCF was in fact sending its own members to a certain death, so there is a close parallel with suicide bombers. Moreover, the Nazis executed hostages in response to attacks by the French Resistance. Sartre commented in 1944 that when he wrote *The Flies*, 'the real drama, the drama I should have liked to write, was that of the terrorist who by ambushing Germans becomes the instrument for the execution of 50 hostages'.[48] Though Sartre saw the necessity for armed resistance, he was not entirely happy about the means advocated by the PCF.

One of the philosophical questions that preoccupied Sartre throughout his life was that of ends and means. His most extensive consideration of the problem occurs in the incomplete manuscript on morality from 1948. Here he was heavily influenced by a reading of Trotsky's short book *Their Morals and Ours*, where Trotsky rejects the formulation that the end justifies the means in favour of an argument that there is a dialectical interrelation between ends and means. Sartre's formulation was very close to Trotsky's.[49] As he put it later, 'We are of those who say: the end justifies the means; adding, however, this indispensable corrective: these means define the end'.[50]

So, for Sartre, the question exists on two levels. On one level the violence of the oppressed may be justified by the greater violence of the oppressor. But there is also the second question: the effectiveness of terrorist methods in achieving the goal of a more just society. Such a distinction is very relevant to today's war on terror.

Sartre's work does not give us a doctrine or a strategy in face of today's world. No organised political tendency can claim his legacy. But in studying Sartre we see a man facing the problems of his own age, a man grappling with the question of freedom and responsibility, of morality and politics, of violence, of the possibility of collective action. The way in which he asked the questions may help those who are still seeking answers.

Note on reading

The main themes of Sartre's work come across most powerfully in his plays and novels. The best plays to read (or see if possible) are *The Flies* (in which Sartre uses a Greek myth to condemn the Nazi occupation), *In Camera* (where three dead souls form an eternal triangle), *The Respectful Prostitute* (for which Sartre was criticised for suggesting that there might be racism in the US!), *Dirty Hands* (a political drama based on the assassination of Trotsky), *Lucifer and the Lord* (a moral and political allegory set in 16th century Germany), and *Nekrassov* (a satire of the right wing press which still rings true today). There is a collection of short stories entitled *Intimacy* (also published under the title *The Wall*) in which 'The Wall' (on the Spanish Civil War) and 'Childhood of a Leader' (on how a middle class adolescent becomes a fascist) are particularly interesting. The three novels of the *Roads to Freedom* trilogy (*The Age of Reason*, *The Reprieve* and *Iron in the Soul*) give a fascinating picture of France before and during the outbreak of the Second World War, where a group of individuals are caught up by the historical process and have to remake their lives.

Sartre's major philosophical works tend to be very long and very difficult. Sartre's 1945 lecture 'Existentialism and Humanism' contains many oversimplifications, but is a useful introduction. It also contains a confrontation with the Trotskyist Pierre Naville (who organised the founding conference of the Fourth International). *Anti-Semite and Jew* is a lucid and thought-provoking study of the roots of racism. While the *Critique of Dialectical Reason* is hard going, the opening section, published separately in English as *The Problem of Method*, is fairly readable and introduces a number of key problems.

Note that many of Sartre's works have been published or performed in English under several different titles. There are various political articles and extracts from the *Critique of Dialectical Reason* at www.marxists.org/reference/archive/sartre The full text of *No Exit* (*In Camera*) is available at www.nyu.edu/classes/keefer/hell/sart.html

NOTES

1: This is a revised version of a lecture given in March 2005 at the Club Voltaire in Frankfurt. Thanks to Mary Phillips and Pete Glatter for comments and encouragement.

2: V I Lenin, 'State and Revolution', in *Collected Works*, vol 25 (Moscow, 1964), p385.

3: For example the bizarre claim that 'Sartre was the wealthy, well-connected chump who so often hangs around revolutionary circles and understands nothing'. Ben Watson in *Radical Philosophy* 129 (Jan-Feb 2005), p44.

4: In recent years a number of Sartre's critics have raised questions about his behaviour under the German occupation, for example the fact that *The Flies* was first performed at a theatre formerly named after the Jewish actress Sarah Bernhardt and renamed by the German occupiers. Such criticisms generally come from people of a later generation, who fail to realise that the institutions of a fascist occupation cannot be boycotted like South African oranges. To survive one had to compromise. In the immediate post-war period Sartre worked with a number of people who had impeccable Resistance records, and some of whom, like Claude Bourdet, had been in German concentration camps. None of them questioned Sartre's conduct. Certainly he was not a Resistance hero—he never claimed to be—but the attacks on his record seem to be motivated by spite rather than fact.

5: At a recent conference I asked Alain Geismar, then a leading Maoist, what Sartre's paper-selling technique had been like. Unfortunately Geismar had been in jail at the time and was not able to observe him in action.

6: B-H Lévy, *Sartre: The Philosopher of the Twentieth Century* (Cambridge, 2003). The French title is simply 'Sartre's Century'. For a critique of this work by the so called 'new philosopher', see I Birchall, 'The Kiss of Death', *Historical Materialism*, 10/3, 2002.

7: J-P Sartre, *The Diary of Antoine Roquentin* [*Nausea*] (London, 1949), p180.

8: Cited in M Winock, *La République se meurt, 1956-1958* (Paris, 1985), p23.

9: J-P Sartre, *Existentialism and Humanism* (London, 1948), p25.

10: J-P Sartre, *Being and Nothingness* (London, 1957), p9.

11: *Le Monde*, 18 April 1964.

12: For a full treatment of Sartre's debates with the anti-Stalinist left see I Birchall, *Sartre Against Stalinism* (New York and Oxford, 2004).

13: J-P Sartre, *The Problem of Method* (London, 1963), p56.

14: L Trotsky, *Fascism, Stalinism and the United Front* (London, 1989), p259.

15: R Garaudy, *Les Fossoyeurs de la littérature* (Paris, 1947), p79.

16: Engels in a letter to W Borgius (and not H Starkenburg as some previous compilations incorrectly have it); K Marx and F Engels, *Collected Works*, vol 50 (London, 2004), p264.

17: J-P Sartre, *Notebooks for an Ethics* (Chicago, 1992), p346.

18: J-P Sartre, *Existentialism and Humanism*, as above, p40.

19: 'Communist Manifesto', section I in K Marx and F Engels, *Collected Works*, vol 6 (London 1976), p482.

20: J-P Sartre, *The Flies & In Camera* (London, 1946), p166.

21: Many younger readers will be unfamiliar with the concept of a bus queue. They should ask their grandparents about the days when people stood in an orderly line at a bus stop rather than clawing their way over other people's bodies to get on the bus.

22: J-P Sartre, *Critique of Dialectical Reason I* (London, 1976), pp256-69, 351-63.

23: B-H Lévy, *Sartre*, pp378, 3.

24: J-P Sartre, *What is Literature?* (New York, 1965), p258.

25: P Robrieux, *Histoire intérieure du parti communiste II 1945-1972* (Paris, 1981), p299.

26: *Sartre on Theatre* (London, 1976), p205.

27: *Franc-Tireur*, 10 December 1948.

28: I was told by Jean-René Chauvin, a veteran Trotskyist who was active in the RDR, that Sartre not only spoke at large public rallies, but attended local branch meetings in the fifth *arrondissement* of Paris.

29: The editorial was drafted by Merleau-Ponty, though fully endorsed by Sartre. The text is reproduced in M Merleau-Ponty, *Signs* (Northwestern University, 1964), pp264-265.

30: J-P Sartre, Ph Gavi, P Victor, *On a raison de se révolter* (Paris, 1974), p41.

31: For details see I Birchall, *Sartre Against Stalinism*, as above.

32: J-P Sartre, *The Communists and Peace* (London, 1969), p62.

33: J-P Sartre, *What is Literature?*, as above, p247.

34: 15, 16, 17-18, 19, 20 July 1954. (This was not the present-day *Libération*, which Sartre helped to found, but an earlier paper of the same name.)

35: 'With total clarity the trials have proved the existence of active conspiracies... All the scum at home and abroad, all the parasites, professional criminals, informers joined them.' R Hayman, *Brecht* (London, 1983), p210.

36: In 1939 just after the Hitler-Stalin Pact, Hobsbawm and Williams wrote a pamphlet defending Russia in the Russo-Finnish War (R Williams, *Politics and Letters* (London, 1981), pp42-43). For Hobsbawm's pre-1956 Stalinism see N Carlin and I Birchall, 'Kinnock's Favourite Marxist', *International Socialism* 21 (summer 1983).

37: 'Yesterday, in the Soviet Union, the Communists were struggling against every difficulty to build up their industry to the level of the leading capitalist powers: today they have before them Stalin's blueprint of the advance to Communism... Thus have the "claims"...of William Morris, the "unpractical" poet, been promised fulfilment!' E P Thompson, *William Morris* (London, 1955), pp760-761.

38: *France-Observateur*, 8 November 1956.

39: For a full study of the role played by Trotskyists in solidarity with the national liberation of Algeria, see S Pattieu, *Les camarades des frères: trotskistes et libertaires dans la guerre d'Algérie* (Paris, 2002).

40: Interview in *Der Spiegel*, 15 July 1968.

41: *Théâtre de la Ville/Journal*, November 1968.

42: J-P Sartre, *Situations VIII* (Paris,

1972), p354.

43: *Der Spiegel*, 12 February 1973.

44: 'Écrire pour son époque', *Les Temps modernes* 33, 1948.

45: See 'The Slow Death of Andreas Baader' at http://www.marxists.org/reference/archive/sartre

46: J-P Sartre, *Situations VIII*, as above, pp34-35.

47: F Fanon, *The Wretched of the Earth* (London, 1965), pp16, 17, 20, 21.

48: *Sartre on Theatre*, as above, p188.

49: *Notebooks for an Ethics*, as above, pp159-68.

50: J-P Sartre, *The Spectre of Stalin* (London, 1969), p87.

Latin America's new 'left' governments

Claudio Katz

This is a slightly edited version of an article by one of Argentina's best known Marxist economists circulated internationally in Spanish earlier this year. Its original title was 'The centre left, nationalism and socialism'.[1] It was written before the most recent upheavals in Ecuador and Bolivia. This translation is by Mike Gonzalez. Footnotes have been added where we thought it helpful; endnotes are Katz's own.

The new governments of Latin America share a critique of neo-liberalism, rampant privatisation, an excessive openness of economies to global capital and of social inequality. They propose to erect more productive and autonomous capitalist forms under greater regulation by the state. But will they form a common bloc and will they offer the people access to power?

The failures of neo-liberalism

Lula came to power in Brazil and Kirchner in Argentina because neo-liberal policies could not reverse the decline in Latin America's role in the world market, a decline shown by the stagnation of investment and per capita GDP, and which contrasted notably with what was happening in China and South East Asia.

Cycles of growth continued to depend on the flows of foreign capital and the price of exports—that is why capitalist profits lacked stability in the 1990s. A falling wage bill did not compensate for the shrinking internal market, and a decline in purchasing power affected capital accumulation. The opening of their economies emphasised the disadvantages of Latin

American businesses vis à vis their competitors. Many capitalists profited from the growing public debt, but the failure to control it hampered the ability of governments to intervene with tax policies to protect them from the periods of recession.

Neo-liberalism did not reduce social struggle, and the ruling classes were not able to achieve the kinds of victories they had won in previous decades; on the contrary, they have had to face risings which have brought down several presidents in the Andean region and the southern cone. Direct action on the land (Peru), an indigenous rising (Ecuador), pressure from the street (Argentina), an insurrectionary climate (Bolivia), land occupations (Brazil), anti-imperialist protests (Chile), a new political movement (Uruguay) and the resistance to military coups (Venezuela) have inspired a new cycle of resistance throughout the region.

The ruling classes have lost the confidence they displayed in the 1990s and many of their principal representatives have withdrawn from the scene (Menem in Argentina, Fujimori in Peru, Salinas in Mexico, Pérez in Venezuela, Lozada in Bolivia). A decade of embezzlement of public funds confirmed the corruption of all regimes that mediate with big capital.

Characteristic behaviour

With Lula and Kirchner the political framework that the ruling classes have controlled for decades has begun to change. The businessmen and bankers who profited from deregulation have now jumped on the interventionist bandwagon. The sectors worst affected by the disasters of the 1990s are especially keen to enjoy the benefits of state subsidies and to put limits on the interventions of foreign competition.

The dominant alliance of financiers, industrialists and agro-export companies which controls the system of power is not the same as the classical national bourgeoisie of the 1960s. They have strengthened their integration into the international financial circuits (as receivers of credit and debtors to the state), they have consolidated their role in exports at the expense of the internal markets, and they have major investments abroad. Yet this increasing transnationalisation has not destroyed their local roots. By maintaining their principal activities within the region, the ruling classes of Latin America remain a distinct sector in competition with the corporations based outside the region. They are the principal support of the new governments and are behind their increasingly conservative direction.

Lula and Kirchner avoid populist rhetoric and avoid any conflict with the US State Department because they share interests with the region's major capitalists. This caution explains why they are prepared to negotiate with the World Trade Organisation and the various 'light' versions of the Free Trade Area of the Americas, and why they have avoided building any real customs union. They implement fiscal reforms, accept funds from the IMF and refuse to consider any joint organisation of debtor nations.

The new presidents have refused to participate in the imperialist occupation of Iraq—but then very few world leaders have supported Bush in his crusade. But they have sent troops to Haiti, allowing the Pentagon to free some of its troops based in the Caribbean for the war in the Arab world. Lula, Kirchner and Tabaré have colluded with the formation of a puppet government which has legitimised the coup against Aristide, regulated drug trafficking and restricted the high levels of emigration to Miami. The fact that Latin American military personnel are wearing UN insignia does not change the fact that they are serving US interests.

The role of the centre left governments has been to soften the resistance movements in the region. That was the role of Lula and Kirchner's envoys during the Bolivian debacle of 2003, for example, when they intervened in the middle of a popular rising to support the establishment of a government that would continue the policies of its predecessor and guarantee the privatisation of oil. Other presidents with progressive credentials have played the same role without need of outside intervention. Gutierrez in Ecuador, for example, promised national independence and instead governed through repression and continued to privatise.

Brazil and Argentina

The new presidents emerged in different conditions. Lula assumed the presidency in the final phase of an economic crisis which accentuated Brazil's urban inequality and rural poverty. Kirchner came to power at the end of the deepest depression in Argentina's history, which had brought the collapse of the banking system, the confiscation of bank deposits and unprecedented levels of poverty, hunger and unemployment.

Lula has won plaudits from Wall Street for maintaining his predecessor Fernando Henrique Cardoso's neo-liberal model. His arguments are the same ('we must win the confidence of the market in order to attract investment') and serve only to strengthen the role of the financiers who run the Central Bank. He has also protected the profits of the banks with a budget surplus of 4.5 percent of GDP and the highest interest rate of recent decades. These methods ensure that creditors will continue to receive repayments that amount to double the level of public spending.

Kirchner avoided this kind of continuity because he was obliged to rebuild the ill-fated circuit of accumulation and so adopted more heterodox policies to restore capitalist profits. He took advantage of an upturn in the economic cycle to combine tax changes with a range of subsidies and re-established the balance between the groups who gained during the period when the Argentinian peso was convertible into one US dollar (bankers and privatisers) and those who lost out (exporters and industrialists).

Both governments defend profits against the interests of workers. The Brazilian president has already imposed a regressive pension reform, frozen agrarian reform and reinforced the fall in the value of wages. His party holds back trade union struggles and has succeeded in holding down the level of popular resistance. Kirchner, on the other hand, is facing a more complex social situation because he came to power amid a popular rising. He has tried to defuse protest through co-optation (giving government jobs to activists), by wearing down the most combative sectors through constant media attacks, and by criminalising many of them—there are dozens of prisoners and thousands facing trial. And he has succeeded in diluting the impact of the picket lines and the *cacerolazos*,[a] although mass mobilisations continue to be the backdrop of Argentinian political life. His administration is conservative, but he is much more careful than his Brazilian colleague to hide his links with the neo-liberal past.

While Lula's rise to power occurred without major institutional fractures, Kirchner reached the presidency unexpectedly after a turbulent sequence of temporary governments. What in Brazil was a calm transfer of power, in Argentina was a delicate operation to restore the credibility of the state in the face of mass rejection of the political system (expressed in the slogan '*que se vayan todos*'—get rid of the lot of them).

Lula marks the final phase of the transformation of the PT[b] into a classic bourgeois party, breaking with its left wing past and becoming

---

a: The militant, saucepan-banging demonstrations that brought down the government in December 2001.

b: Partido dos Trabalhadores (Workers Party), which grew out of working class opposition to the military dictatorship of 1964-1985.

integrated into a bipartisan system. Its patronage finances an army of bureaucrats who upheld the expulsion of those members of parliament opposed to the pension reforms.

This transformation of a popular movement into an appendage of capitalist domination was what happened with Peronism[c] a long time ago. Kirchner was able to renew yet again the party that has guaranteed governability for the ruling class. But he has shown an uncharacteristic duplicity, veiling clientilism with gestures in defence of human rights, the independence of the judiciary and an attack on corruption.

Uruguay and Bolivia

The case of Uruguay is similar to Argentina's in terms of the degree of economic breakdown, but closer to Brazil with respect to a lower level of social struggle and the greater stability of the political system.

Although the GDP and investment levels fell dramatically, the crisis never took on Argentinian dimensions in Uruguay. The Frente Amplio (Broad Front)[d] managed to maintain institutional continuity and to avoid political breakdown or a vacuum. Now its ministers are rushing to implement Lula's orthodox economic orientation. They have promised to pay the debt, introduced a regressive tax system, and they continue to offer a bankers' paradise and sustain the enormous budget surplus that is required to avoid defaulting on debt.

This development can be explained in part by a weakening of resistance through unemployment, emigration and the ageing of the population. But the historical traditions of a country which has never experienced popular uprisings or significant breaks in institutional structures also have an influence.

The Frente Amplio's official line is that 'a small country cannot act alone', as if progressive policies were the exclusive province of big countries. But this discourse justifies inaction and will conflict with the expectations awoken by the coalition's electoral victory. The social base, the cultural hegemony and the mass organisations of the Frente sit uneasily

c: Peronism, the movement named after military president Juan Peron, who ruled Argentina in the postwar years in conditions which enabled him to give big reforms for the working class without damaging capitalism. Overthrown by a coup in 1955 and driven into exile, his movement, the PJ, retained enormous working class support through subsequent decades.

d: Frente Amplio, the coalition of left parties whose electoral victory last year broke the hold which the rival bourgeois parties had always had over Uruguay's government.

with the spurious political realism of its leadership.

In Bolivia the centre left (Evo Morales[e]) is not in government but has supported the unstable presidency of Mesa[f] and is working to replace him in 2007. But this timeline does not square with the breakdown in the regions or the uneasy administration of a ruling class that has neither resources, political tools nor mediating institutions to help it deal with the crisis.

The displacement of the nation's productive axis from the mines of the east to the oil fields of the west has only served to deepen the economic crisis. If the closure of the mines raised the level of unemployment, the attempt to stop coca cultivation sowed devastation among the peasantry. This impoverishment accentuated the tendency to disintegration of the country, which the business sector of Santa Cruz was happy to intensify in order to appropriate petroleum income. Its ambitions clashed with the popular demand that brought down the Lozada government in 2003—the nationalisation of natural gas so that it could be used for industrialisation.

In Bolivia there is a vibrant tradition of popular uprisings. That is why Mesa used a fraudulent plebiscite to mask the continuing privatisation of the energy industry behind promises of nationalisation. The support of Evo Morales allowed him to suggest he was moving towards state owner-ship when in fact he was planning to continue with private contracts for many decades yet.

If they are to govern like Lula the centre left will have to deactivate popular resistance and win the confidence of the ruling class at the same time. The moderate policies and acceptable candidates coming from the MAS suggest that this is their objective. But the territorial integrity of Bolivia is also threatened by a tendency to balkanisation which coexists with the always latent possibility of a new popular insurrection. In these cir-cumstances, it is unlikely that the demobilising formula applied elsewhere in the southern cone can function in Bolivia.

Venezuela: the Bolivarian process

Does Chávez belong to this centre left current? The international press regularly distinguishes his 'populism' from the other 'modernising govern-ments'; and there are indeed significant differences between Lula and Kirchner and Chávez.

---

e: Leader of the coca growers and of the Bolivian MAS (Movement for Socialism)—not to be confused with parties with the same name in Argentina and Venezuela.

f: The vice president who took over the presidency after the uprising of October 2003.

Chávez did not maintain the institutional structures as Lula did, nor did he oversee the rebuilding of the traditional parties like Kirchner. He emerged from a popular rising (the 'Caracazo' of 1989) and a military rebellion (in 1992) which led to a major electoral victory in 1998. He began by making social concessions and introducing a very progressive constitution. His government has radicalised alongside the mass movement and in response to the conspiracies of the right. This dynamic distinguishes him from the other centre left governments because he acted against the bosses (in December 2001), the attempted coup (April 2002), the oil establishment (December 2002) and the challenge of the referendum of August 2004. And there are many other features that distinguish the Venezuelan process.

Chávez displaced the traditional parties of the ruling class which lost their control of the state. His base is the mass movement and there is no sector of the capitalist class who see him as a potential ally. He does not just promise reforms but has initiated genuine land redistribution programmes, extended credit to co-operatives and provided health and education for the whole population. Chávez stands, therefore, in the nationalist tradition of Cárdenas in Mexico, Peron, Torrijos of Panama and Velasco Alvarado in Peru. And this makes him an exception among the centre left responses to imperialism.

The explanation probably lies in the peculiarities of a Venezuelan army which had little contact with the Pentagon but was influenced by the guerrilla tradition, and in the weight of the oil-producing sector with its powerful bureaucracy, its conflicts with its customers in the US and the limited role of private enterprise. But Chávez's anti-imperialism places him at the opposite end of the spectrum from any dictatorship—Chávez has much in common with Peron, but nothing at all with Videla.[g] He shares with the Peron of the 1950s, for example, his social programmes and the redirection of national income towards welfare services. He enjoys the same kind of social support, though if Peron's base was the organised working class. Chávez's support comes from the local organisations of casual workers.

Chávez is different from his South American colleagues, too, in his confrontation with the right. He has scored some victories, but as long as their privileges are under threat, they will not cease to conspire to remove

g: Military dictator of Argentina in the late 1970s responsible for the 'dirty war' that killed 30,000 working class and left activists.

Chávez or to force him into a conservative turn (of the kind taken by the PRI[h] in Mexico).

The US pulls the strings of any coup attempt or terrorist provocation from Colombia, but Washington has no Pinochet to turn to and has to rely on its 'friends in the Organisation of American States' to undermine Chávez. Bush cannot act in too barefaced a way while he is stuck in the Middle East quagmire. He does not dare to compare Chávez to Saddam— and Chávez cannot be tamed like Gaddafi. The US needs Venezuelan oil and it needs to combat Venezuela's active involvement in OPEC and its attempts to redirect crude oil to new clients in China and Latin America.

Chávez supplies oil to Cuba and maintains diplomatic relations with Havana, defying the embargo, which further aggravates the tensions with imperialism. Venezuela sent no troops to Haiti nor will it bend to Washington's demands on trade; and the presence of Cuban doctors and teachers has made Venezuelans very sensitive to the issue. Chávez's understanding of Bolivarianism is sympathetic to socialism.

The country is divided into two camps by income, culture and skin colour. The oligarchy's reaction to the presence of the marginalised in the political process is to manipulate the middle classes, and there are almost daily confrontations. Chávez, on the other hand, has shown great skill in mobilising his supporters against the manipulations of the right wing media. There is much in common between the Venezuelan situation and Nicaragua in the 1980s or Portugal after the revolution of 1974.

Its oil income has allowed Venezuela to raise its public spending from 24 percent of GDP in 1999 to 34 percent in 2004 and to address the external debt without major difficulties. These special circumstances explain the vitality of the Bolivarian revolution compared with other regional centre left governments, but they also raise questions as to how far its experience can be generalised.

A regional bloc?

Chávez's proposals for regional integration met a lukewarm reception from his centre left colleagues, none of whom expressed any readiness to replace the Free Trade Areas of the Americas with Chávez's proposed ALBA (Bolivarian Alternative for the Americas). They echoed his rhetoric, but

---

h: The party that took power in the early 1920s after the Mexican Revolution and ruled without a break for the rest of the century.

showed little will to build anti-imperialist regional organisations. Chávez has proposed three: Petrosur, bringing the oil companies into a single entity; Bansur, a regional bank bringing together national reserves; and a common market (from Mercosur[j] to Comersur).

In some senses, these associations would embrace businesses that already link a number of capitalist enterprises. On the other hand, these agreements will not produce the autonomous integration Chávez is hoping for. That would require social transformations that no centre left government is willing to carry through. For Petrosur to control the region's oil production, for example, would require the renationalisation of oil in Argentina and Bolivia—it would make no sense to link this organism with foreign private oil companies. In any event both Kirchner and Mesa have forged strategic alliances with Repsol to maintain privatisation. The creation of Enarsa (the Argentinian state energy company), with neither resources nor wells of its own, can contribute nothing to integration, any more than the fact that Brazil's Petrobras has bought the shares of an Argentinian corporation (Perez Companc) or that the Venezuela National Oil Corporation has united with Enarsa in acquiring service stations. None of these moves challenges the exploitative character of oil production in the region. Petrosur could expose the profits of some providers but it will not be able to guarantee the energy provision that would make it possible for new industries to develop in the interests of the majority.

The reserves for a regional bank do exist, but are controlled by the IMF. For Bansur to come into being would require first the creation of a debtors' club capable of resisting the IMF's interventions and putting an end to the haemorrhage of funds from the area—and no government in the region is proposing any such thing.

Any attempt to achieve major agreements on trade face the counter-pressure of bilateral agreements encouraged by the US which are favoured by Latin America's ruling classes, who trade more with the metropolis than with their neighbours. Mercosur's difficulties reflect this tension: its customs agreements, for example, contain 800 exceptions. And while 50 percent of European Union exports are between member countries, in Mercosur that figure is only 11 percent. Brazil certainly does not perform an economic role like Germany, nor is Argentina France's political equivalent.

---

j: Mercosur—the free trade agreement between Argentina, Brazil, Paraguay and Uruguay.

Integration is vital to counter the tendencies to fragmentation already visible in Bolivia and Ecuador, for example. But the region's capitalists have other priorities; it is not true that 'the national bourgeoisies that have survived neo-liberalism are drawn towards the formation of a common bloc'.[2] On the contrary, transnationalisation has reduced their interest in integration—hence their hostility to Chávez. The presidential summits issue rhetorical calls to forge a South American Community, but do little practical about it.

Transnational firms, on the other hand, have prospered and they are actively behind moves to ease capital movements in order to cheapen labour, rationalise subsidies and maximise the gains from tariff reductions. But this kind of integration is of no benefit to the people. So Chávez's attempt to spread the Bolivarian spirit has come up against a structural obstacle. No official argument or mass mobilisation has been able to leap this hurdle. While capitalists retain their power the dream of Bolivar and San Martin cannot be fulfilled.

Governments in conflict?

Some analysts have argued that the process of integration will advance through the integration of nationalism and the centre left, on the assumption that Lula and Kirchner will later move to the left.[3] And this opens the second area of debate—can the governments of the centre left bring the people closer to power?

It is a common view that both governments are 'in conflict'—but the clashes with business interests which are normal in any capitalist government are not to be confused with the involvement of popular forces in these conflicts. And they certainly play no role in the clashes between bankers and industrialists that have divided Lula's team nor with the arguments over subsidies that have split Kirchner's cabinet. These clashes arise from capitalism's competitive nature itself. And it is particularly revealing in the case of Lula, who has opted to follow in the footsteps of Blair and Felipe Gonzalez (the former Socialist Party prime minister of Spain) in the absence of any pressure from the right. His working class origins have not held him back from this orientation, and his continuation of previous policies cannot be attributed to 'what he has inherited' nor to the fact that he is leading a government of transition. Some people argue that it is a tactical move on Lula's part because he has not yet conquered power. That would be credible if he showed any signs of opposing the ruling class; control of the state could be a step towards effective control of the economy if he had any intention of transforming the status quo. But today Lula is a close ally of the same capitalist groups that are behind Kirchner.

Unreal options

Obviously Lula is not Cardoso and Kirchner is not Menem—but that only tells us that each new government adapts to the changing needs of the capitalist class. Both governments have strengthened the mechanism of state control—but for whose benefit? The neo-liberals used the state to carry through privatisations and rescue bankrupt banks. Lula's interventions serve to block wage rises, guarantee high interest rates and channel the benefits of economic revival into the pockets of the agro-exporters. This does not contradict the notion of an independent foreign policy, because every Brazilian government has tried to diversify its trade and China today is in the sights of every entrepreneur.

But he introduced the Fame Zero (Zero Hunger) policy at least, some will say, to eliminate hunger; yet the programme never had adequate resources and never got off the ground. Despite the agrarian reform, landowners are still threatening those who occupy land, and while 27,000 oligarchs still control over half of Brazil's land, the promised agricultural settlements are advancing at a snail's pace. Even the modest economic recovery of recent times cannot be ascribed to Lula, since every country in the region is experiencing something similar, the result of foreign investments. The resurgence of the Argentinian economy is often attributed to Kirchner—some even say there are signs of a redistribution of income, though there is no evidence for this. If deepening poverty has been halted in this new cycle, it is worth recalling that the same thing happened in the early 1990s. What is really significant about the recent period is how little unemployment and social exclusion figures have fallen, given the tax surpluses that the government has found to pay off the debt.

Lula's supporters are still hoping that he will 'go back to his roots', and Lula is happy to encourage people to think that way. Kirchner's defenders say much the same thing, but the more secure he is the more he will impose the bosses' model, just as he did during his governorship of Santa Cruz province. And the vigorous advocacy of Mercosur by both presidents is not the sign of change their supporters might have hoped for; in fact they are solely concerned with defending capitalist interests in both countries and protecting the private interests that might be harmed by closer cooperation between Brazil and Argentina. They have no plans to transform Mercosur into a project for integration from below and resisting imperialism.

Contradictions on the right

Some still argue that a defeat for Lula 'would let in the right'—but the reality is that, unlike Venezuela, there is no sign that the right in Brazil have any desire to destabilise Lula. Others affirm that compromise with the IMF and the right is the only way of ensuring reform—but since Lula has adopted the programme of his opponents, those reforms are no longer on the agenda. Lula has changed sides, and the working class now needs to develop its own alternative.

The spectre of the right is also used in Argentina, even though the capitalist class has much to be grateful to Kirchner for.

Some writers[+] have argued the need to form a common front with the government against the right, using Mao's distinction between primary and secondary contradictions as a rationale. But the issue here is not one of socialist strategy. Kirchner is not leading a national bourgeoisie in a conflict with imperialism nor is he involved in a conflict which could lead to an insoluble crisis for capitalism. And even if that were so, it would be wrong to abandon popular demands; pacts with the class enemy can only lead to a disarming of the oppressed and the kind of internal divisions that will destroy the revolutionary project. Addressing only the 'secondary contradictions' simply serves to break the link between minimum and maximum demands and frustrate the development of social struggles.

There are those who argue that the PT has not lost its identity under Lula. But a party that serves the interests of the bankers, while it may preserve an electoral base, can no longer claim to represent the working class. Lula made compromises with neo-liberalism, promoted regressive labour legislation and buried any mention of socialism in the PT's manifestos to ease its alliances with the right. Power has undermined the PT's origins in struggle, just as it did with Peron in Argentina many years earlier.

The 'lesser evil' argument leads to a series of subsequent capitulations. Lula's open collusion with the right is more obvious than Kirchner's development; yet he too has set out to demobilise the mass movement and ensure the dominance of capital.

But however these governments are characterised, there can be no justification for militants or activists to participate in either of them;[5] to be part of the government is to collude directly in the application of policies directed against the mass movement. There is no possibility of representing the people inside a cabinet dominated by the interests of capital, as the history of 20th century social democracy has clearly shown. Progressive ministers end up masking the realities—that is why Lula and Kirchner have appointed well-known figures to the ministries of justice, culture and human rights, leaving political and economic questions in the hands of the establishment.

Comparative justifications

Some Brazilian intellectuals have argued that the lack of the level of struggle that could place socialism on the agenda explains Lula's move to the right. In Argentina the suggestion is that Kirchner is a moderate because the movement did not exist in the first place. In both cases, commentators hypnotised by power have expressed no anger at the sufferings of the people. Instead there is talk of an unfavourable balance of forces—yet there is no mention of the fact that both governments have actively demobilised the movement, reinforcing the trade union bureaucracy through the CUT in Brazil and the Peronists in Argentina. Any reduction in the levels of struggle, therefore, is not an objective fact but the result of government policies. Any discussion of a balance of forces asumes that both presidents have remained within the camp of the oppressed, whereas in fact both have placed themselves firmly alongside business in opposing social reforms.

In these circumstances there can be no defence of Lula or Kirchner. Some argue that this is not the moment to discuss alternatives—when will the moment then be right? We need not await any further signs than the turn that the PT has taken. The danger now is not a premature break, but the effect of growing popular disillusionment. The fatalists in Argentina affirm, 'What do you expect?—Kirchner is a capitalist.' In that case, there is only one conclusion: we should resist government assaults, expose its manoeuvres and build a left alternative. Neither is Uruguay's Frente Amplio a model to imitate: it has just entered government and is already following Lula's path, and the argument that it was an organisation built from below is contradicted by its many years of adaptation to the institutions of capitalism.

Venezuela's dilemma

In Venezuela, by contrast, there does exist a 'government in conflict'; the major struggles in which Chávez is involved bring face to face capitalist interests and those of the masses. Any attempts by business groups to curry favour with Chávez fall foul of this constant confrontation, which in its turn has created a radical anti-imperialist dynamic.

Venezuela has the same levels of inequality and underdevelopment as the rest of the continent: 80 percent of the population lives in poverty and three quarters of the population work in the informal sector of the economy. Any resolution of these problems must begin by going beyond the limits which frustrated all previous attempts at independent national development. Social welfare policies, the distribution of unproductive land and credits to co-operatives can initiate a gradual redistribution of wealth. But it will take massive state investment to reverse the structural unemployment and deepening inequality of recent years. This demands a programme of industrial planning that will eradicate the privileges of the big capitalists and their allies in the bureaucracy. The people who pilfered the national oil wealth will not now become agents of development.

The sacking of the management of the state oil company was a major step forward; the increased level of royalties and the reduction of dependence on the US market (50 percent of exports and eight refineries on US territory) increase the level of economic independence. But there is still manipulation, exploration rights given without permission, and suspect investments to be dealt with. All Chávez's ambitious social reforms require a radicalisation of the process, while Kirchner, Lula (and the new Spanish prime minister Zapatero) are all working to encourage him to build bridges with the opposition—echoing the position of the Organisaton of American States, Jimmy Carter and Human Rights Watch.

Yet the main block on this process lies within the Chávez government itself, dominated as it is by an inept and opportunist bureaucracy which will happily change sides should the wind change direction. One section of Chávez's supporters (the Comando Ayacucho) brought that moment nearer by validating the collection of fraudulent signatures for the referendum.

All this tells us that victories that are frozen get diluted, that a blocked Bolivarian revolution could easily follow the road of Mexico's PRI and become an instrument of the ruling class. The Cuban Revolution followed the opposite path—and while Chávez has often expressed his admiration for Cuba he has not set in motion any break with capitalism as the Cubans did in the 1960s.

The institutions of the Venezuelan state are undergoing a process of democratic radicalisation—although the system has not collapsed as it did in Nicaragua, the possibility of a revolutionary turn is there. It is a mistake to imagine that nothing is happening in Venezuela, and that a populist Chávez will not lead a social revolution. The formation of new trade unions and the growing self-organisation of the missions and the Bolivarian circles suggests that a radical change is already under way.

Globalisation and unipolarity

While it is widely recognised that the climate has changed in Latin America, it is often argued that globalisation has forced the left to retrench.[6] And it is important to discuss the impact of the information revolution, financial globalisation and the internationalisation of production on the region. The reality is that the process that allowed a partial recovery of profit rates in some developed countries has also had a brutal polarising effect. Latin America has suffered deepening impoverishment, decapitalisation and an increasing dependence on primary exports. The question is, can it recover the level of independence that would enable it to reverse that regressive process?

The theorists of the centre left insist that the solution is a model of regionally integrated capitalist production. But this project addresses only those niches that exist for opening up new businesses, without discussing the distortions that global accumulation has produced on the periphery— and neither do they acknowledge that no Latin American capitalism will be able to compete with the imperialist metropolises or reproduce their historical development.

In any event it is difficult to imagine the space in which such a model could operate, given that its implementation would require anti-imperialist measures and a radical break with neo-liberalism. Since no existing government is prepared to do that, it is difficult to know where this 'alternative capitalism' can develop. The new presidents all began with anti-liberal declarations then moved to support the status quo. The only certain route to progress, then, is a radical anti-capitalism with a socialist perspective.

But does the awful power of US imperialism not make any such option an impossibility? This power is not new of course; every 20th century national independence movement has had to confront it and on several occasions has brought the enemy to its knees. The very existence after 40 years of the Cuban Revolution is testimony to that. The US has certainly built up its military potential and recovered its economic dominance in the last decade; but its leadership is unstable and it is facing resistance. Iraq bears witness to the limits of American power. The expansion of Bush's preventive wars is deeply disturbing—but that does not mean that we should accept neo-conservative triumphalism. US aggression is producing both financial and political crises which challenge its global dominance.

The USSR and the balance of world forces

There is a general impression that the fall of Eastern Europe removed an important ally of the left—but in fact it only supported those governments and movements that reflected its strategic interests. The Cuban leadership was fiercely critical in this respect. Latin America was always a pawn in the USSR's diplomacy. So the end of the Cold War had contradictory, and not always negative, effects on the region. If it left the left feeling disarmed on the one hand, on the other it removed the identification in the popular mind of socialism with totalitarian regimes.

This analysis suggests that we move our gaze from what is happening 'above' (between states) to what is going on 'below' (in the mass movements and class consciousness). That is the basis on which to make an assessment of the balance of class forces. The other perspective can only lead us back to the search for an 'anti-imperialist camp' whose membership is unclear—is it Europe, China, the Arab world?

The key question is who is on the offensive in the struggle between workers and capitalists? In general, the initiative has been with the ruling class since the advent of neo-liberalism. But a great deal of water has flowed under the bridge since the 1980s. In many countries there have been popular risings—and here Latin America is in the vanguard. You cannot suggest that the balance of forces is against the popular movement while saying at the same time that the new centre left governments are the products of advances in the mass movement.

Hostile forces, internal and external

It is true that an anti-imperialist victory cannot be limited to one country—though Cuba has shown that it is possible to survive under conditions of imperialist siege. Every revolution has occurred in unfavourable conditions and has begun within a single country before transforming the wider scene by its example. In Central America several countries were involved, though never simultaneously; and though this was a problem it was internal conditions which became the main block, as the Sandinistas' experience proved. Imperialist aggression was a major factor, but what undermined the project was the transformation of the Sandinista leadership into a new wealthy elite which negotiated power-sharing with the right. Twenty five years after this revolution, there remains not a trace of the agrarian reforms or literacy programmes in a country torn apart by poverty and inequality almost equalling the tragedy of Haiti.

Does this mean that the socialist project is no longer viable? Is the centre left project all that we can aspire to? The popular risings in Bolivia, Ecuador and elsewhere give the lie to that, testifying to the readiness of many to develop a radical anti-imperialist solution to Latin America's poverty and degradation. The main obstacles to the growth of that possibility are not found in the international context but in the errors (and betrayals) within the struggle itself.

The popular classes take to the streets and confront the system—but the initiative passes back to the enemy whenever they have to define the future political direction of their country. The centre left governments that accompany the demonstrations in the streets and then betray them in the presidential palaces are the clearest example of this paradox.

The turn to the local

Asserting that the revolutionary cycle has ended leads first to support for Lula and Kirchner and then to a strategy for local activity which privileges the municipal level. Some people suggest that a prefigurative participatory democracy can be built here even if the bourgeois order prevents its establishment at the national level. This idea informed many of the activities of the PT and the Frente Amplio prior to their winning government. Yet in the case of the PT it was a precursor to their absorption into the establishment—and their recent electoral defeats in Porto Alegre and Sao Paulo demonstrate that the citizens will take only so much frustration before they punish them like any other party.

None of this invalidates activity at the local level—indeed it can be an important contribution to the building of a left alternative. The mistake is to imagine that what cannot be built nationally can happen in one municipality, all the more so when local areas are starved of resources and suffering the effects of public spending cuts and regressive taxation, as is the case in most of Latin America. And above all, it is private property which represents the biggest barrier to change.

The PT introduced the practice of 'participatory budgets' in several places, encouraging notions of local self-government. But these experiments were never linked to any struggles against the ruling class—and quickly became an exercise in administering poverty; and they did nothing to stop Lula's drift to the right. For years the municipal reformism practised in Europe transformed fighters into functionaries and dissolved the militant energies of a whole generation. The arguments used then are the same as those used now—gradual reform from within, building consensus, avoiding confrontation and so on.

But this gradualist approach, and the hope of reforms, always foundered on two rocks: first, that accumulation is a crisis-ridden process that does not offer long periods of calm in which to implement this strategy, and secondly, that the crisis drives capitalists to resist social concessions. And in these circumstances the bourgeoisie always reclaims power, unless social democracy has been totally incorporated.

The current scene

As Lula and Kirchner approach the end of their terms they will still be facing a turbulent and unequal region that is economically vulnerable and living in imperialism's shadow. The loss of resources that is implied by debt repayment adds one more factor, because any financial disturbance will tend to produce capital flight. And the multinational corporations will persist in pressing meantime for more privatisation and lower tariffs.

The most explosive factor of all is the increasing militarisation of the continent under Bush's presidency of the US—the public embrace of Bush and Colombia's Uribe is ample evidence of the Pentagon's continuing prominent role in Latin America. The new presidents may respond to imperialist pressures with fine rhetoric and clever manoeuvres, but the reality is that the context is determined by a rightward-moving US administration.

The hopes awoken by the election of Lula and Kirchner remain alive to a greater or lesser extent among the population—and these persistent illusions will have an effect on the strategies of the left. But to recognise popular expectations is one thing; encouraging them quite another. It is and always has been the left's duty to speak the truth however much it hurts, and that includes addressing Castro's and Chávez's support for the centre left presidents. In any event the support is not mutual: Lula and Kirchner have remained silent on events in Venezuela, because neither wants to provoke the enmity of the State Department, while Chávez and Castro support them in order to avoid isolation and to counter imperialist propaganda. But diplomacy does not require a political support which is counterproductive as far as the movement in Brazil and Argentina is concerned. The left should have learned not to adapt its activities to the foreign policy requirements of states; the defence of the Soviet Union produced far too many capitulations for us to repeat them now.

The Latin American left needs now to reaffirm that its field of action is in struggle with the oppressed not in discussing their concerns with the business sector. What matters is not what kind of capitalism we would prefer—be it 'capitalism with a human face' or 'the creation of a society with opportunities for all'—but how to develop a socialist project. The left will have no future unless it marches under the banner of equality and freedom. Today many young people are joining the movement and expressing admiration for the revolutionary legacy of past generations. But they also see how some of those who came from that past have joined the establishment and conceded victory to the powerful. If we are to recover the legacy of the 1970s we will need courage, determination and a deep conviction.

NOTES

1: 'Centroizquierda, Nacionalismo y Socialismo', available on the author's web page www.netforsys.com/claudiokatz

2: See M Rolando, 'Bolivarismo revolucionario y unidad suramericana', *Questión*, September 2004.

3: Representatives of this view include, in Brazil: F Betto, 'Ahora Lula conquistar el poder', *Página 12*, 20 September 2004; P Valter, 'La gauche a l'heure du choix', *Inprecor* 497, September 2004; M Pont and R Rosseto, 'Ideias', Agencia Carta Mayor, 3 May 2004; E Sader, 'Brasil y Lula desde un enfoque de izquierda', *Propuesta*, 10 June 2004; Articulacao de Esquerda e Democracia Socialista, 'Carta aos Petistas', *Democracia Socialista*, no 9, January-February 2005; 'Editorial', *Correio da ciuadania*; 'Un nouveaux parti socialiste', *Inprecor* 497, September 2004. In Argentina: H Tumini, *En marcha*, 14 October 2004; I

Rudnik '¿Quién confronta con el FMI?', *Desde los barrios*, 12 December 2004. In Uruguay: E F Huidobro, 'O estamos fritos', *Página 12*, 25 January 2005.

4: H Tumini, as above.

5: As has happened in Brazil with the DS (Democracia Socialista) current and in Argentina with 'Barrios de Pié'.

6: These issues are discussed for example in M Harnecker, 'La izquierda latinoamericana y la construcción de alternativas', *Laberinto* no 6, June 2001, and 'Sobre la estrategia de la izquierda en América Latina', Venezuela; 'Una revolución sui generis', *Conac*, Caracas, 2004, J Petras, 'Imperialismo y resistencia en Latinoamérica'. S Ellner, 'La situación actual en América Latina', *Los intelectuales y la globalisación* (Abya-Yala, Quito, 2004). 'Leftist goals and debate in Latin America', *Science and Society*, vol 68, no 1 (spring 2004).

China's strike wave

Simon Gilbert

Lots of small incidents have already occurred. There were lots of little incidents [involving worker protests] last year. Whenever a dynasty is ending it is like this. You can put down 99 out of 100 disturbances, but if you don't put down the last one it lights a fuse and there's an explosion.
Wei Jingshen[1]

In March last year demonstrating workers in China's Lanzhou city carried a banner reading 'You want to be "moderately well-off", we just want to survive'.[2] This rejection of the government's claim that China will soon become a 'moderately well-off' (*xiao kang*) society neatly captures the widening gap between the image of increasing prosperity and the harsh reality of working class life. It also shows a growing willingness by workers not only to protest or strike, but also to challenge the priorities of headlong economic growth.

There have also been widespread protests by peasants and laid-off workers. These are generally seen, even by sympathetic observers, as ineffective gestures of despair. But workers' struggles have the potential to develop into a mass labour movement that would be far more threatening to the regime. The purpose of this article is to examine the strengths and weaknesses of this embryonic labour movement, and to argue that a powerful workers' movement offers the best prospects for real democratic change.

The unique history of industrial development in China means that, while one working class is being 'unmade' in the state sector, particularly in the heavy industries of the north east and south west, another is being born in the booming consumer industries of the south eastern coastal provinces. This has led to the emergence of 'two new labour movements'.[3] State sector workers have protested and struck to defend their jobs, while in private and foreign-owned factories, dismal conditions and despotic management are the issues that have provoked revolt.

Resistance to restructuring in state-owned enterprises

The largest and most dramatic labour protests in China have been by laid-off workers against the frequently corrupt and illegal ways in which their enterprises were sold off, or for unpaid benefits to which they were entitled. But their 'radicalism occurs at the moment of exit from the working class' when they no longer have the power to stop production.[4] However, there has been a growing trend for workers to take action before they are laid off, or against the corrupt conditions under which their enterprises are privatised.

The depth of corruption involved in the restructuring process is staggering. Chinese state industry is universally portrayed in the West as hopelessly inefficient and essentially bankrupt. But many enterprises are being helped on their way by management who sell state assets and pocket the proceeds, deliberately running the companies down so that they can buy them at knock-down prices.

A typical example is the Shuangfeng Textile Factory in Dafeng, where managerial corruption caused a 2,000-strong strike and occupation. Workers had been forced to buy what turned out to be worthless shares in the company, using a significant part of their savings. Five years later the company was declared bankrupt and the old management became the new owners, perhaps using the manager's connections in the local party organisation. The workers 'immediately suspected they had been victims of a "fake bankruptcy", a common phenomenon in China in which corrupt managers hide a factory's assets, declare bankruptcy and then purchase the firm themselves at a reduced price, often with money they have embezzled'.[5]

When the new management insisted on pay cuts, the workers struck. The strikers were astute enough not to name representatives, knowing they would be arrested. However, the strike was eventually defeated by mass arrests and the violent eviction of the remaining factory occupiers by the police.

Others have been more successful. When workers at the SL Group in Luoyang, Henan, learned of the conditions they would face under a prospective new owner—extremely long working hours, military style discipline and a series of fines for the most minor mistakes and misdemeanours—they demonstrated and blockaded the factory entrance. Management conceded a referendum which rejected the deal. This case shows how the move towards privatisation means that state employees are beginning to face the same issues as their private sector counterparts.[6]

Just last year, over 6,000 workers at the Tianwang textile factory in Xianyang, Shaanxi, staged a partially successful seven-week strike against the conditions under which their factory was to be privatised. The workers put up a 24-hour picket line which was even defended against an attempt to break it by 1,000 police armed with water cannon.[7]

For many commentators, Chinese workers are seen as a formerly 'privileged' layer or even a 'labour aristocracy', desperately trying to cling on to their privileges.[8] What they ignore is that the cheap housing, medical care and education provided by the *danwei* or work units were poor compensation for their pitifully low wages. And this system of 'low wages and good benefits' only applied to the 42 percent of workers employed in the state sector.[9]

What is more, real wages and average housing space stagnated or declined in the 20 years after 1957.[10] So by the 1960s workers were creating a surplus for the state that was four times what they were paid.[11] In other words, 'by guaranteeing lifelong security...the state could appropriate the bulk of the surplus produced by workers at a very low cost, essentially by promising them a future".'[12]

Resistance was largely prevented by a complex system of factory administration and party penetration:

The significance of this network of political organisation is that it not only makes organised worker resistance and even informal coordination of action difficult, but it creates a cross-cutting organisation into which worker activity is absorbed.[13]

Only when there were splits at the top of the Communist Party did workers' grievances erupt into open resistance. A wave of strikes broke out in Shanghai in 1957 at the height of the 'hundred flowers' movement.[14] And during the confusion of the Cultural Revolution workers could press their own demands by disguising them in Maoist rhetoric.[15]

By the 1970s, under the relentless drive to accumulation, the proportion of output going to investment had risen to 36.5 percent, while productivity growth rates were declining.[16] Workers' demoralisation at their falling living standards had led them to 'withdraw efficiency'.[17] They were also starting to strike more often.[18]

Not surprisingly then, workers have not generally opposed reform in principle or sought a return to the past. Rather, it is the corruption and unfairness with which reform has been implemented that has angered them. As Han Dongfang put it, 'Workers didn't choose the command economy—it was forced on us without anyone asking our opinion, so why should we have to pay for the mistakes of the past?'[19]

Despotic management and unpaid wages in foreign-invested and private enterprises

At the same time as millions of workers are being laid off in the old industrial regions of the north east and south west, millions more peasants are being drawn into the booming consumer industries in the south eastern coastal provinces.

Working conditions in these enterprises are often compared with those in 19th century Europe.[20] An equally valid comparison could be made with factories in 1920s China.[21] Compulsory overtime means that working ten or 12 hours per day and seven days per week is not uncommon. Management is brutal and 'despotic', imposing military-style discipline and arbitrary fines that further reduce already meagre wages. It has also become customary for wages to be withheld for long periods of time. And the work is often extremely dangerous with very high accident rates.[22]

These are the result of what Anita Chan calls a 'race to the bottom' in labour standards as China competes with other developing countries to attract investment. She also compares the *hukou* system, which denies rural migrants permanent urban residence, to South African apartheid.[23]

But this doesn't tell the whole story. Recent reports have described a labour shortage in Guangdong, the province that attracts the largest share of foreign investment. Wages are so low and conditions so bad that migrants are looking for work elsewhere or returning to farming. In order to attract workers, companies are promising to improve conditions and pay wages on time.[24] More importantly, workers are prepared to go on strike even in the face of vicious intimidation.

Many of these strikes involve two groups, migrants and women, who are often seen as the most vulnerable and powerless. Two fascinating and relatively detailed reports from the early 1990s illustrate this.[25] Workers at a Taiwanese shoe factory in Fujian struck when a female worker accused of petty pilfering was beaten and locked up with the dogs kept to guard the premises. At a Guangdong textile factory the workers went on strike over unpaid wages, despite some of the strikers being threatened with their lives.

Though the disputes were caused by the workers being pushed to the limit on one particular issue, once the strikes began other grievances were aired, such as low pay, sexual harassment and safety. Clearly in both factories a lot of resentment and frustration had built up, and came pouring out once given an outlet.

In both cases the local authorities sided with management, but the workers were able to get some satisfaction by appealing to higher level authorities. This tactic was more successful in the urban shoe factory, where the city and provincial authorities may have carried more weight and been nervous about the example the strike might set, than in the rural textile factory.

A number of these features have also been seen in other strikes and protests. A manager of the Japanese-owned Ricoh factory was forced to apologise for verbally abusing female employees after they struck in protest. The workers were also reported to be working long hours for low pay which may have helped to fuel their anger.[26]

In 2001 a group of female workers from the South Korean owned Baoyang Industrial Corporation in Shenzhen protested after being illegally body searched on management orders. This case also illustrates another feature of recent labour unrest: the workers called for the company to be punished for violating China's labour law, enabling them to get support from the Shenzhen Federation of Trade Unions, the deputy mayor and the local media.[27]

Unpaid wages are a frequent cause of industrial unrest. In 1998 workers from the Chong Xing Qiu spectacle factory in Guangdong protested outside government offices after failing to get support from local labour officials. A protest earlier the same year had successfully secured them a month's owed wages.[28]

Migrant construction workers are a common sight in China's major cities, but they too are often unpaid for long periods. In 2002 they were owed 2.2 billion yuan (£14.5 million) by construction contractors in Beijing alone. As the 2003 New Year festival approached, a group of several hundred of these labourers staged a protest outside a luxury compound in the capital, claiming to be owed a full year's pay. The difficulties faced at this time of year by workers who had been away from their families for long periods was poignantly described by one of them: 'I feel frustrated, baffled and humiliated. What can I tell my wife and son now? They are expecting me to bring home enough cash for the whole family.' Another explained that he no longer had the money to phone home to talk to his children.

The police did not intervene to break up this protest, while similar protests were also reported in a number of other cities. The government seemed to be tolerating the protests in order to put pressure on local officials to be stricter with property developers. This had opened up a space for one of the most exploited groups of workers.[29]

Another strike by construction workers at the state-owned No 4 Bureau of China Railway Engineering Corp had similar features to the private sector conflicts. The migrant workers, who were building a new underground line as part of developments for the 2008 Olympics, explained that they had 'no choice' but to strike after being unpaid for over six months.[30]

A strike at the Xinxiong shoe factory in Dongguan, Guangdong, was caused by a change in overtime arrangements which would reduce the salary of most workers. However, a local official described the working conditions as 'very harsh' and thought that 'the strike was an almost inevitable outbreak of collective anger against the management'.[31]

An earlier dispute at Canon's Zhuhai factory in 1993 illustrates the potential for a much higher level of industrial unrest should the economic situation change. Despite being relatively well paid, workers went on strike for more pay after the high inflation of the early 1990s had undermined their standard of living.[32]

Containment and the role of the trade unions

With few exceptions, however, these disputes have remained at the level of individual enterprises and have not yet created anything that could be called a national labour movement. The government has so far managed to contain labour unrest by showing some tolerance to enterprise-level strikes while acting to prevent generalisation or independent organisation.

After the shock of 1989 the Chinese leadership moved to regularise industrial relations. The Trade Union Law of 1992 and the Labour Law of 1994 defined minimum conditions for workers and gave the unions a role in enforcing them.[33] The point was to 'institutionalise conflict resolution' through the official grievance procedure and 'pre-empt labour agitation'.[34]

Where this fails, enterprise-level protests and strikes, though in a legal grey area, often gain concessions.[35] This toleration is often combined with punishment of the organisers.[36] But actions which involve more than one workplace or attempts to form independent organisations are ruthlessly repressed.[37] The most obvious examples are the mass protests in Daqing and Liaoyang.[38]

In other words, the regime has realised that it is impossible to prevent all labour protests and would probably be counterproductive to try. So protests that remain fragmented and specific are tolerated, while anything that threatens to lead to a mass movement is suppressed.

The official trade unions have played a central role in this process. Although a number of writers on Chinese labour believe that the unions are moving towards a more genuine representative role, this seems to be little more than wishful thinking.[39] With the withdrawal of the state from direct economic control, the unions have moved from promoting production to implementing the government's containment policies on the factory floor.

In order to do so, they have at least to appear to address their members' problems. For instance, at a mine in Liaoning province 'siding with the workers was critical in order to win their trust, and only with their trust could the union persuade them to channel their discontent into the official grievance procedure'.[40] During enterprise-level strikes they usually try to mediate. But they firmly oppose any signs of wider generalisation or attempts to form independent unions. Not surprisingly workers seldom turn to the unions when they take action.

The failure to effectively implement labour legislation and the often blatantly illegal behaviour of managers in both the state and private sectors has led to the emergence of 'legal activism' by workers. Many protests explicitly or implicitly demand greater compliance with the law by management. But this is a 'double-edged sword' for the government.[41]

On the one hand, it can channel workers' activity into legal avenues that fit with its stated aim of moving to the rule of law. And in several cases the workers found that, although the local authorities sided with management, they could get more sympathy from higher level authorities. On the other hand, it requires what in China is essentially extra-legal protest or strike activity for the law to be enforced. This has a clear risk for the government of leading to greater unrest, while encouraging cynicism about the law. One victim of a forced share-buying scheme thought that 'the law is just a means by which the dictatorship controls ordinary people'.[42]

A strike by over 10,000 workers at the Japanese-invested Uniden Electronics factory in Shenzhen was aimed at enforcing their entitlement to a union under the trade union law. At the same time they demanded sick pay, paid maternity leave and permanent contracts for long term employees. This was just the latest phase in an ongoing struggle to improve their lives involving four or five strikes since 1987.[43] Workers are clearly learning the lesson that 'a small disturbance leads to a small solution, a large disturbance leads to a big solution. No disturbance leads to no solution'.[44]

Workers and democracy

The official trade unions' role as 'an arm of the party state' means that 'few workers seek union help' with their problems.[45] Strikes and protests are always organised by the workers themselves without union involvement.[46] So the question of independent unions inevitably arises.

For instance, Cao Maobing, an electrician at the Funing County Silk Mill, Jiangsu, explained why they had petitioned (presumably unsuccessfully) to form their own union: 'The factory does have a union, but it exists in name only... The current union takes no responsibility for the workers... So we told them we'd set up a trade union ourselves'.[47]

The high point of recent labour organisation in China came in

1989 with the formation in several cities of Workers' Autonomous Federations. Their experience suggests that there is a direct link between workers' economic struggles, independent organisation and political reform. As Walder and Gong explained of the Beijing WAF:

> From its earliest pronouncements, *gongzilian* [the Workers' Autonomous Federation] focused heavily on bread and butter economic issues, and its demands for political reform were invariably ones that would allow workers to pursue their interests more effectively in the future.[48]

Most writers on China either look to gradual change from within the regime or the pressure of an emerging 'civil society' to produce democratic reform. While there has been political change since the economic reforms began in 1978, it has been geared towards maintaining the dominant position of the Communist Party as it loosens its control of the economy, not to greater democracy.

The term 'civil society' usually refers to the new private business class. But this group has done well out of the reforms, and their dislike of Communist Party rule is generally outweighed by fear of 'chaos' if it were removed.[49] At the same time the opportunities offered by a booming economy and the far greater options for foreign study have helped to defuse student opposition. Indeed the recent anti-Japanese demonstrations highlighted a growing class divide in protest activity. While students joined the protests against Japan, tolerated if not encouraged by the government, peasants in the Zhejiang village of Huankantou were fighting a pitched battle against 3,000 riot police.[50]

That is not to say that students may not return to pro-democracy protests in the future, but at the moment it is the losers in China's economic boom, peasants and workers, who are on the streets. If these demonstrations, riots and strikes are to develop into a mass movement, workers will be central. The working class has both a vested interest in democratic change and the economic muscle that derives from its productive role in the new workshop of the world. In other words, it has the potential to play the same galvanising role that its counterparts in South Africa and South Korea did in the 1980s.

Conclusion

Deng Xiaoping understood, as many western academics apparently do not, that not only is there no necessary connection between economic and political liberalism, but the success of China's economic boom has been dependent on political repression to suppress the inevitable discontent. When the tanks rolled into Tiananmen Square in June 1989, he described the chilling logic behind the decision: 'Even if we sacrifice ten to 20 thousand people, we must exercise control over the situation of the whole country and get 20 years tranquillity in return'.[51]

However, workers proved to be far more resilient than Deng anticipated, with strikes reported even in the second half of 1989.[52] The most significant aspect of the growing industrial unrest is that for the first time since 1949 strikes have become a permanent feature of Chinese society. And, unlike in the past, this has happened at a time of consensus among the Communist Party leadership.

There is every sign that the pressures leading to labour unrest, restructuring of state industry and the promotion of China as a cheap labour economy will continue for the foreseeable future.

In the export sector the competitive pressures that force down wages and conditions are also being felt within China, so that, 'as a region becomes more prosperous, it violates the national guidelines and seeks to maintain its attractiveness to foreign capital by keeping its minimum wage level low'.[53]

Some argue that the development of a social security net to assist laid-off workers could defuse labour unrest.[54] However, attempts to implement social welfare measures have been largely ineffective because the decline in state-owned industry is simultaneously reducing government revenues and increasing the numbers of unemployed.[55] While central government can set welfare policies, it is up to local government to implement them, and they simply do not have the funds. The endemic corruption in the restructuring process is also undermining attempts at reform as the embezzlement of Xiangfan workers' premiums shows.[56]

Meanwhile, the prospects for laid-off workers are not getting any better. As the economy has continued to grow, the rate at which it creates new jobs has slowed.[57] In fact, the problems may be about to intensify. Having restructured many of the smaller State Owned Enterprises, the government now needs to deal with the bigger ones, whose 'large number of workers are more able to stage resistance'.[58]

The high points of Chinese labour activity in the past have occurred when the ruling group was divided. Should these sorts of cleavages emerge again, perhaps as a result of an economic crisis, then 'those forms of unobtrusive struggle and public resistance' could be transformed into a 'Chinese labour movement powerful enough to

NOTES

1: Quoted in J Miles, *The Legacy of Tiananmen: China in Disarray* (Ann Arbor, 1996), p211.

2: 'Hundreds of Chinese Textile Workers Protest Over Lay-off Threat', Agence France Presse, 31 March 2004.

3: A Chan, 'The Emerging Patterns of Industrial Relations in China and the Rise of Two New Labor Movements', *China Information* 9:4 (1995), pp36-59.

4: C K Lee, 'From the Specter of Mao to the Spirit of the Law: Labor Insurgency in China', *Theory and Society* 31:2 (2002), p219.

5: P P Pan, 'High Tide of Labor Unrest in China', *Washington Post*, 21 Jan 2002.

6: F Chen, 'Industrial Restructuring and Workers' Resistance in China', *Modern China* 29:2 (2003).

7: Several reports relating to this strike can be found on *China Labour Bulletin* http://www.china-labour.org.hk

8: See for instance Lee, 'From the Specter of Mao' in A Liu, *Mass Politics in the People's Republic: State and Society in Contemporary China* (Boulder, 1996), or M Blecher, 'Hegemony and Workers' Politics in China', in *China Quarterly* 170 (2002).

9: A laid-off worker interviewed by Dongfang Han, in 'Reform, Corruption and Livelihood' (1998), available on the *China Labour Bulletin* website at http://www.china-labour.org.hk/iso/

article.adp?article_id=1008. This is a fascinating collection of interviews conducted by Han on a phone-in programme for Hong Kong based Radio Free Asia.

10: A Walder, *Communist Neo-traditionalism: Work and Authority in Chinese Industry* (Berkeley, 1986), p194.

11: B Naughton, 'Danwei: The Economic Foundations of a Unique Institution', in Xiaobo Lu and E J Perry (eds), *Danwei: The Changing Chinese Workplace in Historical and Comparative Perspective* (Armonk, 1997), p174.

12: Wang Yi, 'From Status to Contract?' in Chaohua Wang (ed), *One China, Many Paths* (London, 2003), p192.

13: A Walder, as above, p95.

14: Some workers struck against their companies being taken into state ownership as it actually threatened to worsen their conditions. See E Perry, 'Shanghai's Strike Wave of 1957', *The China Quarterly* 137 (1994).

15: J Sheehan, *Chinese Workers: A New History* (London, 1998). This is the best book on labour in the Communist era, covering the whole period from 1949 to the early 1990s.

16: C Riskin, *China's Political Economy: The Quest for Development Since 1949* (Oxford, 1987), pp261-271. I disagree somewhat with Charlie Hore's emphasis ('China's Century?', *International Socialism* 103 (summer 2004), p6). There is a consensus in popular writing on China that the Communists' economic policies were a complete failure before being rescued by free market reform from 1978. But, with the exception of the disastrous Great Leap Forward period, China's economy grew at historically high rates from 1949 right up to the 1970s, including the Cultural Revolution period. Reforms were initiated because those policies were increasingly ineffective, and were provoking discontent. For the growth figures see A Eckstein, *China's Economic Revolution* (Cambridge, 1977), pp204-205 and p219.

17: A Walder, as above, pp197-201.

18: Strikes were reported in 1974, in Hangzhou in 1975, the April 5th movement in 1976 was dominated by young workers and that summer saw another strike wave. See J Sheehan, as above, pp144-154.

19: D Han, 'Reform, Corruption and Livelihood', as above.

20: See for example B Taylor, Kai Chang and Qi Li, *Industrial Relations in China* (Cheltenham, 2003), p163.

21: J Chesneaux, *The Chinese Labor Movement, 1919-1927* (Stanford, 1968), pp71-112.

22: A number of the worst cases reported in the Chinese press are translated in A Chan, *China's Workers Under Assault: The Exploitation of Labor in a Globalizing Economy* (Armonk, 2001). See also C K Lee, as above, and B Taylor et al, as above, p98.

23: A Chan, 'A "Race to The Bottom": Globalization and China's Labour Standards', *China Perspectives* 46 (2003).

24: T Johnson, 'China's Factories Go Short on Labor', *Charlotte Observer*, 10 September 2004. The labour shortage is also giving workers more confidence to strike: 'Female Workers at Wal-Mart Supplier in Shenzhen Demand Union', *China Labour Bulletin*, 21 December 2004 http://www.china-labour.org.hk/iso/news_item.adp?news_id=3790

25: A Chan, as above.

26: 'Insulted Workers End Strike After Japanese Manager Apologizes', Kyodo News Service, 14 June 2004.

27: 'Workers Humiliated by Body Searches', *China Labour Bulletin*, 3 Aug 2001 http://www.china-labour.org.hk/iso/news_item.adp?news_id=1538

28: H Luk, 'Protest at HK-run Factory Over Pay', *South China Morning Post*, 16 July 1998.

29: 'Hundreds of Workers Protest at Luxury Compound in Beijing', Agence France Presse, 17 January 2003, and 'China's Unpaid Migrant Workers Vent Anger as New Year Approaches', Agence France Presse, 28 January 2003.

30: 'Several Hundred Rural Workers Strike in Beijing for Back Wages', AFX News Limited, 4 August 2004.

31: 'More than Ten Workers Detained after Rowdy Protest Against Unfair Overtime by Several Hundred Guangdong Shoe Factory Employees', *China Labour Bulletin*, 30 April 2004 http://www.china-labour.org.hk/iso/article.adp?article_id=5347

32: K Chen, 'Canon Unit in China Provides Picture of Workers Chafed by Market Economy', *Wall Street Journal*, 9 April 1993.

33: D Z Ding, K Goodall and M Warner, 'The Impact of Economic Reform on the Role of Trade Unions in Chinese Enterprises', *International Journal of Human Resource Management* 13:3 (2002), and G White, 'Chinese Trade Unions in the Transition from Socialism: Towards Corporatism or Civil Society?', *British Journal of Industrial Relations* 34:3 (1996). The Labour and Trade Union laws are available online at http://www.acftu.org.cn

34 F. Chen, 'Between the State and Labour: The Conflict of Chinese Trade Unions' Double Identity in Market Reform', *The China Quarterly* 176 (2003), p1012. The number of official dispute cases has grown exponentially from 19,098 cases involving 77,794

employees in 1994 to 184,116 cases involving 608,396 employees in 2002. More than three times as many disputes were resolved in favour of the employees than the employers. These 'dispute' figures are sometimes confused with strike figures: there are no national strike statistics for China. See C K Lee, 'Pathways of Labor Insurgency', in Elizabeth J Perry and Mark Selden (eds), *Chinese Society: Change, Conflict and Resistance* (London, 2003), p75, and *Zhongguo Laodong he Shehui Baozhang Nianjian* [*China Labour and Social Security Yearbook*] (Beijing, 2003).

35: The 'right to strike' was removed from the constitution in 1982, although strikes are not explicitly illegal either. In practice it is probably easier for workers to strike now than it was before 1982.

36: M J Blecher, 'Hegemony and Workers' Politics in China', *China Quarterly* 170 (2002), p286.

37: C K Lee, 'From Organized Dependence to Disorganized Despotism: Changing Labour Regimes in Chinese Factories', *China Quarterly* 157 (1999), p68 and 'Pathways of Labor Insurgency', as above, p85.

38: These were probably the most significant labour protests in recent years, but they were covered by Charlie Hore, as above, and my focus here is on employed workers. For more details see T Leung, 'The Third Wave of the Chinese Labour Movement in the Post-Mao Era', *China Labour Bulletin* 5 June 2002 http://www.china-labour.org.hk/iso/article.adp?article_id=2397 and T B Weston, '"Learn From Daqing": More Dark Clouds For Workers In State-Owned Enterprises', *Journal of Contemporary China* 11:33 (2002).

39: A Chan, 'Revolution or Corporatism? Workers and Trade Unions in Post-Mao China', *The Australian Journal of Chinese Affairs* 29 (1993). Chan's article became a reference point for several other writers arguing in the same vein. However, Chan herself has more recently described the unions as 'an

arm of the party-state'—see A Chan, 'A "Race to the Bottom",' as above, p48.

40: K Chen, 'Between the State and Labour', as above, p1021.

41: C K Lee, 'From the Specter of Mao', as above, pp219-220.

42: Quoted in D Han, 'Reform, Corruption and Livelihood', as above.

43: 'More Than 10,000 Striking Workers At Japanese-Invested Wal-Mart Supplier Firm In Shenzhen Demand Right To Set Up Their Own Trade Union', *China Labour Bulletin*, 22 April 2005 http://www.china-labour.org.hk/iso/article.adp?article_id=6326

44: E Rosenthal, 'Workers' Plight Brings New Militancy In China', *New York Times* 10 March 2003.

45: A Chan, 'A 'Race to The Bottom', as above, p48; C K Lee, 'From Organized Dependence', as above, p59.

46: B Taylor et al, as above, p176.

47: E Eckholm, 'Silk Workers In Standoff With Beijing Over Union', *New York Times*, 15 December, 2000.

48: A G Walder and Xiaoxia Gong, 'Workers in the Tiananmen Protests: The Politics of the Beijing Workers' Autonomous Federation', *The Australian Journal of Chinese Affairs* 29 (1993).

49: This attitude was reflected in Zhang Yimou's recent film *Hero*, where a plan to depose a despotic emperor was abandoned for fear that lack of a strong leader would plunge the country into chaos.

50: 'Chinese Village Protest Turns Into Riot Of Thousands', *The Guardian*, 12 April 2005 http://www.guardian.co.uk/international/story/0,,1457243,00.html.

51: Quoted in J L Wilson, '"The Polish Lesson": China and Poland 1980-1990' *Studies in Comparative Communism* 23 (1990), p272.

52: See M J Blecher, 'Hegemony and Workers' Politics in China', as above, pp284-285; Liu, *Mass Politics in the*

People's Republic, as above, p120; and J L Wilson, 'The Polish lesson', as above, p278.

53: A Chan, 'A "Race to The Bottom", as above.

54: F Chen, 'Subsistence Crises, Managerial Corruption and Labour Protests in China', *China Journal* 44 (2000), p62; and C K Lee 'Pathways of Labor Insurgency', as above, p89.

55: S Cook, 'Readjusting Labour: Enterprise Restructuring, Social Consequences and Policy Responses in Urban China', in M Warner (ed), *Changing Workplace Relations in the Chinese Economy* (London, 2000), pp240-243.

56: '10,000 Workers from Xiangfan Block Roads to Uphold Their Rights During Factory Privatisation', *China Labour Bulletin* 21 Nov 2003 http://www.china-labour.org.hk/iso/article.adp?article_id=5123

57: S Wang, 'The Social and Political Implications of China's WTO Membership', *Journal of Contemporary China* 25 (2000), pp383-384.

58: Y Cai, 'The Resistance of Chinese Laid-Off Workers in the Reform Period', *China Quarterly* 170 (2002), pp343-344.

59: C K Lee, 'Pathways of Labor Insurgency', as above, p89.

Rediscovering the revolution

Mike Haynes

A review of Kevin Murphy, **Revolution and Counterrevolution: Class Struggle in a Moscow Metal Factory** *(Berghahn Books, 2005),* £45

A book on the history of Russia which begins by asserting that 'the Marxists got it right. Leon Trotsky and Tony Cliff provided the theoretical groundwork for much of my understanding of the Russian Revolution while Victor Serge acted as the "conscience" of the revolution by giving it such an inspirational and principled voice' is bound to be of interest to readers of this journal. And this is a book to beg, steal or borrow, for it is in a sense the missing volume in the analysis of how state capitalism developed out of the degeneration of the Russian Revolution.

Revolution and Counterrevolution explores the lives of workers in Moscow's largest metalworking factory—the Guzhon factory, which became the Hammer and Sickle works—in the years between 1900 and 1932. It marks a double first in writing on the Russian Revolution. It breaks the implicit taboo that has seemed to prevent historians tracing the experience of these workers across both the rise and fall of the revolution, and it is based on the most intensive research in the Moscow archives.

Chapter one describes the emergence of an organised working class in the Guzhon works, the heady days of 1905, the repression after the defeat, and the pre-war radicalism that followed the massacre of workers on the Lena Goldfields in 1912. This marked the start of an upturn bringing large-scale industrial conflict back to Russian factories on the eve of the First World War. Chapter two tells the story of the 4,000 Guzhon workers involved in the revolution, complementing the city-wide accounts of Petrograd and Moscow that were written by Western historians in the 1980s. In 1917 factory committees were created in the works, workers won the eight-hour day, management was forced back and the level of class consciousness rose to new heights.

'In the Marxist sense of a working class conscious of its collective strength, 1917 marked the zenith of proletarian power in the 20th century,' writes Murphy. It is at this point that his analysis strikes out on its own to establish 'how...a movement based on egalitarianism and freedom transformed into a system based on exploitation and repression'.

The argument that the Russian Revolution degenerated from the high point of 1917 under the blows of foreign intervention and civil war will be familiar to readers. But what kind of country was Russia between this point and Stalin's consolidation of power? Although Trotsky discredited the concept by stretching it to cover the era after 1928, the idea of a degenerating workers' state captures an important part of the reality. Lenin used a slightly different formulation describing Russia as a workers' state with bureaucratic deformations in a peasant country. Those of us who have written about this have often been so fixated on the degeneration aspect that we have neglected to analyse enough the extent to which, despite the poverty and penury, there were positive gains and evidence of a still vibrant, if more attenuated, culture below.

Here Murphy makes three important contributions. Firstly, he rejects the legend of the Civil War—that Bolshevik labour policy at this time anticipated Stalinism through 'its iron discipline and brutal terror'. The extreme collapse during the Civil War affected the Hammer and Sickle works just as badly as other factories, but he finds no evidence in the archives to support 'grossly inflated estimates about early state repression, concentration camps and coercion'. The Civil War unravelled the working class and so undercut class consciousness in favour of 'a desperate and apolitical individualism in the factory'. In 1921 the factory nominally had 1,412 workers with conditions so bad that they were producing only 4 percent of the pre-war output. Yet these remaining workers 'were almost completely unfazed by a state that had virtually ceased to exist'. This was very different then from what came later.

Secondly, whatever the deficiencies of Russia in the NEP period, and they were many, Murphy argues that early on there was a positive attempt to narrow the gap between the revolution and its base that had resulted from the Civil War. In the early 1920s workers had real material grievances in a situation of great difficulties, but they articulated them within the context of a regime with which they had an 'uneasy compromise' and felt some identity. Certainly they went on strike, they held boisterous mass meetings, but they also joined the party for positive reasons and saw factory committees and trade unions as vehicles

for the expression of their grievances. This led to the creation of a system of arbitration for disputes that came to involve 6 million workers and which gave real weight to workers' interests:

'The early Soviet participatory institutions differed markedly from those of both the Tsarist and Stalinist eras. It was workers' trust and involvement in workplace institutions that gave the factory regime an essential degree of legitimacy.'

Thirdly, Murphy shows how this was undercut in the second half of the 1920s and how Stalin was able to rise to power on this increasing separation of the state from the workers. This partly reflected the pressures forcing the state towards industrialisation, but it also reflected the changing position of workers, traced by Murphy in the case of the Hammer and Sickle works.

Although the power of the workers to resist the bureaucratic degeneration towards counterrevolution was weakening, Murphy supports the argument of Michael Reiman in his *The Birth of Stalinism* that there was something of a crisis in the factories in late 1927. It appeared briefly that there might be a surge in support for the opposition to the leadership. But this was overcome and after 1928 any independent working class expression was increasingly suppressed. In the Hammer and Sickle works a minority of workers were co-opted but most were forcibly squeezed by the state to help provide the resources for industrialisation. 'Management coercion rested on social pressures by a milieu of hardened state loyalists to bully other workers and utilised control over food as its most effective weapon to discipline the workforce.' So far from Stalinism having popular mandate, it was based on repression beneath which there was 'simmering but fractured discontent' among the workers of the Hammer and Sickle factory.

Murphy's book will not be popular in academic circles. Each of the arguments he presents involves a challenge to the orthodoxy which stresses the continuity between 1917 and Stalinism. It will be less popular still because it is based on such serious research: 'Fifteen years after the doors of the archives swung open, not a single source-driven study has supported either of the contending arguments—that the workers were either terrorised by the early Soviet state or impressed with Stalinism.'

But if his book is disliked because it stands out against the mixture of eclecticism and confusion that passes for wisdom in the study of Russian history these days then so much the better. The pettiness of the academic world sometimes seems to know no bounds and the pressures to conform are great. We should be grateful that Kevin Murphy has had the courage to write a book which ends so confidently with the argument that 'Karl Marx and Frederick Engels were correct... The history of the Russian Revolution is the history of class struggle.'

Leadership battles
Megan Trudell

A review of Alexander Rabinowitch, **The Bolsheviks Come to Power: the Revolution of 1917 in Petrograd** *(Pluto Press, 2004), £12.99*

During the 1970s and 1980s a 'social history school' of writers challenged both official Soviet histories of the Russian Revolution which regarded the Bolsheviks as the architects of the revolution, and the

US Cold War historians who were hostile to the revolution and the Bolsheviks. The social historians' work concentrated on showing that 1917 was not a coup, nor the action of a blind mob, but was based on a genuine mass movement led by workers who were increasingly politically conscious of their own actions.

First published in 1976, *The Bolsheviks Come to Power* is one of the best of these histories. Now republished, it offers a new readership an involving and convincing account of the revolution which has at its heart the self-activity of workers and soldiers, led by a responsive and flexible Bolshevik Party that bears no resemblance to the rigid, disciplined faction of right wing myth.

Rabinowitch's history traces the 'development of the revolution from below'. He uses minutes of meetings of local and city-wide soviets, the Provisional Government and the Bolsheviks, resolutions and newspapers, to carefully assemble a compelling account of the complex and fluid relationship between the Bolsheviks and Petrograd's workers and soldiers throughout the course of 1917. In the process he decisively demolishes the idea of the revolution as a highly organised coup forcibly imposed on the population.

Rabinowitch begins with the July Days in Petrograd, with the Bolshevik retreat from a premature challenge for power and the ensuing repression against the left. He examines the attempted right wing coup in August, the steady draining away of support for the Provisional Government that followed, and the rise of Bolshevik support in the Petrograd Soviet which preceded the October revolution.

Rabinowitch emphasises the impact of the First World War on driving the revolution forward in February, and in continuing to push soldiers to the left as the government's continuation of the war alienated the army. He reveals the extent of this radicalisation—despite the July accusation that Lenin was a German agent most soldiers sided with the Bolsheviks because they were opposed to the death penalty at the front which Kerensky, the head of the Provisional Government, had reinstituted. By the time of the October insurrection, Kerensky was unable to mobilise any troops from the rear *or the front* in defence of his government against the forces of the Bolshevik-led soviet.

The increasing polarisation between the right wing forces of the Provisional Government and the revolutionary forces of the soviets from February to October is rigorously drawn out. The government installed by the February revolution had given in to right wing forces that threatened the revolution, and increasingly the strong impulse to unity that held the masses of workers and soldiers to the government became focused instead on the creation of a revolutionary soviet.

Rabinowitch traces how these tensions within dual power in Petrograd were played out, and demonstrates the necessity of the October insurrection to prevent another counter-revolutionary attempt.

Many social history accounts, in stressing the independent action of workers and soldiers, dilute the important role that the Bolshevik Party and the individuals in it played. Rabinowitch shows that, while October was clearly no coup or conspiracy, the Bolshevik role was central, and was intimately related to the independent action of the masses. The relationship between the party and the workers and soldiers in the soviets, trade unions and, indeed, the other socialist parties, was a dynamic and sensitive one. The Bolsheviks were not imposing their desires onto the 'masses', but were part of the collective shaping of a concrete strategy for the reali-sation of collective desires. The February demand for 'bread, peace and land' became more radical as workers and soldiers found their hopes for reform from the Provisional Government frustrated. They found their desires expressed in the Bolshevik slogan of 'All Power to the Soviets'.

Rabinowitch attributes the Bolsheviks' success to the intense debate within the party and to the strength of democratic centralism—the leadership was often corrected by the membership in the workplaces and local soviets, and indeed was often itself divided. In explaining the Bolsheviks' growth and influence, Rabinowitch emphasises 'the party's internally relatively democratic, tolerant, and decentralised structure and method of operation, as well as its essentially open and mass character'.

He also points to the growth of the party as contributing to its flexible and accessible nature—the thousands of new members who joined the party in 1917 were 'by no means without influence, so that to a significant degree the party was now responsive and open to the masses'.

There are weaknesses with *The Bolsheviks Come to Power*. Rabinowitch's narrow focus means he spends little time on wider events and processes, which makes some prior knowledge of the revolution and its context essential. He constrains his account to events and social changes in Petrograd with no reference to the rest of Russia or the international context, which can be frustrating. His approach 'from below' provides much less sense of the view of bourgeois forces at the time. However, within these limitations, the cumulative power of the evidence Rabinowitch uses is thorough and convincing without being dry—the atmosphere in Petrograd is vividly transmitted and the sense of dynamism and development in people's actions and ideas comes through very well. There is even a map with all the key buildings marked enabling the reader to follow the revolution through the streets.

At a time when histories of the revolution are dominated by a new 'revisionism'—like Orlando Figes' *A People's Tragedy* and Anne Applebaum's *Gulag*, both of which cloak their return to traditional, hostile accounts of the revolution in more liberal and populist language—this book is a

reminder of the strengths of social history writing at its best.

The collapse of Stalinism disoriented many on the left, in some cases leading to dramatic political reversals. Consequently today there is little resistance to the revisionist picture of the revolution. This, and the renewed importance of debates over the nature of leadership within the movement against capitalism and war, in which interpretations of the Russian Revolution are crucial, make the re-publication of this classic book timely and very welcome.

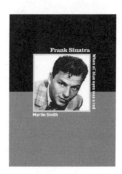

More than the mosque

Hassan Mahamdallie

A review of Humayun Ansari, The Infidel Within: Muslims in Britain since 1800 (Hurst & Company, 2004), £16.50

Can history teach us anything about a political approach to Britain's Muslims, and how we should regard them in terms of race and class? Ansari's fascinating and wide-ranging book *The Infidel Within* has pointers to the answers we need.

The book, subtitled 'Muslims in Britain since 1800', is a historical, political and social survey of Muslims touching on many aspects, including the position of Muslim women in society, the founding of early mosques, Muslims and education, Muslim religious and political movements, and the vexed question of British Muslim identities.

The first point Ansari makes is important—the diversity of those who describe themselves as Muslims. Today there are maybe as many as 1.8 million Muslims in Britain. If you go to the big mosques, such as Regents Park Mosque, you will observe a simple truth: to be a Muslim is not a racial classification. There are Muslims in this country from up to 50 different ethnic backgrounds—from Arabs to Somalis to Bosnians to Indonesians to white English converts, North Africans and so on.

Some are rich migrants from the Gulf, but most are South Asian, working class and economically disadvantaged, with groups such as Bangladeshis very poor. (Government figures show one in eight of Pakistani male workers drive cabs, while 50 percent of Bangladeshi men work in the restaurant trade.)[1]

As Ansari writes:

'Any presumptions of Muslim homogeneity and coherence which claim to override the differences between rural and urban, rich and poor, educated and illiterate, do not necessarily correspond to social reality. A Sylheti from Bangladesh, apart from some tenets of faith, is likely to have little in common with a Mirpuri from Pakistan, let alone a Somali or a Bosnian Muslim. Values, symbols and aspirations, approaches to issues of identity, strength of adherence to ritual and loyalty to kin networks, and the form and nature of institutions are likely to be extremely varied, making Muslims in Britain a very heterogeneous population'. (p3)

British Muslim Asian ethnic groupings are targeted both for their race and their religion. This duality is one that, for example, the BNP have sought to exploit. Ansari shows that historically hatred towards Muslims centred on racism has also been sometimes expressed as religious hatred and vice versa—often simultaneously. (In the BNP's eyes you can be guilty of the dual 'crime' of being a 'Paki' and a 'Muslim'.)

Islam came out of 7th century Arabia and as a highly successful social, political and economic formation spread its empire into Europe and Asia. At that time Britain was not important. The odd Arab sailor or pirate landed on the south coast to take provisions—or sometimes to snatch captives back to North Africa. One of the first recorded Muslim visitors was a traveller called Al Idrisi—a North African Arab patronised by Sicilian kings who toured the West of England in the early 1100s.

With the rise of the Ottoman Empire there began more formal links. In 1588 Elizabeth I offered a treaty to ally with Ottoman Sultan Murad III against Catholic Spain. Elizabeth considered Islam closer to Protestantism than the Catholics were, whom she considered idolaters (for worshipping statues). Under Elizabeth, Muslim traders were given protection in England, and in return English traders were given free passage in Muslim territories.

So the English were not unaccustomed to Muslims, and writings from the time, including Shakespeare, burst with both fascination and fear for these traders, soldiers and diplomats.

Thousands of English mercenaries served under rulers in North Africa and Turkey where they might convert to Islam. Muslims could be feared (for their armies), objects of curiosity (for their religion and cultural ways), admired (for their trading skills), and so on—but they were never regarded as inferior. In fact, if anything, they were resented because of their superiority.

Small groups of Muslims began to settle in Britain. We know that by 1627 there was a 'community' of poor Muslims living in central London. They mingled with poor whites and became tailors, shoemakers, pedlars and button makers. (p27)

The British Empire changed this fluid situation in two ways.

Firstly, it encouraged a larger flow of people across the globe. These included Muslims from the region around the Suez Canal, particularly Yemenis, Adenese, Sudanese and Somalis from the north of their country (which was then the British protectorate of Somaliland). Many began to settle in Britain.

By 1911 Cardiff was the 'black' capital of Britain with 700 African and Arab residents who were mostly Muslim. Muslims (Arabs and Indians) could also be found in Scotland, in areas such as Dundee, Ben Lomond, Aberdeen, Dumbarton and Clydebank. Many were ex-sailors turned door to door salesmen and small traders. The Scottish urban

areas were 'where these disciples of the prophet of Mecca wander'.

Brick Lane and Cable Street in London's East End used to be the haunt of African Muslim sailors, with attendant coffee houses and boarding houses, as late as the 1950s. They were then joined by a new and larger wave of Muslim migration from Bangladesh.

Secondly, as the British Empire grew the ruling class shifted in the middle of the 19th century from propping up the fading 400 year old Ottoman Empire to challenging it and taking it over. This produced differing, changing and sometimes violent attitudes to Muslims from the establishment.

Imperialists began to consistently portray the fading Ottoman Empire as the enemy and its official religion as part of the problem. The only solution therefore was to take them over—colonise them and purge their religion. This bred at home a chauvinist reaction against Muslims and their identity became transformed into the 'heathens in our midst'.

Where Islam was regarded as a challenge to Christian colonial rule it was denigrated and its followers abused. In 1835 Macaulay wrote his infamous 'Minute on Education' over British policy in India and demanded total assimilation of Muslims to English 'taste, opinions, morals, and intellect'.

William Muir wrote his notorious diatribe against Islam, *Life of Mohamet*: 'The sword of Mohamet and the Koran are the most fatal enemies of civilisation, liberty and the truth the world has ever known.' Muir believed Islam a false religion that kept Muslims in 'a backward and…barbarous state'. (p61)

British rulers used anti-Muslim prejudice to justify their imperial adventures. Later on in the 19th century—when Britain came into direct military conflict with Turkey over control of the Middle East—the Liberal prime minister, William Gladstone, deliberately stoked up anti-Muslim feeling to justify war. He called the Koran 'that accursed book' and branded Muslims as 'anti-human specimens of humanity'. In the First World War the Turkish ruling class sided with Germany. Muslims in Britain were looked upon suspiciously as 'un-British', while the Liberal prime minister, Lloyd George, dubbed military operations in Palestine as 'the British Crusade'(p80):

'We are undertaking a great civilising duty—a mission which Providence had assigned our race, which we are discharging to people living under the shadow of great tyranny, trembling with fear, appealing with uplifted hands for our protection. Turkish misgovernment…shall come to an end now that Britain and the Allies have triumphed'. (p90)

One spin-off from the First World War was the 1919 'race riots' against black sailors. The underlying condition that led to the riots was economic competition. Sailors discharged back into civilian life from the Royal Navy found black sailors, including Arabs and East Africans, employed in the merchant navy. The 1919 riots are commonly described as against 'black' people, but closer scrutiny shows that within that umbrella term there were many Muslim victims, including Somalis hunted down by mobs in Cardiff.[2]

After 1919 the National Union of Seamen (which was at this time very right wing) and the shipping bosses did a deal to keep out black sailors. The NUS had a 'British First' policy, stating that black sailors be picked last and that they go on a forced rota, which meant they had to take any job (most often the worst) offered them or lose all rights to a job and residency.

Arab and African sailors launched a campaign to smash the rota, saying that no one should sign up to it, and picketed shipping offices trying to get the union's position changed, but their pickets were broken up and many arrested were deported. They were blocked in the union, despite the fact that their union subs kept the NUS afloat.

Some sailors began to search for political allies. They looked to radical forces in the union and British society and joined the Communist Party Seamen's Minority Movement and the Colonial Defence Association (also CP-dominated). Ultimately the black sailors lost the battle after the NUS successfully lobbied that shipping bosses be given a government subsidy for every white sailor they hired. However, the Muslim sailors were so radicalised that one moderate anti-racist campaigner complained that Cardiff was full of black Communists! (p113)

The authorities went further on the attack on the very citizenship of the sailors—despite the fact that most of them were from the British Empire and 'entitled' to come to Britain. New laws demanded strict proof of identity. Sailors had to carry ID cards with a photo and a fingerprint on it (apparently a picture wasn't good enough because the police said they couldn't tell blacks apart!). (p109)

Even though they were herded into ghettos, that didn't stop those hostile to them claiming that they were self-segregating (living in a comfort zone in today's parlance), and it was their religion, Islam, with its rigid social code, that was at fault.

A Muslim youth leader, H Hasan, rightly protested, 'We were born in this country and we expect to enjoy all the privileges afforded other British youth and are opposed to discrimination on account of colour or race.'

Ansari shows how these early struggles anticipated and prefigured later and larger movements and political interventions in the 1960 and 1970s, and today.

He shows us that Muslims have always made an impression on Britain; that they have been here a long time; that they carried their religion with them, but were prepared to enter the social and political arena to fight for their rights, despite being victims of racism and prejudice transferred from the world stage.

Muslims in Britain have always been very active, ready to form alliances, by and large integrated on a class-conscious basis. Today we see them organising themselves through the anti-war movement and subsequent political formations on a scale that the Somalis in Butetown could only dream of. Yet the struggle is the same.

NOTES

1: See H Mahamdallie, 'Racism: Myths and Realities', *International Socialism* 95 (summer 2002).
2: See P Fryer, *Staying Power: A History of Black People in Britain* (London, 1984).

It can't stop Blair
Mike Haynes

China Miéville, **Between Equal Rights: A Marxist Theory of International Law** *(Brill, Historical Materialism book series, 2005), Euro 69*

Did Tony Blair break international law in his support for the American invasion of Iraq? Could he be successfully prosecuted in an international court? As evidence accumulates of the murky dealings that led to war more and more people are coming to the conclusion that there is a legal case to answer. China Miéville would disagree, not because Blair's actions weren't 'criminal', but because international law does not work in this way. Moreover it is an illusion, he argues, to think that it

could ever be made to function in a fundamentally different way.

Miéville will be well known to readers of this journal as a leading writer of science fiction in the UK. Here he pioneers something quite different—the Marxist critique of international law. The result is a significant book which, if parts are not for the fainthearted, nevertheless establishes some very important ideas that will influence not only the debate about Iraq and other Western interventions but the whole approach to international law.

An obvious question to those who want to see Blair in court is, who would arrest him and try him? But even if this could be answered it by no means follows that there is a strong legal case against him. This is not simply because of the ambiguities of the evidence but also the ambiguities of the law itself. This does not mean that Blair was right. It means that trying to condemn him in terms of international law is not the right way to attack him. Miéville points out for example that if there is ambiguity in the law about Iraq there might well be other wars which were less ambiguous in law but no less objectionable politically. But if the argument is left simply at the level of law then we might be forced to support them. The same applies to Iraq. No one has put the legal doubts about Iraq more eloquently than Robin Cook, but suppose for a moment (a fantasy!) that these were tested in some international court and there was found to be no case to answer. Would Cook then hold his hands up and say, 'I was wrong and you were right Tony, it was legal, I should have supported you…'? As Miéville puts it, 'A lawful war is not necessarily a just, prudent or humanitarian war.'

A supporter of international law would argue that Blair and Bush would have to be found guilty because the evidence and law to interpret it is so clearly against them. But Miéville suggests that this is not the case at all. Any state could find a basis in law for almost any action, because 'for every claim there is a counter-claim, and legalist opposition to war is therefore ultimately toothless'.

Why should this be so? Three main positions commonly influence the discussion of this problem. Realists see the basis of global relations in the clash of state power. They are sceptical of ideas like globalisation and sceptical of the idea of international society. For them international law is no more than 'a moralistic gloss on power politics'. It plays a useful role in obscuring the extent to which power is still the central determinant of how the world works. If a conflict emerges between the 'gloss' and state needs then realpolitik dictates the impotence of international law before power.

Against this supporters of international law argue that it exists above states and can therefore constrain their actions. It must represent some natural conception of what is right or it must develop into a rational set of rules that states can be persuaded to agree to. In either form it can be a force of stability and progress. If this is not yet fully the case then this is because the law needs to be further strengthened and then enforced.

The third and most critical view is associated with the left. This is less idealistic. It largely accepts the role of power and it looks at the way in which all law is conditioned by social interests and not least capitalist interests. But it still aspires to use law for progressive ends. Law, writes Susan Marks, is 'a strategic tool, which can be used for both good ends and bad ones, to constrain violence

and to legitimise it'. The task for the left is to struggle to use and expand this space.

Miéville recognises the importance of this critical approach to the understanding of law but he argues that it does not go far enough. It especially fails for international law. This is not because international law is not real law (as a realist might suggest) and can therefore be dismissed. International law is essential to the way global capitalism works. When, for example, Robin Cook writes that 'for the neo-conservatives around George Bush it was a guiding principle that the US should undertake no policy that conferred validity on the concept of international law' (*Guardian*, 25 March 2005) he is simply wrong. The US wants and needs international law— consider the issue of patent protection or intellectual property rights, and so on. Yet it also needs its own freedom of manoeuvre. Because the US is the world's most powerful state it has a greater capacity to manage and twist things to its own advantage, but all states reflect this ambiguity and thus so does international law. Miéville notes, for example, that all states have a right to exist and war is only justified in terms of self-defence, but he also notes that there is an equally long history in international law where (and this must give Blair comfort) 'great powers have always asserted a right of intervention in the affairs of small countries'.

To understand why this is we have to appreciate how international law emerges at the intersection of two processes. One was the development of the nation-state system, the other was the rise of capitalism. Miéville argues that these are not separate or autonomous processes but developments that fed off and supported one another. He thus has much to say of historical interest on the way in which law developed in the context of the shift from feudalism to capitalism and the nature of that shift. But his central theoretical point is that capitalism is a system of both commodity competition and inter-state competition and this must be reflected in both the existence and the ambiguity of the international order and its legal expressions.

One thread here is the contribution of the great Soviet legal theorist Evgeny Pashukanis before he became a victim of Stalin. Miéville builds on his analysis to show the role of commodity production in the development of law. The rise of law, Miéville suggests, has to be understood in the context of 'market relations generalising globally, in the transition to capitalism'.

Because capitalism is a global system of commodity production organised through competing states, international law can only partially contain states. Inter-state competition is also the instrument through which international law develops. Demonstrating this involves Miéville in a valuable historical analysis of the way international law evolved in the context of colonialism, imperialism, unequal treaties and the like. International law was not only a means by which global capitalism incorporated non-capitalist parts of the world; it was also an expression of the dominance of the powerful imperialist nations. Thus those supporters of international law who try to counterpose it to imperialism misunderstand its historical roots—imperialism made international law, and international law helped make imperialism and it continues to do so today. 'Coercive political violence—imperialism—is the very means by which international law is made actual.'

International law cannot therefore transcend the system which gives rise to it. The legalistic argument is not only wrong because it cannot work. It is also wrong because those who support it fail to reflect on why international law is so ambiguous and limited. As capitalism changes so will international law, but it cannot be the means to overcome the major contradictions of the system from within. In this sense, says Miéville, international law is 'fundamentally unreformable... I see no prospect of a systematic progressive political project or an emancipatory dynamic coming out of international law.' This is an important conclusion based on a deep and impressive analysis of the law, its origin and history and current state and it makes a major contribution to the way we think about the world. It is well worth ordering through your library.

Pioneer of liberation
Hazel Croft

*A review of Barbara Taylor, **Mary Wollstonecraft and the Feminist Imagination** (Cambridge, 2003), £16.99 and Lyndall Gordon, **Mary Wollstonecraft: A New Genus** (Virago, 2005), £25*

Over 200 years after her death at the young age of 38 the life, writings and ideas of Mary Wollstonecraft still provoke interest, fascination and debate. Successive generations of socialists, feminists and radical thinkers have turned to her writings—most famously *A Vindication of the Rights of Woman* (1792)—and adopted them for their cause. But who was the real Mary Wollstonecraft? The latest biography to hit the bookshops and review columns is *Mary Wollstonecraft: A New Genus* by Lyndall Gordon. It's a racy account of her life, love affairs and her involvement in radical causes. But Gordon has a very shallow understanding of how Wollstonecraft's ideas developed in the context of the momentous revolutionary events of the late 18th century and their impact in Britain.

If you want a much greater insight I would recommend instead Barbara Taylor's recent thorough and serious examination of Wollstonecraft's thought. Taylor has produced some of the best writings on women's history: some readers of this journal will have read her wonderful history of women's involvement in the Owenite movement, *Eve and the New Jerusalem*. Taylor applies a similar rigorous historical approach to Mary Wollstonecraft, attempting to rescue her writings both from her opponents but also from those admirers who, in adopting her for their own causes, have misrepresented and distorted her thinking.

As Taylor puts it, 'Perched on her pedestal, Wollstonecraft has acquired a mythic patina that blurs and distorts her historical contours. Every feminist generation reinvents her.' But for Taylor, 'ripping her from her own intellectual world to claim her for ours has had the paradoxical effect of reducing her real intellectual significance'. Taylor does Wollstonecraft the service of treating her array of writings—theory, philosophy and novels—as works to be held up to scrutiny as much as those of Rousseau, Tom Paine and other male figures of the Enlightenment and of the movement of radical dissent in Britain.

Wollstonecraft lived through a period when the American and then the French revolutions totally reshaped the world. Wollstonecraft hailed these revolutionary upheavals as harbingers of a 'glorious future'. The French Revolution, in particular, had a momentous impact on her and she travelled to revolutionary France in 1793, 'glad' to be there during 'the most extraordinary event that has ever

been recorded'. She was, as Taylor says, 'a proponent of revolutionary democracy'. She visited Paris and defended the revolution during the height of the 'Terror' when other figures, such as the poet William Wordsworth, were turning their backs on the revolution. She took on the most vociferous British opponent of the French Revolution, Edmund Burke, and published a marvellous defence of the revolution in her *A Vindication of the Rights of Men* (1790).

Taylor's study examines in great detail Wollstonecraft's debates with Rousseau and other Enlightenment philosophers, looks at her relationship to the tradition of radical dissent in Britain, and puts her ideas alongside other women writers of the day. The central theme of Taylor's book is that Wollstonecraft's ideas were much more contradictory and complex than is often portrayed, and steeped in the ideas of the Radical Enlightenment, a movement following the Dutch and English revolutions which challenged the reactionary churches—and the very basis of societies that let them flourish.

There is a long and detailed examination of the contradictory role of religion in her thought: Taylor argues that Wollstonecraft never lost her belief in a personal god and was not the atheist some portray her as. She looks at how feeling, emotion and fantasy were seen to be as much a part of the 18th century 'Enlightened Mind' as reason. There is also a very interesting examination of the sexual imagery and eroticism which infused Wollstonecraft's writings.

Although Taylor uses the label 'feminist' in the title of her book, she argues it should be applied only with extreme caution. It was not a word or concept used at the time Wollstonecraft lived, and it attaches to her the ideas and beliefs of her successors.

Wollstonecraft was motivated by her hatred of all injustice and hierarchy and regarded women's liberation as part of a historic movement towards 'a new age...of perfect harmony between the aspirations of the individual and the collective needs of humanity as a whole'. Wollstonecraft deliberately linked women's freedom, argues Taylor, 'to the elimination of all hierarchical divisions of rank, sex, age, race and wealth' and so 'stands well to the left of the feminist spectrum'.

She hated the barriers put upon women, especially the often miserable fate of women who had to struggle to survive without men—a struggle which Mary herself endured as a young woman, trying to survive as a teacher, a governess and a writer. She hated the Marriage Laws which treated women as the property of men. Above all she argued that women's 'neglected education' was the 'grand source' of their oppression: 'Let the practice of every duty be subordinate to the grand one of improving our minds.'

But, Taylor argues, Wollstonecraft's writings are full of invective against idle rich women who played on and used their supposed 'feminine' attributes for their own gain. As Taylor writes, 'The *Rights of Woman* castigates its female readers in the harshest terms for classic feminine follies: vanity, irrationalism, intolerance, frivolity, ignorance, cunning, fickleness, indolence, narcissism, infantilism, impiety and, above all, sexual ambition.' Taylor seems to imply that this signifies a very ambivalent attitude towards women. But I feel that while so many subsequent feminist writers have lumped all women together in a mythical sisterhood, Wollstonecraft is simply not doing this. Wollstonecraft's rage seems by and large directed against rich women, who idle away the hours reading sentimental trashy novels, and who do not have to struggle for a living.

And Wollstonecraft herself pointed out, 'Considering the length of time that women have been dependent, is it surprising that some of them hug their chains and fawn like a spaniel?'

This is an in-depth academic study, and I wouldn't recommend it as a first read for those who haven't previously come across Wollstonecraft. But for anyone familiar with her work and the ideas of the Enlightenment, this is an interesting and thought-provoking read. And why does it matter? Well, says Barbara Taylor, as much as it would 'be good to be able to bury Mary Wollstonecraft', history won't let us. It is the reality of women's oppression that continues to breathe life into Mary Wollstonecraft. Her call for women's liberation and for an end to sexual injustice speaks to us still across two centuries, and her life's work deserves the kind of serious examination undertaken in this book.

From markets to massacres
Dragan Plavsic

A review of Michael Barratt Brown,
From Tito to Milosevic: Yugoslavia, A Lost Country *(Merlin Press, 2005),*
£14.95

During the Cold War, Tito's Yugoslavia held a special place in the hearts of many on the left who regarded it as a potentially viable 'socialist' alternative to both Eastern Bloc totalitarianism and Western capitalism. Today this may well seem outlandish, but there were reasons why many once thought like this. After all, did not Tito's partisans liberate Yugoslavia from Nazi occupation without direct

Soviet help, build a multinational federation, break with Stalin, introduce 'workers' self-management' and help lead the Non-Aligned Movement? By the 1990s, however, as war engulfed Yugoslavia, an insistent question had to be faced: where did it all go wrong?

Michael Barratt Brown is a socialist for whom Tito's Yugoslavia was special for both personal and political reasons, and so it is fitting that this book[1] attempts to answer that insistent question by interweaving personal testimony with economic and political analysis of Yugoslavia's slide into catastrophe. The author's long acquaintance with the country began during the Second World War when, serving in Egypt, he met Yugoslav partisans fresh from the anti-Nazi struggle. So impressed was he by them that he abandoned his pacifist Quaker beliefs for the British Communist Party, to which he was recruited by James Klugmann, a notorious Stalinist propagandist. From 1944 until 1947 he worked in Yugoslavia for the United Nations War Relief Mission, and remains justly proud of its achievements. Failing, much to his regret, to break with the party in 1948 over the Tito-Stalin split, Barratt Brown finally broke with it over Hungary in 1956, subsequently helping to found New Left Review and authoring several books.[2] He continued to visit Yugoslavia and has maintained an interest in its fortunes ever since.

Barratt Brown's central argument is that we cannot understand Yugoslavia's collapse without understanding the long term impact on the country of an increasingly market-based economic policy introduced after the split with Stalin in 1948. This policy loosened the chains of a state centralist economy in favour of a more decentralised market one that gave companies and republics the

'freedom' to keep profits and invest them. The result was a steadily widening wealth gap between the stronger economies of the north—Slovenia and Croatia—and the weaker economies of the south—Bosnia, Serbia (especially Kosovo) and Macedonia—cementing what might be called a two-tier Yugoslavia. This gap widened with the opening up of the country to foreign trade as Yugoslav firms sought cheaper manufacturing products and raw materials abroad rather than at home. As imports grew, Yugoslavia turned to IMF loans, paying a heavy price when the IMF demanded, as elsewhere, more market reforms that further raised unemployment and cut living standards. By the 1980s, Yugoslavia was in a severe economic crisis that laid the basis for much of what later followed.

Barratt Brown's purpose here is to show that the seeds of future discord were sown early by a policy commitment to the market internally and to Yugoslavia's integration into a global market economy externally. In its essentials this argument is a strong one and draws on now classic works such as Susan Woodward's Balkan Tragedy. But it is at this point that Barratt Brown's belief in the socialist credentials of Tito's Yugoslavia obliges us to confront a profound irony at the heart of his position. What he celebrates as the country's experiment in 'economic democracy'—the 'workers' self-management' in factories and workplaces the Titoists claimed as their unique hallmark—was, in practice, the regime's cover for the introduction of the very market mechanisms Barratt Brown rightly deplores.

This point will be clearer if we draw a parallel with the market reforms of the NHS so favoured by Tony Blair. Here too the idea is to replace a centralised state-run system with a more decentralised market-based one that gives so-called foundation hospitals the 'freedom' to keep surpluses and attract private sector finance. And here too the reform proposals come ready-wrapped in the seductive language of self-management. They will, Blair says, put 'power in the hand of the patient' and 'power into the hands of [healthcare] professionals'.[3] But such rhetoric is only cover for the introduction of market mechanisms that are set to create a two-tier NHS as potentially divisive as a two-tier Yugoslavia. It is also cover for the fact that real power is vested not in patients and staff as claimed, but in that contemporary hate figure, the NHS manager; just as in Yugoslavia, as Barratt Brown himself acknowledges, 'self-management gave great power to those who became managers', with the Communist Party often ridiculed by his Yugoslav friends as a 'managers' club'. When viewed in the cold light of day, this is really self-management for market managers, not workers.[4]

Barratt Brown does not of course rest his argument solely upon the impact of the market on Yugoslavia's collapse. He describes the fact that Tito's regime was a one-party state as 'a fatal flaw'. He argues that what lay behind US interventions in Bosnia in 1995 and Kosovo in 1999 was NATO's drive eastwards towards Russia and the oil reserves of the Caucasus. And he deplores 'the appeal of nationalist leaders offering some protection on a communal nationalist basis'. Much of this will be familiar to readers who have followed the left's critique of events in the Balkans. At the same time, Barratt Brown seeks to defend Milosevic from some of the charges made against him, seeing him as a 'victim' of imperialism. What is lost with this approach is an objective appreciation of how Milosevic was the author of his own misfortune. For all his anti-imperialist rhetoric, Milosevic's

nationalist politics helped to entrench imperialism in the Balkans by driving Serbia's opponents into the supportive arms of the imperialist powers. By contrast, for all their fatal flaws, Tito's partisans, essentially revolutionary nationalists of an all-Yugoslav kind, momentarily grasped something on this all-Yugoslav level Milosevic never could: that only unity based on equality between peoples can protect against imperialism.

NOTES
1: Unfortunately this book is sloppily edited. Yugoslav names are frequently and sometimes bizarrely misspelt and some footnotes are out of sync with the text.
2: Among which is a useful pamphlet entitled *The Yugoslav Tragedy: Lessons for Socialists* (Spokesman, 1996) rehearsing similar arguments to those used here.
3: Blair's speech at the Labour Party Conference, 1 October 2002.
4: This is borne out by the best empirical studies, some of which appeared in the Yugoslav journal *Gledista* in the mid-1960s. One such study concluded that workers were a 'voting mechanism' used to approve decisions already made by managers.

Digging the wrong way
Helen Salmon

A review of John Landers, **The Field and the Forge** *(Oxford University Press, 2005), £22.50*

This book is an account of the transition from what John Landers calls the 'organic economy', that is an economy based on agrarian production with little mechanisation fuelled almost entirely by animal and human muscle power, to a 'mineral economy' of towns and industry. Landers argues that political centralisation and war were the primary motors of the transition from an organic economy to a mineral economy and that the military revolution, rather than the rise of capitalism was therefore the stimulus to the creation of the modern state.

Readers of this journal will be more familiar with this process being called the transition from feudalism to capitalism. Marxists see the economic transition as being the motor of change, leading to the rise of a capitalist class that came to politically challenge the feudal order in the English and French revolutions. Landers sees the forming of the modern state as being state-led, under the impetus of the age of mass war that came with the use of gunpowder.

In the organic economy the vast majority of the population had to be food producers. Populations were very thinly spread across land masses. There was little incentive to create a usable transport infrastructure because the small development of markets meant there was never a high volume of traffic on one particular route. All transport was driven by animals' muscles, which limited what could be transported. Food commodities were bulky, so they were only carried short distances. Therefore each area had to produce all its own food, which impeded the regional specialisation that could have led to a more developed economy.

Landers argues that this organic economy limited the consolidation of political power. He defines political power as the extent to which a ruler can exercise coercion beyond the geographical seat of power. Power was therefore limited by the scattered nature of population settlement. The scarcity of resources endemic to organic economies limited the effectiveness of armed forces. Rulers' lack of finance meant responsibility for land seized in wars was often devolved to local warlords. Similarly, the raising and payment of armies was often contracted out to local chieftains. This meant that even where states grew through conquest the power of the central government was weakened and threatened by civil war.

For Landers, the gunpowder revolution of the 17th century was a pivotal point in the development of warfare and therefore of economic and political change. The use of gunpowder massively enlarged the scale of warfare. Wars lasted longer, killed many more people and cost enormously more, but the potential returns on military expenditure for rulers were now multiplied out of all proportion to the costs of war. Consequently the use of public finances for war grew hugely.

Landers argues that the Napoleonic Wars between Britain and France represented a battle between two economies. France, operating with a wholly modern form of raising an army—ideological zeal and compulsion—expected each war to pay for the next one. Britain's ability to revolutionise production in the 18th century allowed a new, modern system of public credit and taxation to be established that enabled it to stave off the fiscal collapse that had felled other European states and win the war with France.

The massive growth of London was key to this breakthrough to a mineral economy (or industrial revolution, as the process is more widely known). London required fuel, which was transported by sea from the Newcastle coalfields. The need to make the coalfields more efficient led to the use of steam pumps, and the need to transport coal to the docks led to the first railroads. The needs of war forced this breakthrough, creating the apparatus of a modern state.

This view of the transition from the agrarian to the industrial economy states that the revolution in military technology was the prime factor in creating the modern state, rather than the rise of the capitalist class. Landers does not talk about which class controlled the new economy, or the systems of public credit, as important factors. The change in the nature of economic power enriched a new class that pushed against the political barriers of feudalism.

As Landers says, it was in Britain that the industrial revolution was born. However, far from it being the state that drove this process, of all the European powers, Britain had the weakest level of state control over the economy. The industrial revolution was driven by private capital, not the state. It was the mismatch between the growing economic power of this rising capitalist class and the lack of political power afforded to it that led to the political revolutions against feudalism and the growth of the modern state.

Picking up the pieces
Tony Staunton

A review of Iain Ferguson, Michael Lavalette and Elizabeth Whitmore (eds), **Globalisation, Global Justice and Social Work** *(Routledge, 2005), £22.99*

Neo-liberalism has enormously increased global immiseration over the last 40 years. For those of us involved through that period in the fight against poverty and for the promotion of welfare rights anywhere in the world, the experience has been dispiriting.

There has always been a recognition that social work is necessary for maintaining social cohesion, even if this has laid the basis for accusations of us being social pacifiers, a role most of us rejected. An atomised

society is not a prerequisite for revolution, and the suffering of the poor and those disabled by society has to be addressed, whatever broader political goals we are also striving for. Today, neo-liberalism is taking the world in the opposite direction from the aims of social work, let alone socialism.

So what is the role of social work today, in a world of increasing conflict, poverty and alienation? Our traditional advocacy of social rights and redistribution to meet need has been replaced with the more ambiguous notion of social welfare and has meant, in practice, the replacement of a determined drive towards universal provision with defence of emergency responses only to dire need.

In the West, the growth and domination of non-governmental organisations of social support over the organs of the welfare state has ensured the rationing of provision through means-testing and crisis intervention. In the UK the privatisation of the majority of care provision has led to the marketisation of social work itself. Government-driven competencies have replaced the theory and skills base of social work, de-skilling and regulating the ever-dwindling elements of support to those in need. And we're being 'managed' to death, with many social workers spending more than 80 percent of their working life form-filling and dealing with bureaucracy for the protection of agency, not 'client'.

Any attempt to find a way forward for radical social work in this situation is to be welcomed. Ferguson, Lavalette and Whitmore's contribution is even better—a breath of hope and fresh direction. Indeed, a new perspective. Globalisation and all it conveys requires a reassessment of global forces for social justice, and inside that, the implications for social work. Just as transnational corporations invade the lives of all humanity, so the counter-assertion of human rights becomes an international movement.

It is in any case refreshing to look in from the outside and observe social work across five continents in the 21st century. The globalisation of social work offers a new way of seeing our day-to-day tasks, and naturally links the theories of social development to the practice of the global social movements.

As John Harris points out, there is a contradiction resulting from the economic globalisation of capital. Just as there is greater mobility of capital, investment and new forms of technology, all of which is increasing and compounding class polarisation and poverty, so there is greater sharing of ideas and actions across the world. What he terms the 'increased spatial freedom' offered by international debate allows a sharing of strategies and 'what works' in mediating between the exploited and oppressed, and the nation state.

The export of social work methodology was one-way in the 20th century, with the colonial imposition of ideology and philosophy from the West, and particular Britain and the US, to the rest. Now we have much to learn from experiences in India, South America and Africa about the project of neo-liberalism in ensuring the retreat of the state from tackling social problems through welfare.

Indeed, there is more that unites our social work experience internationally than separates us. This collection of articles details, for example, the rise (or for us the return) of voluntary grant-funded agencies, charities or Non-Governmental Organisations (NGOs) substituting for the state and the greater reliance of social work upon specific external funding that requires evidence of 'positive' outcomes, thereby falsifying the true situation and masking the issues and methodology of social work practice.

There is discussion of social development, often funded and promoted without sufficient critique. Who defines what constitutes positive social development or what power and strings are attached to aid? These issues are not only live in the poor South but in every country. Here in the UK, to what degree does the transfer of resources for children to Sure Start and Children's Centres, or the development of Direct Payments for services for adults, constitute the destruction of principles of universal welfare provision?

In reality social work has suffered a continuing assault from neo-liberalism. Chris Jones documents the disillusionment that is the day-to-day experience of social work in the UK, while Fraser and Briskman detail the war on asylum seekers in Australia. But this is not a collection of horror stories. The final third of the book explores our potential. Marxist concepts of collective participatory opposition from below share space alongside strategies for reform from above towards a comprehensive challenge at least to the logic of the free market, and at best to capitalism itself.

Eerily for those of us with 30-plus years experience, the obvious conclusions mirror our best strategies from the mid-1970s, updated to reflect the globalised world. Then, the bible of radical social work by the time of the Thatcher offensive was offered by Brake and Bailey's *Radical Social Work and Practice*. The book detailed methods for social work skills facilitating and joining with the oppressed, exploited, unemployed and abused to collectivise their struggles for social justice and decent life through mutual support and political organisation. The importance of social workers as active trade unionists was a required conclusion.

Similarly, Ferguson, Lavalette and Whitmore conclude the need for 21st century social work to be an active section of the global anti-capitalist and anti-war movements. Many people engaged in social work attended last January's World Social Forum, there to debate strategies for social justice, debt cancellation and preventing conflict and war. The opportunity is definitely there.

The question left dangling as we return to the social work office Monday morning is: where is the space and energy to link our personal commitment to social justice with our daily practice? This book can be the social work bible for the next generation of radical social workers, and should be widely read, but just as last time around we need to acknowledge the urgency and put ourselves out to participate in the wider struggle.

Booms, slumps and theory
Chris Harman

A review of Pavel V Maksakovsky, **The Capitalist Cycle** (Brill, Historical Materialism book series, 2004), Euro 59

There was a flourishing of Marxist intellectual life in the Russia of the mid-1920s that was wiped out with the final triumph of Stalinism in 1928-1929. Maksakovsky, a working class revolutionary in 1917 and a Bolshevik activist in the civil war of 1918-1921, was part of it, trying to clarify Marxist economic understanding in critical confrontation with non-Marxists like Kondratev (best known for his still fashionable notion of 'long waves'). This is the only book he completed before he died of natural causes in 1928 (almost all the other participants in the debates were victims of Stalin's Terror).

Maksakovsky's concern was with what he called the 'conjuncture', meaning the concrete development of the capitalist boom-slump cycle. Marx, he argued, never turned his fragmented insights into a single account of the cycle, while bourgeois economists looked at it only in a superficial manner.

Maksakovsky insists on the need to abstract from immediate appearances so as to locate the fundamental features of the capitalist economy in the operation of the law of value.

Under capitalism, the rate at which goods exchange with each other and for money (their 'exchange value') is determined by the amount of labour required to produce them using the average level of techniques and skill operating in the system as a whole ('abstract labour'). But their production involves concrete human labour bringing physical objects ('use values') into interaction with each other. The correct relations between different exchange values and different use values must exist for production to take place.

The more industry develops, the more complicated these relations become. Cars cannot be produced without steel; steel without iron ore and coal; coal without cutting machinery, winding gear and so on. But the chains of physical interactions depend on a chain of buying and selling, in which coal firms sell to steel firms, steel firms to car firms and car firms to consumers—people who get wages or profits to spend from other firms so long as they can sell their goods.

Such long, intertwined chains linking acts of production to final consumption only function if two completely different conditions are fulfilled. There have to be the correct physical relations between things that go to produce other things, determined by the laws of physics, chemistry and biology. But, at the same time, each act of production has to expand the amount of value (ie the amount of average abstract labour) in the hands of the owners of the particular firm. The physical organisation of the production of use values has somehow to correspond with the capitalist determination of prices by exchange values.

That is not all. Production will not take place at all unless capitalists think they can sustain themselves in competition with other capitalists by getting a rate of profit at least equal to the average in the system as a whole. To guarantee this they have repeatedly to reorganise production, using more advanced techniques so as to increase productivity per worker. But as all the capitalists try to do this, they continually reduce the average amount of labour needed to produce goods—and therefore the value of the goods. The physical quantity of goods produced by the system will tend to rise, but the value of each individual goods to fall. The two things necessary for the system to function, the physical organisation of production and the flows of value through the system, both change repeatedly—but without there being any automatic compatibility between the changes taking place.

Firms undertake production by buying physical equipment (machines, buildings, computers and so on) at prices dependent on the average amount of labour needed to produce them at a particular moment in time. But even as production is taking place, increases in productivity elsewhere in the system are reducing the value of that equipment and of the goods the firm is producing with it. The firm's profitability calculations were based on the amount it had to spend on this equipment in the past, not on what its present value is (attempts to refute Marx's arguments by people like Okishio and Steedman do not grasp this simple point): it is its initial investment that the firm has to make a profit on.

Not only do the values of goods keep changing, but, Maksakovsky shows, the reaction of capitalists to these changes leads to calculation in terms of prices to diverge from those in terms of values. As profits fall, some firms stop new investments for a period. This reduces the demand for other firms that supplied them previously; they try to maintain their sales by cutting their prices below the levels as determined by value considerations, and to protect their profits by sacking workers and cancelling their own investments. A wave of contraction goes through the economy, and with it a general reduction of prices below values.

The contraction does not last forever. Some firms go bankrupt, allowing other firms to buy new plant and equipment on the cheap and to cut the wages which workers are prepared to accept. Eventually, a point is reached where they can expect to get higher than average profits if they embark on a new round of investment; other firms to sell them goods they have stockpiled; a new wave of expansion to take off as capitalists rush to take advantage of the better business conditions. Competition leads firms to undertake levels of investment which, temporarily, exceed the existing output of new machinery, components and raw materials. The 'overproduction' of the downturn is replaced by 'under-production' in the upturn, and just as prices before were below values, now they are above values.

But this only lasts until all the new plant and machinery passes into operation, increasing output at the same time as cutting values, making some investment unprofitable and giving rise in time to yet another downturn.

Maksakovsky's central point is that the cycle is not a result of mistaken decisions by individual capitalists or their governments, but of the very way value expresses itself in prices. This takes place through a continual oscillation, with prices rising above and falling below values, not through some continuous equilibrium.

This cannot be grasped without starting with the objective contradictions expressed in the notion of value. Only by dialectically drawing out these contradictions was Marx able to provide an overview of the system's dynamic.

There is only one fault in Maksakovsky's reasoning on these matters. He sees over-production in relation to demand as precipitating the crisis, rather than over-accumulation of capital in relation to the surplus value, as Marx does in Volume Three of *Capital*. Overaccumulation expresses itself on the one side as a fall in the rate of profit; on the other side as the production of more goods than consumers can afford to buy. Hence the difficulties of getting out of the crisis in the short term. Attempts to raise the rate of profit by the classic means of wage-cutting reduce consumer demand still more and deepen the crisis; attempts to increase demand (through Keynesian-type measures) cut into profits and also deepen the crisis. Not until some firms have gone broke, leaving room for other firms to resume profitable expansion, can such measures be effective.

Maksakovsky recognises that the capitalist state or bankers can prolong the phase of expansion through controls on credit—although, he insists, only to make the eventual eruption of crisis more profound. He argues against economists who believed that state capitalism was doing away with crises in the 1920s by pointing to the international character of the system: 'State capitalism, on the scale of capitalist production in its totality and transcending "national limitations", is historically impossible.' He could not, of course, foresee conditions in the aftermath of the crisis of the 1930s when a collapse of international trade and historically massively high levels of arms expenditure enabled states to intervene to prevent overaccumulation (and 'underproduction') precipitating a slide into slump. Not until the mid-1970s in the West and the late 1980s in the USSR did they find themselves unable to intervene.

There are some gems in Maksakovsky's analysis. His devastating onslaught on Kondratev's long waves theory is still relevant today when many economists, influenced by Ernest Mandel, somehow see this theory as part of Marxist common sense.

The work limits itself to the cycle and so does not look at the long term trends in the system: the impact of increased investment per worker (the 'rising organic composition of capital') on profit rates, and the impact of the concentration and centralisation of capital on the crisis—questions which are important for anyone trying to understand present-day capitalism. It is, however, very useful within this limitation—and a reminder of how alive Soviet Marxism was before Stalin strangled it.

Novel insights

Esther Leslie

A review of Julian Markels, **The Marxian Imagination: Representing Class in Literature** *(Monthly Review Press, 2003), £15*

Julian Markels' book participates in a long-standing debate about the relationship between Marxism, class and literature. It sets itself apart, however, from many contributions, by junking virtually all Marxist cultural theory to date, in order to focus instead on an undervalued issue: imagination.

Markels restarts Marxist literary theory by going backwards, aligning himself with an unfashionable figure from the liberal-humanist tradition of literary criticism, Lionel Trilling, whose book title *The Liberal Imagination* (1950) is echoed here. Trilling insisted on the importance of private and individual human *sensibility*. Markels, a Marxist humanist, agrees with Trilling that the novelist's task is to imagine a particular consciousness as it responds to the circumstances of life, drawing cultural energies from the realm of sentiment and emotion, rather than ideas. Consigned to the dump are unimaginative novels, devoid of emotions, inadequate novels of ideas or 'political-tendency' novels. Such books, according to Markels, can never contribute to Marxism's cause, for Marxism is so closely connected to questions of the imagination.

For Markels, Marxism imagines the enlargement of life via the extension of human possibility. The crucial terms of Marxism are also imaginative categories, in the sense that they have to be concocted. Class is not written on the body. It is not a

visible, tangible quality of a human being, in the way that gender or race may be visible, physical or 'geographical', as Markels terms it. Class's defining aspect, according to Markels, is its processual nature, variously described as exploitation, expropriation and the extraction of surplus value. Class denotes a transient process of producing, appropriating and distributing surplus labour. As a transient process, class cannot be assumed to be especially significant in the formation of identity. Many contemporary Marxists have forgotten this, insists Markels. Fredric Jameson for one, in his assertion that the working class is defined by its *ressentiment*, a psychic structure characterised by feelings of envy and hatred. In such a reading, class becomes an identity, an all-consuming stance vis-à-vis the world.

The book's motto is 'class is an adjective, not a noun', a statement taken from Markels' 'mentors', Stephen A Resnick and Richard D Wolff. This indicates that class is something acted out, experienced, lived, suffered and resisted in a variety of ways, none of which are determined or predictable in advance. For Markels, much Marxist cultural theory has been deterministic. For example, Raymond Williams and Fredric Jameson assume a deterministic sense of class, and correspondingly exclude imagination from their purview.

For Williams, a writer is unable to reach beyond an ascribed 'structure of feeling'. Writers and characters, and by extension workers, are condemned to experience the world only in relation to a series of stages, identified as emergent, dominant and residual. Fredric Jameson is labelled equally determinist: Markels quotes Jameson on Flaubert. Hopelessly incarcerated in his historical moment, Flaubert is 'no longer Balzac, not yet Zola'. The novelist (as much as the weaver or baker) is trapped at a certain point in time and cannot see beyond his immediate environment. In contrast, Jameson elevates the theorist's perspective, who is somehow assumed able to step outside his time and its prevailing ideologies.

EP Thompson's historical writings are key for Markels' Marxism. Thompson rejects the determinist idea of a tight fit between economic forces and the ideas that humans hold in their heads. Workers live their lives and develop their ideas within a 'fluent social process'. To capture this dynamic, Thompson sets his imaginative powers to work, conjuring up contradictory and complex lived realities. Like characters in a novel, his historical subjects respond to experience in 'class ways', but these are not predictable or determined in advance. There is nothing inevitable about modes of experience.

For Markels, literature can go even further than history in imagining and portraying the complexity of classed lives in all their variety. He selects a diverse range of writers to examine in greater detail: Shakespeare, Charles Dickens, Henry James, Meridel Le Sueur, Alexander Saxton, Grace Lumpkin and Barbara Klingsolver. Few of these are Marxists or even socialists, and yet Markels' contention is that their writing can generate a cogent sense of working class existence, the inequities and consequences of expropriation and the possibilities of collective human action. They do this not by bypassing imaginative creativity and reflecting the world as it is or seems, but rather by producing or constituting the world imaginatively.

Only from this perspective is it possible to understand how Shakespeare, in *King Lear*, might imagine modes of experience and types of emotion theoretically more relevant to a later age. Class conflict and capitalist entrepreneurship interweave with

kingship, nature and gender to produce the rich web of the play's meanings. Though Shakespeare cannot conceive directly the material process of feudal and capitalist expropriation, he is still able, through his extraordinary imaginative powers, to depict a range of responses in opposition to the hegemonic culture of the time, and these prefigure what is later theorised in Marx.

The focus on imagination might appear anti-theoretical, an assertion of something intuitive, spontaneous and analysable. However, Markels does have his own theoretical armoury, notably two concepts from Resnick and Wolff. The first is 'overdetermination'. People are classed, but they are also gendered, are parents or sports fans, animal lovers or poets. All these factors impact upon the way they experience class. Marxism cannot claim a monopoly on interpretation of life experiences. The literary form of this is echoed in George Eliot's sense of her novels as tracing the ravelled web of human lots. The second concept from Resnick and Wolff is 'point of entry'. The tight webs of overdetermination among social processes can never be comprehensively analysed. Any mode of explaining the world must choose a point of entry to organise the data. Darwinism has the narrative of 'survival of the fittest', while Freud has the libido. Marxism has class as expropriation, and so literary works can be interpreted along Marxist lines by sensitivity to the question of expropriation.

This book is concise but challenging. Its criticisms of deterministic Marxism are cogent, but its insistence on open-endedness, points of entry and overdetermination seem too much of a compensation for any past bad Marxist cultural theory. Subtle and original interpretations of diverse works are made here, but the overarching schema sets writing confusingly adrift in a sea of historical relativism, and the emphasis on imagination derives writers' powers solely from their own personal awareness. In the process, the Marxist emphases on the importance of history and the way in which, at particular historic moments, individuals (including writers) are shaped, dialectically, by economic, social and historical forces are largely lost.

A fighter who got lost
John Newsinger

A review of Hugh Purcell, **The Last English Revolutionary: Tom Wintringham 1898-1949** *(Sutton, 2005),* £20

'You probably have not heard of Tom Wintringham,' writes Hugh Purcell, 'but by the time you have finished this book I hope you will agree that you should have.' And he is absolutely right. Wintringham is one of those people who was well known when he was alive, but subsequently disappeared from view. His falling out with the Communist Party (CP) in 1938 meant that he was effectively airbrushed out of their history and his refusal to embrace the Labour Party until just before his death excluded him from theirs.

Instead, according to Purcell, he stands alone, as someone who attempted 'to explore a distinctively English way to revolution'. This is, however, not the case. What Wintringham really stood for at the height of his influence was a popular front politics that never really took off in Britain. This is the real reason for his neglect. Nevertheless, Purcell does make a very good case for a sympathetic re-examination of the man and his politics.

Wintringham was born in Grimsby in

1898, the son of one of the town's most prominent families. He was educated at private schools before joining the Royal Flying Corps during the First World War. Here he broke decisively with his family background by serving in the ranks as an air mechanic. After the war, he went to Oxford University, but as someone who had moved dramatically to the left. He visited Soviet Russia in 1920 where he worked as a translator, meeting John Reed among others. As Purcell notes:

'Moscow 1920 remained in Tom's mind as the practical affirmation of his faith in socialism. This was not the Moscow of the 1930s with its paranoia, purges and misery. The mood was youthful, idealistic and free. It was still the revolution of the Soviets rather than the dictatorship of the Communist Party.'

Wintringham returned from Russia a committed revolutionary socialist and in 1923 he joined the Communist Party. Within the party, Wintringham was associated with Harry Pollitt and Rajani Palme Dutt in their efforts to 'bolshevise' the party, to turn it from a propagandist into a fighting organisation. He was appointed assistant editor to the party newspaper, the *Workers' Weekly,* and was considered dangerous enough by the authorities to be one of the 12 party leaders imprisoned in the run-up to Britain's 1926 General Strike. Wintringham served six months and was only released weeks before the battle began. He was responsible for the covert publication of the party's *Workers' Bulletin,* the mere possession of which could earn a prison sentence.

Purcell begins to have difficulties with Wintringham's transformation into a Stalinist apparatchik in the aftermath of the General Strike. He went along with the Communist International's Third

Period turn and its ultra-left sectarianism without a word of complaint. Purcell suggests that he kept his head down during this period, but this is not really credible. One feature of the Third Period was precisely that party members could not keep their heads down, particularly if they had Wintringham's class background. Moreover, Purcell acknowledges that he 'penned his share of "class against class" agitprop', attacking both the Labour Party and the left wing Independent Labour Party as fascist organisations.

More important, he played a key role in launching the *Daily Worker*, and only someone fully on board the Third Period madness would have been in such a responsible position. Purcell, it has to be said, never really gets his head around the way that men and women like Wintringham, in many ways admirable, nevertheless willingly subordinated themselves to the dictates of Moscow, no matter how disastrous. He is not, of course, alone in this.

Wintringham clearly welcomed the Communist International's 1935 popular front turn. The embrace of the broadest possible alliance against fascism seemed to offer the CP a way into the political mainstream. Wintringham was very much to the fore in this endeavour, becoming the party's military expert and commentator. He put his money where his mouth was by going out to Spain to serve with the International Brigades fighting against Franco in 1936.

As Purcell makes absolutely clear, Wintringham wholeheartedly endorsed the Communist line in Spain, including the repression of the revolutionary left, most notably the POUM. Indeed, he joined in the slander of the POUM, whose leader, Nin, was tortured to death by the Communist secret police.

Nevertheless, it was in Spain that he began to fall out with the party.

Wintringham seems to have believed every lie that the CP told about the POUM, every lie that they told about the victims of the Great Terror in Russia, and every lie that they told about Trotsky and the Trotskyists and their collaboration with the Gestapo. What he refused to swallow was the denunciation of his American lover, Kitty Bowler, as a Trotskyist. His refusal to break with her led to his expulsion from the party in October 1938. In Russia, of course, such a stance would have cost him his life, but Wintringham never grasped this. His disagreement was with the British party and he never uttered a word critical of Stalin. Purcell has difficulty with the way that Wintringham's experiences never actually led to him denouncing the Moscow Trials or Stalin's murderous regime. Indeed, he was to remain an admirer of Stalin right up until his death in 1949. Purcell does not adequately get to grips with the remarkable hold that Stalinism had on so much of the left, even outside of the Communist Party.

Wintringham rationalised his break with the CP with the argument that whereas he had wholeheartedly embraced the popular front as the way forward, for the CP it was merely a tactical manoeuvre to be cynically taken up and just as cynically put down. He argued that Communist conduct in Spain demonstrated how skin deep the party's popular frontism really was. And, of course, the Hitler-Stalin Pact of 1939 which led to the popular front being unceremoniously thrown overboard bore this out.

Purcell is much too uncritical of the popular front politics that Wintringham was to try to sustain throughout the

Second World War. Far from offering a way forward, they were to inevitably end up with his joining the Labour Party after the war. To be fair, however, there was some way to go before this result became clear.

A good case can be made that Wintringham actually achieved his greatest influence during the Second World War. He was one of a number of individuals (George Orwell, a great admirer of his at this time, was another) who believed that Britain was approaching a revolutionary situation in the summer of 1940.

Defeat had completely discredited the old order and growing resentment at continuing inequalities and injustices in wartime was fuelling widespread unrest. The organisation that Wintringham saw as potentially decisive in any revolutionary outbreak was the Home Guard. To a generation raised on *Dad's Army* this seems positively ludicrous, but at the time there were significant numbers of people for whom the Home Guard was the arming of the workers and for whom this was a guarantee against any compromise peace with Hitler. Wintringham established a training school for the Home Guard at Osterley Park and taught revolutionary guerrilla warfare to thousands of volunteers, much to the alarm of the government. His *New Ways of Warfare*, published in 1940, sold 75,000 copies in a couple of months.

The revolution proved stillborn, however. If Britain had been invaded or if a collaborationist government had taken power the Home Guard might have become an important part of the British resistance, but instead Churchill's Conservative-Labour coalition government successfully contained the unrest.

The authorities took over Osterley Park and Wintringham and his fellow thinkers were pushed aside.

He continued his campaign for 'the imperialist war to be turned into an anti-fascist war', arguing the case in his book *The Politics of Victory*, published in June 1941. This coincided with Hitler's invasion of Russia, which saw the CP turn from opposition to the war to enthusiastic support for it. This support extended to the Churchill coalition government and involved ferocious opposition to the sort of regrouping on the left that people like Wintringham were trying to bring about. He was one of the architects of Commonwealth, a loosely organised movement that attempted to challenge the coalition. For its pains Commonwealth was denounced by the CP as 'crypto-fascist'. Although it achieved some success at wartime by-elections, Commonwealth was never to overcome its middle class origins. If Labour had remained in a coalition with Churchill in 1945, as the CP had urged, the movement might have achieved some sort of breakthrough. As it was it never managed to go beyond middle class radicalism.

In 1945, Wintringham published his best-selling attack on the Tories, *Your MP*, which sold over 200,000 copies—but it actually helped Labour into power. Only one Commonwealth MP was elected and Wintringham subsequently joined the Labour Party. His popular frontism led relentlessly to the embrace of reformism. Wintringham was to die prematurely in 1949 and was, sad to say, soon forgotten on the British left.

Clearly Wintringham is an interesting figure, someone who had a considerable impact during his lifetime, but whose politics, in the end, were found wanting. Purcell sees him, if he had lived, as a future Eurocommunist, a contributor to *Marxism Today*. This seems most unlikely: Wintringham was much too much a man of the left to have ever been comfortable in that particular milieu. Much more likely is that his failure to break intellectually with Stalinism together with his continued popular frontism would have seen him embrace some sort of Third Worldism. This would probably have been irresistible in the aftermath of the Chinese Revolution of 1949.

Of course, this is all so much speculation. Whatever he might have become, his life provides a useful case study of the impact of Stalinism on one of the more independent thinkers on the left in the period between the two world wars.

Pick of the quarter

The May issue of **Monthly Review** is the best for a long time. It contains an outstanding article on Albert Einstein's Marxist politics (by John J Simon and available at www.monthlyreview.org/0505jjs.htm); a very useful piece commemorating the 20th anniversary of Levins' and Lewontin's pathbreaking *The Dialectical Biologist* (by Brett Clark and Richard York); an account of the international experience in organising informal sector workers (by Fatma Ulku Selcuk); and an account of how the US AFL-CIO union federation's international department has continued its long history of working for an agenda laid down by the CIA and the State Department—which has had its effect on TUC policy as regards Latin America.

In the previous issue Michael D Yates provides a thorough going 'Statistical Portrait of the US Working Class' (available at www.monthlyreview.org/0405yates.htm)

Hidden away in the back end of the March-April **New Left Review** (number 32) is an article which complements very well Simon Gilbert's piece on China's workers in this journal. Yan Lian reviews a survey of peasant life by Chen Guidi and Wu Chuntao that has been banned by the Chinese government. It provides a devastating account of the desperate plight and sporadic rebellions of half the population as neo-liberals exalt the country's embrace of the market as the model for the whole third world.

Also of interest in this issue of NLR are the first part of a long piece by Giovanni Arrighi arguing that the US is losing its global hegemony, a piece by Wang Chaohua on Taiwan and a review by John Newsinger of two recent books telling of the barbarity of the British crushing of the Mao Mao movement in Kenya half a century ago.

John Newsinger also appears in a debate with Andy Croft over George Orwell in issue 26 of **Socialist History**.

A useful follow-on for readers of Claudio Katz's article in this issue will be the April **Science and Society**. It contains a symposium on left strategy in Latin America, with pieces by the former Mexican foreign minister Jorge Castañeda, the left wing academic specialist on Venezuela, Steve Ellner, the Cuba-based Chilian activist and journalist Marta Harnecker and veteran left wing commentator James Petras.

Recent issues the **Journal of Agrarian Change** have carried a three part book-length study of the rise of capitalist agriculture in Scotland by Neil Davidson (whose review of Pierre Broué's *The German Revolution* will appear in our next journal). It is very relevant to the debate over the rise of capitalism with Bob Brenner which took place at the day school we organised with **Historical Materialism** last year. The issues also contain what look like interesting articles on the effect of the neo-liberal turn in Vietnam, Jamaica and elsewhere.

Anyone interested in controversies in Marxist economics should look at Rick Kuhn's long piece (using previously unpublished and untranslated material) on the German Marxist of the 1920s Henryk Grossman in **Research in Political Economy** 21 (available at http://eprints.anu.edu.au/archive/00002400/01/Economic_crisis_and_socialist_revolution_eprint_secure.pdf).

The **Marxists Internet Archive** have recently announced that they have created and massively expanded their online Marxist writers archive in Arabic, including a lot by Lenin and Trotsky (they say, much of it for the first time). http://www.marxists.org/arabic/index.htm

Finally, the issue of **Revolutionary History** that comes out around the same time as this journal looks to be a real treat. It is devoted to the Russian revolution of 1905, with translations of eyewitness reports and workers' leaflets, accounts of the mass strikes and preparations for uprisings, unpublished pieces by Rosa Luxemburg and much more.

CH